John,

I hope you find this book good "food for thought".

Mary Lou

"In a time of widespread confusion and uncertainty about the meaning of life, Sohrab Ahmari makes a strong case for the truth and
relevance of traditional values, virtues, and beliefs. This is a unique
and hopeful book that reminds us that the human person is made for
great and beautiful things—far more than the vision of life offered
by our society today."

—Most Reverend José H. Gomez, Archbishop of Los Angeles

"Drawing on the deepest wells of ancient and modern wisdom from
around the world, *The Unbroken Thread* weaves together essential
lessons desperately needed to guide a new generation into an uncer-
tain future. Written with love as a legacy for his young son, Sohrab
Ahmari has produced a gift for all of us."

—Patrick J. Deneen, professor of political science,
University of Notre Dame, and author of *Why Liberalism Failed*

"Sohrab Ahmari has been thinking for himself since arriving from
Iran as a youth. Paradoxically, he has thought himself back into the
heart of our best traditions and has seen, with striking clarity, that
the modern quest for total liberation of the intellect and will is both
quixotic and damaging, individually and collectively. This clever and
engaging work is the result; the dozen questions it asks are fresh,
and the answers it gives are powerfully persuasive."

—Adrian Vermeule, Ralph S. Tyler, Jr. Professor
of Constitutional Law, Harvard Law School

THE
UNBROKEN
THREAD

THE
UNBROKEN
THREAD

DISCOVERING THE

WISDOM OF TRADITION

IN AN AGE OF CHAOS

SOHRAB AHMARI

CONVERGENT
New York

Published in the United States by Convergent Books, an imprint of Random House,
a division of Penguin Random House LLC, New York.

CONVERGENT BOOKS is a registered trademark and its C colophon is a trademark of
Penguin Random House LLC.

Library of Congress Cataloging-in-Publication Data
Names: Ahmari, Sohrab, author.
Title: The unbroken thread / Sohrab Ahmari.
Description: First edition. | New York : Convergent, [2021] | Includes index.
Identifiers: LCCN 2020047382 (print) | LCCN 2020047383 (ebook) |
ISBN 9780593137178 (hardcover) | ISBN 9780593137185 (ebook)
Subjects: LCSH: Christian ethics—Catholic authors. | Christian life—Catholic authors.
Classification: LCC BJ1249 .A453 2021 (print) | LCC BJ1249 (ebook) | DDC 241/.042—dc23
LC record available at https://lccn.loc.gov/2020047382
LC ebook record available at https://lccn.loc.gov/2020047383

Printed in Canada on acid-free paper

crownpublishing.com

2 4 6 8 9 7 5 3 1

First Edition

Design by Fritz Metsch

To Don Javier.

To Rusty.

To beloved Libo and Feng-Qiao.

Do not free a camel from the burden of his hump; you may be freeing him from being a camel.

—G. K. CHESTERTON

Continuity is a human right.

—CHARLES DUPONT-WHITE

CONTENTS

A NOTE ON SCRIPTURE

EXCEPT WHERE OTHERWISE noted, all Scripture quotations are from the Revised Standard Version of the Bible, Second Catholic Edition (San Francisco: Ignatius Press, 2006).

THE
UNBROKEN
THREAD

INTRODUCTION

———

An immigrant isn't supposed to complain about the society that gave him refuge. That is what I am: an immigrant, a radically assimilated one at that—who nevertheless harbors fundamental doubts about the society that assimilated him.

I spent the first thirteen years of my life in Iran, a nation many in the West associate with traditional backwardness, with black chadors and dour clerics, severe sexual mores and teeming multitudes that fill the streets on Fridays to pray and to chant, "God Is Great!" As a boy growing up there, I had already absorbed this judgment and made it my own: I blamed all that ailed my native land, its repressiveness and the double-thinking and double-living it engendered, on our hidebound traditions.

Once I immigrated to the United States, I reveled in the chance to remake myself anew each day. My moral opinions were as interchangeable as my clothing styles and musical tastes. I could pick up and drop this ideology or that. I could be a high-school "goth," a college socialist, a law-school neoconservative. I could dabble in drugs and build an identity around my dabbling. I could get a girlfriend, cheat on her, dump her willy-nilly, and build a pseudo-identity around that, too. All along, it outraged me to recall that there were people still trapped in societies that didn't permit such experiments in individual self-definition.

But lately, my mind has taken an unexpected turn. When I soberly examine the West as it really is, I find much wanting in its worldview and way of life. More than that, I have come to believe that the very

modes of life and thinking that strike most people in the West as antiquated or "limiting" can liberate us, while the Western dream of
autonomy and choice without limits is, in fact, a prison; that the quest
to define ourselves on our own is a kind of El Dorado, driving to
madness the many who seek after it; that for our best, highest selves
to soar, other parts of us must be tied down, enclosed, limited, bound.

These are the paradoxical arguments at the heart of this book. To
explain why I believe in them so dearly, I need to tell you about two
people, both of whom happen to be named Maximilian.

THE STORY OF the first Maximilian begins in Poland before World
War II and reaches its climax in 1941 at the Auschwitz-Birkenau concentration camp. Maximilian Kolbe, a resident of that camp, ranks
today among the greatest of modern Christian martyrs. The Catholic
Church recognized him as a saint in 1982. Each year, thousands of
pilgrims flock to the Auschwitz punishment bunker where the Nazis
murdered him.

Kolbe was born in 1894 to a poor, pious family in central Poland.
As a boy, he had a vision in which the Virgin Mary visited him bearing
two crowns. One crown was white, signifying purity; the other red,
the color of martyrdom. The mother of Jesus asked young Kolbe
which of the two he would prefer. "I said that I would accept them
both," he later recalled.[1] That vision would serve as Kolbe's interior
compass for the rest of his life, pointing his way to the two crowns.

The crown of purity, or priestly chastity, was easier to obtain. After
flirting for a time with a military career, Kolbe entered the Franciscan
Order as a novice at age sixteen, pouring himself into a life of rigorous study, prayer, and self-discipline. The year was 1910. Europe tee-
tered at the precipice of a century of war and totalitarianism, though
almost no one saw how close to the edge the Continent had drawn.
The Europe of the great empires appeared solid.

Following doctoral studies in Rome and ordination as a priest,
Kolbe returned to his homeland, head brimming with big plans. He

started newspapers, a radio station, and a monastic community outside Warsaw called Niepokalanów ("City of the Immaculate Mother of God"). He campaigned against communist ideology, Freemasonry, and other forms of militant secularism and anticlericalism then in vogue. In between, he went on missions to far-flung places: India, China, and Japan. He endured periodic bouts of tuberculosis, but the sickness couldn't put a stop to his various projects.

The Nazis, however, succeeded where illness failed. In September 1939, the German war machine rolled into Poland from the west, while the Soviets invaded from the east. When the Luftwaffe bombed Warsaw, the printing presses at Niepokalanów temporarily ground to a halt. The Germans occupied the community, expelled most of its residents, and arrested Kolbe.

"I do not know exactly what will happen in Poland," he warned his followers, "but we must expect the worst. There is no corner of this world that is without the Cross. Let us not run away from it and, if necessary, let us take it upon our shoulders for the sake of the Immaculate"—that is, the Virgin Mary.[2]

By December, Kolbe regained his freedom and returned, undeterred, to Niepokalanów. He published anti-Nazi literature, broadcast a steady stream of anti-Nazi propaganda from his amateur-radio station, and sheltered some fifteen hundred to two thousand Jews in the monastery.[3]

On February 17, 1941, a Gestapo convoy entered Niepokalanów and arrested Kolbe again, this time for good. In May, the Nazis sent him to Auschwitz, shaved his head and beard. Father Maximilian Mary Kolbe became Prisoner No. 16670. The red crown was within his reach.

At Auschwitz, Kolbe continued his ministry as if he were still free. He heard confessions, urging penitents not to give in to hatred. "Hate," he said, "is not creative." He gave alms to the poor, though now the poor were the other inmates, and the sustenance he gave them came from his own paltry rations. And he preached. "No, they

will not kill our souls," the emaciated priest told a gathering of his
Auschwitz parishioners, as one of them later recalled. "When we die,
then we die pure and peaceful, resigned to God in our hearts."[4]

One night in July, a prisoner escaped from Kolbe's block. When
the authorities discovered the escape, they alerted the camp's deputy
commandant, Karl Fritzsch, and he ordered the inmates to line up
outside the block. Fritzsch had a genius for cruelty. It was he who first
had the idea of using Zyklon B gas to exterminate inmates, including
the one million Jewish men, women, and children murdered at Auschwitz as part of the Final Solution. That night, Fritzsch carried out his
protocol for when inmates escaped: selecting ten men to die of star-
vation as collective punishment for the one who went free.

The priest in the bunch wasn't selected. But when he heard one of
the condemned cry out, "My wife, my children!," Kolbe took off his
cap and quietly stepped forward from the line.

"What does this Polish pig want?" the deputy commandant asked.

"I am a Catholic priest from Poland. I would like to take his
place"—here, Kolbe pointed at his fellow prisoner—"because he has
a wife and children."[5]

Fritzsch accepted Kolbe's offer.

The Nazis stripped the ten men naked and huddled them into a
punishment bunker, where one of the worst forms of death known
to humankind awaited them. Eyewitnesses later reported that Kolbe
confronted his ordeal with calm, prayerful resolve. While the other
men broke down, the priest was never heard to complain. Instead, he
passed much of the time kneeling and saying the Rosary.

Days went by. Hunger and dehydration felled one after another.
After two weeks, six of the ten had died, and the sound of men begging for bread and water no longer emanated from the bunker. Of
the four still alive, Kolbe was the only one still fully conscious when
the camp authorities entered the bunker on August 14 to finish the
job.[6]

When an executioner approached with a syringe full of carbolic
acid, the priest said a prayer and offered his own arm. A camp worker

later recalled seeing Kolbe after the injection "with his eyes open and his head drooping sideways. His face was calm and radiant."[7]

I WAS THIRTY-ONE years old, on the cusp of becoming a father and a Christian, when I first learned the story of Maximilian Kolbe. It floored me utterly. It wasn't the kind of account one could read and then calmly set aside.

I could, if I tried hard, put myself in the shoes of the condemned men. I could imagine myself standing in front of their prison block as Fritzsch walked up and down the line, casually deciding who should live and who should die. I could feel my heart pounding in my throat, my breath speeding up, my mouth drying up, while my fate seesawed on the whims of a demon. I could also imagine sighing a deep sigh of relief when Fritzsch passed me over and allowed me to live.

As a father-to-be, I could imagine how it would have felt to be the prisoner Kolbe saved. But to be the man who volunteers to step into the shoes of one condemned—now, that was something else.

What gripped me the most, what I couldn't get out of my head once I learned about Kolbe, was how his sacrifice represented a strange yet perfect form of freedom. An ordinary man, once Fritzsch had passed over him in the line, might be stunned by his luck and gobble up the night's rations all the more eagerly, knowing how close he had come to death. Kolbe, however, climbed the very summit of human freedom. He climbed it—and this is the key to his story, I think—by binding himself to the Cross, by denying and overcoming, with intense spiritual resolve, his natural instinct to survive. His apparent surrender became his triumph. And nailed to the Cross, he told his captors, in effect: *I'm freer than you.* In that time and place of radical evil, in that pitch-black void of inhumanity, Kolbe asserted his moral freedom and radiated what it means to be fully human.

This form of freedom is at odds with the account of freedom that prevails in the West today. Plenty of people still carry out great acts of sacrifice, to be sure. Witness the heroism of physicians, nurses, and other front-line health workers in response to the novel-coronavirus pandemic. But the animating logic of the contemporary West, the intellectual thrust of our age, if taken to its logical end, renders the actions of a Kolbe insensible.

Our version of freedom sprang from the European Enlightenment, a philosophical movement that "sought to liberate man from the dead hand of tradition," as one historian of ideas has written.[8] Beginning in the late eighteenth century, men and women inspired by Enlightenment ideas swept violently through the West, assailing every source and symbol of authority that stood in the way of the sovereign individual and his autonomous exercise of his reason and his rights.

The assault was especially fierce in France. There, the rebels inaugurated the reign of the "goddesses" of Reason and Liberty with one swift guillotine chop after another. In 1789, the (routine) sight of a revolutionary mob parading the severed head of the local governor through the Paris streets famously prompted the writer and diplomat François-René de Chateaubriand to cry out: "You brigands, is this what you mean by liberty?"[9]

Chateaubriand raged against an abominable instance of revolutionary violence and lawlessness. Yet behind his anger lay a perceptive critique of the new philosophy: For the Enlightenment thinkers, *what* people did with their freedom mattered far less than their being generally unrestrained: to marry or divorce; to worship or blaspheme; to serve others or hoard wealth.

The Enlightenment took hold. Three centuries later, most of us take it for granted that liberty means being able to select how we live from the widest possible range of options. Our goals are self-gratification and "well-being," usually defined in material, utilitarian terms, and we are free to the extent of being unhindered to pursue the life we think will gratify us best. But if that is the ideal, then why should anyone voluntarily accept a life of poverty, vow absolute obedience to a religious superior, and embark on arduous foreign missions to preach his faith, as Kolbe did? Why should he lay down his life for a complete stranger?

Our conception of freedom can't make good sense of a vast range of ties that bound traditional peoples: folkways and folk wisdom, family loyalty, unchosen religious obligations such as baptism and circumcision, rule-bound forms of worship, and, above all, submission to moral and spiritual authorities. Any one of us might choose to accept such commitments, to be sure, but the key word is "choose": To live in accord with tradition is one more option or "lifestyle," little different from our choice of which book to read next or which diet to follow.

If sacrificial love and freedom persist today, they do so in spite of, and no thanks to, our reigning worldview. We have abandoned Kolbe's brand of freedom—freedom rooted in self-surrender, sustained by the authority of tradition and religion—in favor of one that glories in the individual will.

WHICH BRINGS ME to the second Maximilian.

As I write, this other Maximilian is a little more than two years old. He has been walking for some time, though his waddling gait resembles a penguin's more than it does that of a boy. Not long ago, he was a screaming bundle of primordial needs: breastmilk, cuddles, sleep. But now he takes delight in goods he likes ("I want cooo-key," "I want watch-tee-vee"), while scorning other things that are good for him (meat, bedtime).

He has also become aware, if dimly, of his personality and sense of humor. If he eats his fill of dinner on a given night, he might use the leftovers to fashion symbols: A pair of string beans makes an alligator; string cheese can be twisted to form the alphabet. If he is feeling more voracious, he devours everything, leaving only crumbs, which he offers to his parents, only to renege at the last second and finish them off himself, his idea of an uproariously funny joke.

He is just old enough to act out in self-consciously naughty ways. He knows it irritates his mother when he throws his sippy-cup to the floor, and he is far more likely to do the dastardly deed if she warns him not to. He knows, too, that all her upset melts away if he intones the magic words "sowwy, Mama" in a meek tone. He watches his parents, especially his father, and he tries to imitate their words, gestures, and facial expressions. He is instinctively drawn to cars, trucks, bulldozers, tractors, and tools, as if pulled by some mysterious boyhood gravity.

The second Maximilian, as you may have already guessed, is my son. We usually call him Max.

He was born in the West to immigrants from Iran (me) and China (his mother). We hail from two ancient civilizations, but at the point when we became Max's parents, neither of us could be said to have been deeply rooted in those civilizations. In the case of my wife, this wasn't entirely of her doing: By the time she was born in Xi'an, in central China, Mao Zedong's Cultural Revolution had attempted to snuff out much of traditional Chinese thought and culture on the Mainland.

With me, it was different. I deliberately rejected my homeland's inheritance while I was still enmeshed in it. Iranian culture came with a long historical memory and a set of robust, if often particularistic, truth claims: about the noble origins of our nation, the supremacy of the Shiite branch of Islam over the Sunni, and much else of the kind. I received this inheritance not through rational, systematic argument, but while sitting cross-legged at my great-grandmother's feet and listening to her stories—personal stories, national ones, religious ones, all blended together as if by the musky smoke of her domestic-brand cigarettes.

To my great-grandmother, objecting to the established fact of tradition would have seemed about as futile as arguing with the weather. But my parents—my father a postmodernist architect, my mother an abstract-expressionist painter—sure tried. People in my parents' milieu venerated the West, and the West meant secularity. It meant freedom from the Islamist regime that ruled us. It meant underground parties where women went unveiled, the mullahs were mocked, alcohol was served, and taboo watchwords like "liberal democracy" flowed with the booze. For a boy of twelve or thirteen, just becoming somewhat socially and politically conscious, the choice wasn't hard to make.

The then-nascent Islamic Republic claimed the mantle of tradition, but it was, in fact, a ruthless revolutionary regime in the Bolshevik or fascist mold. As a child, I heard about public executions, watched as the morality police repeatedly interrogated my family, and saw the welts left by judicial flogging on the back of a family friend. "Tradition," to my boyish mind, was the portrait of the Ayatollah Khomeini scowling at me from every billboard and in every classroom.

I had an overriding urge to slash through these webs of tradition, and the machete I picked up was called "America." In Tehran, I watched American television via an illegal satellite dish we had installed on our roof. The colorful, sexualized culture of the 1990s was irresistible: Which ancient and intricate Persian poem could beat the opening credits of *Baywatch*? Which black-clad clerical authority could survive Bart Simpson's ruthless mockery?

These were childish intuitions, yes, but they turned out to be correct. Thanks to the family-preference visa program, a.k.a. "chain migration," I immigrated to the United States in 1998 and became an American by choice a decade later. Since then, America has fulfilled its promise to me—and then some.

I'm a member of the global creative class, free to move anywhere, work anywhere, party anywhere. I live in Midtown Manhattan in a doorman building with a Whole Foods one block over and easy access to restaurants that serve every kind of cuisine on earth. I edit the op-ed pages of a major tabloid. I get invited to all sorts of media shindigs and feted by P.R. agents. Any cultural event is an Uber ride and a free press ticket away.

And I enjoy greater moral choice than any of my ancestors could possibly have imagined. If I so chose, I could declare myself a woman, insist on being called "Sabrina," and my subjective state of mind would suffice to make it so, as far as many elite institutions are concerned. More mundanely, I could put my aging mother in a nursing home and abdicate all the duties entailed in being an Iranian son, without anyone thinking less of me for it.

A radically assimilated immigrant isn't supposed to complain about his freedom. Yet as I grow into my faith and my role as a father, I tremble over the prospect of my son's growing up in an order that doesn't erect any barriers against individual appetites and, if anything, goes out of its way to demolish existing barriers.

The fear had been with me, inchoate and unarticulated, ever since my wife and I learned we were expecting our first child. But it found concrete form, I think, in a set of ads we spotted during a routine ride on the New York subway when Max was one. The now-notorious 2018 campaign for the dating site OkCupid featured the vulgar acronym "DTF" (for "down to fuck") alongside colorful images, the "F" leading into jokey sayings. "DTFour-Twenty" showed a smiling couple sitting on a couch that was levitating in midair ("420" is slang for marijuana); "DTFall Head Over Heels" showed two women embracing to kiss, with an extra pair of hands holding one of them (suggesting polyamory). The messages seemed to subvert the meaning of "DTF," even as they enticed straphangers to get DTF the old-fashioned way.

Now, I have spent most of my life in large cities, and I know that prudes and prigs will never exactly belong in Gotham. Still, I couldn't help imagining Max turning to me if he were a little older to ask, "What does 'DTF' mean, Baba?"

Parents have had to contend with kids' awkward questions since time immemorial. No doubt, I could come up with an answer, honest or not, or direct his attention somewhere else. But what bothered me was the *banality* with which these ads treated one of life's most intimate dimensions. It was that corporate banality, not even the sexual vulgarity itself, that stuck with me. What messages were the ads communicating—about human sexuality, about men and women and their relations? How had a realm of life once treated as hidden and profound become the casual space of an Internet firm that facilitates one-night stands?

The conclusion I drew from that incident, and many others of the kind, seemed inevitable: American civilization comes with plenty of *procedural* ideals, all more or less aimed at maximizing individual rights and ensuring the smooth functioning of a market economy. Those procedural norms and historic liberties are no small blessing. They guard against terrible governmental abuses and are the reason countless families like mine yearn to immigrate from unfree societies to free ones, the United States especially. But the fact remains that American order enshrines very few *substantive* ideals I would want to transmit to my son.

Max's very existence is a product of the autonomy-maximizing, barrier-dissolving impulse that animates modern America. Only in America, as they say, could an Iranian-born journalist meet and marry a Chinese-born architect—a union that would eventually produce a child given the delightfully Hapsburgian name Maximilian. But no amount of gratitude can allay the anxiety that grips me when I ask myself: What kind of a man will contemporary Western culture chisel out of my son? Which substantive ideals should I pass on to him, against the overwhelming cynicism of our age?

MY BAD DREAM runs something like this. Max returns home after finishing college at some elite university. He plans to spend two weeks with his parents before striking out on his own as a junior associate at an investment bank (or hedge fund or publishing house or advertising agency—it really doesn't matter which meritocratic colony he chooses).

Two decades of good nutrition, proper schooling, and rich extracurricular activities have yielded a winsome, "well-rounded" young man. Max has clear skin, an easy smile, and the confidence that comes with knowing life's material fruits are ripe for his picking. One night, Max's friends stop by for dinner. One is a Southern congresswoman's glad-handing son, bound for Yale Law School. Another has just secured seed funding for a tech startup she launched as an undergrad. Still another, an environmental-engineering graduate, has won a sustainable-design award and been named an "Emerging Visionary" by a prestigious foundation in Davos, Switzerland. At this dinner, Max's mother and I take an obvious pleasure in our son. In him, we see our own love embodied and projected into the future. And let's be honest, the fact that *this* is the company he keeps reassures us that we have minimally succeeded as parents; Max looks set to be a "winner" in life.

Yet the moment he and his friends open their mouths to speak, they talk mostly about money. They boast about entry-level salaries at their dream firms, how long it will take them to make partner, the Fifth Avenue apartments owned by senior associates not much older than they are, and so on. They might be well-read, but to the extent they discuss ideas at all, they concern themselves with the latest TED Talk about the power of making eye contact in meetings or the power of genetically personalized steroids to push your workout to the next level.

Max pays a certain obeisance to his father's ancient faith. "Sure," he tells me, he heard the Mass at the college chaplaincy when he "wasn't too busy." But if I push past this polite condescension to his father's sensibilities, he admits that while the Catholic faith might have some social utility, he doesn't think it should be taken "too seriously."

Most of his friends consider themselves to be "very spiritual." In between semesters, they have taken trips to India, where they meditated for days and subsisted only on bananas; they use meditation apps on their smartphones; they do hot yoga; they find consolation, of a kind, in the endorphin rush of long-distance running. These forms of spirituality provide temporary solace from the hectic pace of their lives—without making any absolute moral demands.

"Well-being" and "self-care" and "authenticity" are their mantras when it comes to dealing with others, not least members of the opposite sex. Attachments are to be avoided, because they encumber the true self, who longs for maximal independence across life's realms. They all "play around," even if they don't openly boast about it.

Career ambition and relentless competition punctuated by chances to blow off steam: Max and his buddies may not admit that *this* is what they take to be the meaning of life. Yet the choices they make, and will continue to make as they grow older, attest that it is, indeed, the meaning they hold most dear. And they are far from alone: All across the developed world, many people, elites especially, are making similar choices as we speak.

Fast-forward my bad dream: Max is now forty-seven years old— the same age at which his patron saint laid down his life for a stranger at Auschwitz. Having retired early from his firm with a tidy sum in his investment account, my Max is now touring Europe with his girlfriend in a luxury electric RV. The two of them have been cohabiting on and off for nearly a decade now, yet they have no intention to marry, much less have children.

On the road, they seek out Michelin-starred restaurants for feasting—followed by nights browsing Tinder (theirs is an open relationship). And this is the relatively *optimistic* scenario. It assumes that Max hasn't succumbed to opioids or high-end synthetic drugs. It assumes he hasn't become one of those young men who spend months and years shut in their bedrooms, playing videogames and browsing the Web. The Japanese call them *hikikomori,* though the phenomenon sadly spans the whole developed world.

"Dad, I'm happy!" he insists, if and when he permits us to talk about his life. And the worst part of it is, he might be telling the truth, by his own lights. He may not even know what he has missed: the thrill of meditating on the Psalms and wondering if they were written just for him; the peace of mind that comes with regularly going to Confession and leaving the accumulated baggage of his guilt behind; the joy of binding himself to one other soul, and only that one, in marriage; that awesome instant when the nurses hand him a newborn baby, his own.

Having kept his "options open" his whole life, he hasn't bound himself irrevocably to anything greater than himself and, therefore, hasn't exercised human freedom as his namesake understood it. Maximilian Kolbe dreamt of acquiring the crowns of virtue and sacrifice. The dream—or rather, the nightmare—that haunts me is one in which my Maximilian spends a lifetime reaching for other "crowns."

WE NAMED OUR firstborn after Maximilian Kolbe, because naming one's children after saints is what Roman Catholics do. We believe doing so wins the newborn the patronage of the saint in heaven. But there was more to it than that: I picked the name, with his mother's assent, to bind my own Max to the absolute ideals that stretch backward from Kolbe's sacrifice, through the whole Western tradition, all the way to the Gospels and the Hebrew Bible. The name was to my mind a sort of thread, tying my progeny to tradition.

But can such symbolism alone overcome the West's centrifugal forces? I'm not so sure. All things being the same—and it remains to be seen if the COVID-19 pandemic will effect deep, long-term change in our way of life—the United States will remain on its current trajectory, and Max is bound to inherit an even more disordered society and way of life than we have today. Thus, America's bequest to him will be even less certainty and fewer Permanent Things. Soon, I fear, there won't be anything solid upon which he might base his life.

Here, then, is the dilemma of a young father: How do I transmit to my son the value of permanent ideals against a culture that will tell him that whatever is newest is also best, that everything is negotiable and subject to contract and consent, that there is no purpose to our common life but to fulfill his desires? How do I reinforce that fragile thread linking my son to a life of humane obligations and responsibility? To a life anchored in stable and unchangeable ideals? To a life, in other words, filled with the goods secured by tradition?

The book you are holding is my answer to this dilemma. And I suspect it is a shared dilemma, for the symptoms of cultural disorder affect us all: from precipitous demographic decline to astronomical divorce rates; from the opioid epidemic to explosive racial, sexual, and class animus; from the unprecedented rate of people spending their twilight years without any loved ones to hold their hands to our increasingly dysfunctional politics; from obscene wealth inequality to a pandemic whose spread was made possible, in part, by a global economy lacking barriers and limits. If any of these phenomena have even marginally touched your own life, then chances are, you share my anxieties. You, too, fret about the fate of that thread.

THE PLAN OF THIS WORK: A BOOK OF QUESTIONS

The writer who bangs on about tradition, especially religious tradition, risks looking ridiculous. This isn't a novel predicament. As Rabbi Joseph Soloveitchik, the father of Modern Orthodox Judaism, wrote in 1965, the traditional believer has suffered from a kind of existential loneliness and been scoffed at, going back "to the times of Abraham and Moses." Even so, he observed, the *contemporary* man of tradition

> lives through a particularly difficult and agonizing crisis. . . . He looks upon himself as a stranger in modern society, which is technically minded, self-centered, and self-loving, almost in a sickly narcissistic fashion, scoring honor upon honor, piling up victory upon victory, reaching for the distant galaxies, and seeing in the here-and-now sensible world the only manifestation of being.[10]

The message of tradition runs counter to "the fundamental credo of a utilitarian society." Why? Because, Soloveitchik taught, traditional belief "speaks of defeat instead of success, of accepting a higher will instead of commanding, of giving instead of conquering, of retreating instead of advancing."[11] The whole of the Psalms can be summed up as finding joyous liberation in binding oneself to the Mosaic law, which the psalmist treasures as a guide to the inner structure of the cosmos. Jesus's entire teaching, meanwhile, might be encapsulated in his Gethsemane prayer, recorded in all three of the Synoptics: "Not what I will, but what you will" (Mk 14:36; cf. Mt 26:39; Lk 22:42). This logic of deliberate surrender is at work in all the great religious traditions. Five times a day, the devout Muslim shopkeeper in Cairo drops whatever he is doing at the *adhan,* the call to prayer, to prostrate himself before Almighty God. The demands of raising six children might overwhelm a traditional Catholic mom in suburban Milwaukee, yet she still finds time to say five decades of the Rosary every night. Both she and the shopkeeper practice fasting and abstinence at different times of the year; both are religiously obligated to serve the poor; both submit to regulations that, while differing somewhat in content, aim to bring the adherent's life into harmony with an objective moral order; both profess that God, not men and women, is ultimately in control.

It is precisely this emphasis on surrendering instead of advancing, binding instead of loosening, that most repels our age from tradition. We don't want to surrender. We want to keep shopping, no matter the liturgical hour. We "fast" and accept other bodily deprivations, yes, but for the sake of our own bodily perfection, not in submission to a higher power. The only moral regulations we accept are those that prevent physical harm to others, and not even that in the case of unwanted children in the womb. We believe we are in control, that our lives are ultimately our own individual projects.

As a father, I'm acutely aware of the urgency of this problem. Unlike my Iranian ancestors and my spiritual forebears in Catholic Christianity, I made a conscious, deliberate decision to submit to tradition. I chose to work my way back, to grasp at the thread until I could feel the fabric it was part of in the palms of my hands. Handing on what I found to my Maximilian, over against a reigning worldview that disdains retreat and surrender, is a difficult business. The modern world, after all, can seem so awfully *confident.*

Modern people go about their lives according to predictable routines, though, crucially, ceaseless change and discontinuity are part of the routine. Fashions come and go. Ideas suddenly take hold of society, are forgotten, resurrected, and forgotten again. The market conjures and fulfills previously unimagined desires, until still-newer desires supplant the old. Imposing structures of glass and steel replace marble and brick. The natural world likewise appears pliant. Calamitous disruptions caused by natural mysteries (a novel virus, for example) only throw into relief the extent of our mastery over nature under "normal" conditions.

It all just *works,* and that suffices to legitimate our way of life. Or so we think.

"In the past," wrote Joseph Ratzinger (the future Pope Benedict XVI) in 1968, tradition "embraced a firm program; it appeared to be something protective on which man could rely; he could think himself safe and on the right lines if he could appeal to tradition." But now, we regard progress "as the real promise of life, so that man feels at home, not in the realm of tradition, of the past, but in the realm of progress and the future."[12]

In the realm of tradition, truth is something that precedes individual human beings, something we inherit and must hand down, in turn. We can discover truth and reason about it, to be sure, but we can't change it. In the realm of progress, however, truth is what individuals or groups can articulate or build on their own, through scientific inquiry and their acts in history. Truth thus becomes an ongoing project, a malleable thing. In our realm of progress, tradition is viewed as not only antiquated and inefficient, but as an impediment to achievement.

But what if that confidence of the modern world is an illusion, the product of a determined resolution not to confront the fundamental dilemmas of what it means to be fully human? Or what if beneath the moderns' complacency lurks a deep soul-soreness?

Pick your favorite negatively trending social indicator—loneliness, alienation, addiction, polarization, etc.—and the dire message is the same: The realm of progress can't fulfill our soul yearnings or satisfy our urge to put ourselves right with the sacred. In vain we seek substitutes for that "firm program" of the past. We idolize politics and politicians, indulge in drugs or consumer extravagance, try out do-it-yourself spiritualities, and seek meaning and community online.

Even if these balms temporarily assuage the pain, the wounds don't heal. We can't integrate our own lives, as a personal project, without a vision of the whole that has endured the test of time: precisely what the great traditions promise. Yet given that superficial confidence of an anti-traditional age, the man of tradition in the twenty-first century can't start with the "firm program." Rather, he must begin by restating the fundamental human dilemmas his contemporaries have forgotten or would prefer to ignore. He must, in other words, assume the role of the critic, the interrogator of modern certainties.

That is the plan of this book. I simply ask questions—twelve timeless queries that a confident, progressive modernity should readily be able to answer: questions about the nature and scope of reason; our responsibility to the past and the future; how and what we worship; and how we relate to each other, to our bodies, and to suffering and death. Across long centuries, some of the greatest philosophical and religious minds grappled with these questions and offered answers upon which generations of people based their lives. Yet we moderns have heedlessly discarded many of the answers, simply because they are distant in time from us or because we arrogantly assume we have "evolved" beyond them.

Many of the questions touch on "hot-button" issues, but I pose them in a way that steers us away from our tired and tiresome quotidian disputes and points to larger possibilities beyond. Each question challenges one tenet of our contemporary dogma, with its ingrained, reflexive hostility to tradition. Building on each other, the questions reveal how some of the most ancient theological, philosophical, and moral problems are as urgent to our age as they were to our ancestors. These questions can't easily be squared away, and that is the point: Their bedeviling quality humbles the false sense of superiority that the realm of progress enjoys over the realm of tradition.

The effect is meant to be unsettling at first but ultimately reassuring. Unsettling, in that these questions impel us to confront the poverty of our reigning worldview. But reassuring in the end, because by laying out tradition's attempts to grapple with what it means to be fully human, the questions allow us to see that we aren't alone. The past can lend us a hand amid our modern misery, and we can retrace a path out of the current chaos and confusion.

WE WON'T UNDERTAKE our inquiry alone. On the far side of our modern habits and dogmas there lies a whole constellation of dissident thinkers. Some are squarely and emblematically identified with religious tradition, while others would utterly reject any such association. Even among those figures identified with tradition, there is wide disagreement over *which* source of tradition offers the best way. What makes them useful is the fresh light and air they inject into narrow and musty intellectual spaces.

Some are premodern thinkers. Some are moderns, and among these, some are typically associated with the political left, others with the right. Yet as we will see, these labels don't do full justice to these figures. For our purposes, what matters is that even those who lived closer to our time had one foot in the past. Others might be said to be open to a premodern critique of what came after. As the medievalist scholar C. F. J. Martin has noted, "The great benefit to be derived from reading pre-modern authors is to come to realise that after all we [moderns] might have been mistaken."[13]

That's my primary purpose: not to offer definitive answers, drawn from any one particular tradition, but to explore the possibility that our contemporary philosophy might be wrong in crucial respects— that we may have too hastily thrown away the insights of traditional thought and too eagerly encouraged the desire for total human mastery.

The choice of tradition (or traditions) is bound to rankle some readers. Catholics familiar with my work as a public Catholic might reproach me for granting too much to other traditions (including the Jewish, Protestant, Muslim, Confucian, and feminist) and thus betraying Tradition with a capital T, which in the Roman church is a very specific source of authority. Non-Catholic Christians and other believers, meanwhile, may see in it a stealthy attempt to nudge them Rome-ward.

I have already laid bare my own commitments, and I don't mean to suggest that every tradition is equally valid so long as it challenges modernity's anti-traditional reflexes. Still, in our current situation, thoughtful followers of different traditions can find more in common with each other than any of them might with secular-liberal-technocratic modernity.

As for skeptical or nonbelieving readers, I don't try to persuade them to change their opinions about God. At the same time, I can't make a case for reconsidering tradition while somehow sidestepping God. When God appears in the book, he does so not merely as a sociological or historical fact (e.g., "people have believed X about God with Y and Z social consequences, etc."), but in full: This is the God of tradition, the God who lives and makes claims on us in the present day.

At each step, I pose a deceptively simple question and then plumb its depths: Here is what modernity tells us about this problem, or here is why modernity tells us that this *isn't* a problem—when, in fact, it eminently *is*. Traditional thought helps reveal how deep the problems go. And we will trace the working out of the question through the biography of each thinker, on the principle that the greatness of any idea can't be truly appreciated apart from the real-world joys and agonies, the personal triumphs and defeats, that gave rise to it.

I'm neither a philosopher nor a theologian. I'm a journalist and storyteller. The bulk of this book is devoted to telling the stories of great ideas and of the men and women who brought them forth, and highlighting the lessons we can take from each of them. By centering each chapter on the life and work of one great thinker in this way, I steer clear of any pretense to scholarly originality.

Not every question will resonate with every reader. If I can spur you to rethink even a few of them, I will have succeeded in my task: revealing that the thread tying us to the past, while indeed fragile, is yet unbroken. We aren't as unbound as we might imagine.

PART I

THE THINGS OF GOD

HOW DO YOU JUSTIFY YOUR LIFE?

————

Senator Daniel Patrick Moynihan (1927–2003) captured one of the axioms of modern public life when he said that "everyone is entitled to his opinion, but not to his own facts."[1] A generation later, the conservative commentator Ben Shapiro articulated something similar with his spunky battle cry: "Facts don't care about your feelings."[2]

At first glance, the idea strikes us as eminently reasonable: Insofar as our feelings or biases reflect our volatile passions, they can distort our grasp of reality. We should try to tune out that volatility, then, and base our judgments on the real truth of things, which can be found in cold, hard *facts:* calculations of gross domestic product, crime statistics, medical data, indubitable historical events, not to mention the findings of basic science.

Scratch beneath the surface of what seems like common sense, however, and you will find a philosophical claim that by no means is beyond doubt: namely, that truth is limited to these facts—in other words, to only that which can be observed with our senses, measured with our instruments, and generally expressed in mathematical language. All other claimants to the name truth, in this view, amount to less-than-trustworthy "values," opinions, myths, emotions, or superstitions.

This way of strictly equating truth with "facts" is a relatively recent development in the history of ideas. It emerged roughly four hundred years ago out of the natural sciences but soon came to color most people's approach to life as a whole. This scientific outlook *isn't* itself a scientific claim, mind you, yet it rests on the prestige of natural science and commands the allegiance of many top scientists and science popularizers.

Granted, the same four centuries have seen advanced, technological societies make tremendous strides in mastering the physical workings of nature. But the downsides should also be obvious by now: The reduction of truth to facts has degraded many of our public debates to rancorous and tiresome contests over who can marshal the most data, or who can best shoehorn political or philosophical claims into pseudo-factual statements ("Brexit Spells Disaster, Experts Say"). The great war of facts entrenches us in a narrow range of issues and statistics, and we don't step back from it to examine our political systems as a whole. Our discourse rarely even reaches questions about what *ought* to be the shape, nature, and goal of our society.

When we talk about beauty, love, grace, the virtues, and so on—the things that give life meaning and make it worthwhile—we are dealing with the seemingly nonfactual. These things are real enough, to be clear, but they can't be rightly understood using the scientific method. Therefore, academic disciplines that treat such topics are held to be somehow provisional or second-rate; the quest for "real" knowledge, in this view, takes place nearby in the engineering, chemistry, biology, computer-science, physics, and astronomy departments.

But if love, grace, and other "subjective" experiences of the kind are as unreliable as proponents of the scientific outlook claim, then what is left to help us keep going? Can facts tell us why we should continue living when faced with moments of existential despair? Can scientific inquiry answer why, for humans, being is preferable to non-being? Why should my children think that life is worth passing on? Why should you and yours? In short, *can the language of "facts" justify our lives?*

"The Good of Humanity and All That"

On a walking tour of England, Elwin Ransom, a scholar of languages at the University of Cambridge, comes across an eerie-looking, seemingly deserted country estate. The gate is locked. But the hour is late, Ransom is thirsty and exhausted, and besides, an old woman he met earlier on his journey had implored him to find her intellectually disabled son, who works as a servant at the estate.

No one answers when Ransom rings the bell, and he would soon leave—but for a sound of men struggling and shouting that suddenly crashes from somewhere behind the house. He races to follow the sound to its origin and finds three men fighting outside, though in the darkness he can barely tell what the silhouettes are up to. One of the voices screams: "Let me go! I'm not going in there!" Ransom figures that must be the old woman's son, the one she asked Ransom to fetch. The two other men, one brawny and the other less so, seem to be bullying the boy somehow.

When the professor introduces himself as Ransom, he utterly surprises the smaller of the boy's two bullies, a man named Devine, who turns out to be a fellow alumnus of the professor's prep school. Ransom never liked the knave. Devine and the other bully, named Weston, drop whatever they were up to and invite Ransom over to the estate for a rest and a drink. They then proceed to drug him, huddle him into a spaceship hidden in their yard—and lift off.

Destination: the planet Malacandra.

So begins C. S. Lewis's 1938 science-fiction classic, *Out of the Silent Planet*.[3] The novel, and *The Space Trilogy* it launched, showcased speculative fiction's power to explore philosophical ideas and critique real-world trends. In the hands of Lewis, science fiction was no longer boyish schlock but serious literature in service of serious thought.

Lewis began developing the story in the late 1930s, with the encouragement of his friend and fellow Oxford don J. R. R. Tolkien. The science fiction of the time promoted the enthusiastic and uncritical view of science then in vogue. Writers like H. G. Wells "used fictional narratives to argue that science is both prophet and saviour of humanity, telling us what is true and saving us from the human predicament," as the Lewis biographer Alister McGrath has written.[4] Wells, for example, imagined an extraterrestrial utopia where widespread scientific education has rendered government, politics, and faith entirely obsolete (*Men Like Gods*, 1923). Wells also wrote a fictional "history" of the future, in which an enlightened, science-worshipping world state delivers humankind from war and chaos by abolishing all organized religion, including by shuttering Mecca and other Muslim holy places and gassing the pope and the entire Catholic hierarchy (*The Shape of Things to Come*, 1933).

Lewis worried that science fiction "exaggerated" the benefits of science and was "naïve concerning its application," that the "triumphs of science might have run ahead of necessary ethical developments that could provide the knowledge, self-discipline, and virtue that science needed."[5] If a novel could push science boosterism, Lewis wondered, couldn't it also be used to cast doubt on the science triumphalism then gathering strength in the West?

Out of the Silent Planet and its two sequels were his answer to that question. The book's villain, Weston, is the very type of the 1930s scientist-ideologue. His sidekick, Devine, introduces him as "*the* Weston. You know. The great physicist. Has Einstein on toast and drinks a pint of Schrödinger's blood for breakfast." Devine is just a sort of crude profiteer: "I am putting a little money into some experiments he has on hand. It's all straight stuff—the march of progress and the good of humanity and all that, but it has an industrial side."[6] Weston is far more sinister. He believes sincerely that scientific facts, the kind produced by repeatable experiments, are the only kind of knowledge worth seeking—indeed, the only kind of knowledge worthy of the name. And he is thoroughly and coldly amoral.

Once Ransom recovers from his drug-induced haze aboard the spaceship, Weston lets his prisoner in on his plans. The ultimate goal, he tells Ransom, is nothing less than the total conquest of time and nature through space exploration and colonization: "Infinity, and therefore eternity, is being put in the hands of the human race."⁷ And if the conquest demands the death of one or even a million innocents—so be it. Weston and Devine thus have no compunction about kidnapping Ransom and taking him on an involuntary journey to another planet.

There, the professor begins to gather, he is to be sacrificed some-how, to appease the planet's terrifying native inhabitants, called *sorns,* with an eye toward ultimately colonizing their world and extracting its mineral resources. If Ransom hadn't fallen into the duo's hands, they would have instead taken their servant boy. "In a civilized com-munity," Weston coolly declares, such boys "would be automatically handed over to a state laboratory for experimental purposes."⁸

But doesn't a moral law, the kind recorded in the ancient books Ransom studies for a living, prohibit such inhumanity? Not for Weston, and not, he suggests, for the scientific-philosophical elite he represents. "All educated opinion—for I do not call classics and his-tory and such trash education—is entirely on my side."⁹

Weston's opinions might strike people today as implausibly ghoul-ish. We know about Josef Mengele's experiments on prisoners and about Nazi eugenics; medical procedures carried out on the vulnera-ble will forever be associated with these crimes. But some of the most eminent men of Lewis's age—men celebrated for their liberality and dedication to "progress"—thought the disabled were suitable sub-jects for all sorts of compulsory procedures and openly advocated eugenic "purification" of the human race.

In an essay published in 1927, the prominent British geneticist and "humanist" J. B. S. Haldane warned that "civilization stands in real danger from overproduction of 'undermen'" and called for a "ratio-nal program" of eugenics to avert that catastrophe.¹⁰ Two years later, the philosopher and Nobel Prize winner Bertrand Russell suggested sterilizing "feeble-minded women"—an effort whose moral "dan-gers," he argued, "are probably worth incurring, since it is quite clear that the number of idiots, imbeciles, and feeble-minded could, by such measures, be enormously diminished."¹¹ In the United States, many elites sounded a lot like Lewis's fictional Weston. "Chloroform unfit children," declared the famed progressive lawyer and civil libertarian Clarence Darrow (of Scopes Monkey Trial fame). "Show them the same mercy that is shown beasts that are no longer fit to live."[12] The Harvard social Darwinist Earnest Hooton saw the involuntary euthanasia of the "hopelessly diseased and the congenitally deformed and deficient" as essential to America's demographic health.[13]

Lewis's Weston similarly sees himself advancing the cause of superior, rational, intelligent men, the torchbearers of true civilization, only on a much grander scale. As it soon becomes clear, his destination is none other than Mars. "Malacandra" is the name given the Red Planet by its inhabitants—the aliens Weston intends to subdue and, if necessary, eliminate in the course of his project of interplanetary colonization. For advanced, scientific civilization to survive, he believes, it needs space to roam and expand. Weston sees himself as the pioneer who would secure such space. Total scientific mastery is both the end goal of Weston's vision and the means with which he intends to achieve it.

Few of us would put things quite so bluntly today, but our society is structured around similar ideas. If science *can* achieve some new feat of labor automation, for example, our elites, progressives and conservatives alike, struggle to explain why we *shouldn't* go ahead with it, even if a side effect might be mass joblessness. The introduction of new technologies for screening fetuses for Down syndrome has led to widespread termination of such pregnancies, with some nations in Northern Europe boasting of having all but eliminated DS.[14]

Still, we can see the appeal of the elite consensus on science. Scientific inquiry, after all, presents an indubitable way of knowing the world that has made possible space travel, high-energy astronomy, self-driving vehicles, genetic engineering, and many other marvels. And for this reason, it is entitled to our unrivaled esteem, especially when other claimants to knowledge—ethics, for example—simply can't produce the kind of experimentally verifiable discoveries yielded by the scientific process.

Well, then, doesn't Weston have a point? The author of *Out of the Silent Planet* would have answered emphatically: No. But it hadn't always been so with Lewis. The story of how he came to reject the Weston worldview formed the central drama of the author's own life of the mind.

ENCHANTMENT AND DISENCHANTMENT

Clive Staples Lewis was born on November 29, 1898, in Belfast, the younger of two sons of Albert and Flora Lewis. His father, a lawyer by profession, had strong literary inclinations and preferred his study to the courtroom. His mother, Lewis wrote later, was a clergyman's daughter, "a promising mathematician in her youth and a [bachelor of arts] of Queen's College," making her a women's-education pioneer of sorts.[15]

The Lewises were members of the Ascendancy, the Protestant minority favored by Ireland's colonial rulers in London. By the time Lewis was born, the Ascendancy felt increasingly squeezed by rising Irish nationalism. Rare for the time, however, the Lewis family had a Catholic housemaid, a fact that, as McGrath speculates, may have contributed to his "long-standing aversion to religious sectarianism."[16]

Lewis was well and truly Irish, even if he later formed his deepest attachments to Oxford and the republic of letters. Ireland bequeathed to him the sensibility of a people in love with language—and with stories. Lewis's Ireland, McGrath tells us, was "the broad sweep of Belfast Lough, the Cave Hill Mountain, and the little glens, meadows, and hills around the city."[17] He wove the fantastical landscapes of his later children's books from this quintessentially Irish fabric.

When Lewis was ten, his mother fell gravely ill. He recalled one night feeling sick himself, and his mother not coming to comfort him, as she usually would have. "And then my father, in tears, came into my room and began to try to convey to my terrified mind things it had never conceived before. It was, in fact, cancer and followed the usual course": treatment, operations, remission, return, death. "With my mother's death, all settled happiness, all that was tranquil and reliable, disappeared from my life."[18]

Still, there was Joy, which, when he wrote about it in capitalized form, wasn't for Lewis just a synonym for "delight" or "happiness," but something much more profound, linking memory and sensation with deep but intangible spiritual insights. It came when he remembered standing by a "flowering currant bush on a summer day," and "suddenly arose in me without warning, and as if from a depth not of years but of centuries, the memory" of playing with his brother, Warren, in their nursery. Joy flashed in his heart after reading three verses in an epic poem, or when contemplating the feeling or idea of a season—autumn—as it was evoked in his mind by the turn-of-the-century children's book *The Tale of Squirrel Nutkin.*[19]

Where, he wondered, did these sudden "stabs of Joy" come from?[20] And why were they so damned fleeting? Was Joy an illusion, glittering bits of folly flitting through his mind, or did it reflect an underlying reality? Was there some way to permanently align his life with Joy at its source? These were the questions that haunted Lewis's young life after his mother's death, as his relationship with his father became ever more strained.

In his own way, Albert Lewis was a devoted father: He cared very much that his two sons should succeed careerwise, and he took what he considered prudent steps to secure their material happiness. But he was an emotional illiterate and not exactly loving. Just when his younger son needed companionship, he had dispatched the older son to boarding school; the younger boy was left alone in a big old house with nothing to console him but the piles of books he read voraciously.

Then, his father did something worse, from the perspective of a boy desperate for security: He sent the young Lewis to a series of boarding schools in England, which he picked with the help of an agency tremendously successful at recruiting young men but with scant good sense about placing them—or at least, placing a sensitive, curious, decidedly unathletic boy like Lewis. In his memoir, Lewis remembered the worst of these, in an admittedly overwrought way, as "the concentration camp." Education, such as it was, meant throwing kids into "a jungle of dates, battles, exports, imports, and the like, forgotten as soon as learned and perfectly useless had they been remembered," as Lewis wrote. Despite this brute stuffing of minds with facts, he retained his love of learning. But as he grew into a teenager, Lewis began what he called his "slow apostasy": the loss of his faith, the disenchantment of his world.[21]

Left alone to navigate schools where young men who couldn't play sports were ruthlessly ostracized, Lewis was bound to feel enchantment dissipate. Then, too, he imbibed from science writers like Wells and Sir Robert Ball a picture of the cosmos as vast and indifferent, "menacing and unfriendly," denying any meaning to human beings.[22] He still loved literature, loved Norse and Anglo-Saxon myth and epic poetry. And these things supplied him with a kind of pseudo-religion animated by a pagan, nature-loving *sensibility*—but lacking any of the metaphysical beliefs and moral demands of traditional faith, which now stretched his credulity. The mythic, Northern sensibility also pointed him to his literary vocation: As he approached the end of secondary school, he resolved to pursue the life of the mind as an Oxford academic.

Oxford admitted him in 1917—but soon after he began his studies, he had to join his brother and some 5.5 million other subjects of the British Empire on the Western Front of World War I. The industrial-scale slaughter of the trenches forced Lewis to strike what he later called a "treaty with reality": He would serve his nation with his body but not permit the war to touch his mind.[23] The terms of the treaty extended to his memoir of his youth, *Surprised by Joy*, which barely discusses Lewis's wartime experience. What we do know is that he suffered a shrapnel wound in April 1918, during an assault on a German-held village in northern France. His condition was serious enough to require evacuation to England.

Lewis's father didn't visit him while he convalesced. For family feeling, he drew close to Jane Moore, the mother of a fellow officer-school cadet. Moore's son and Lewis had vowed to care for each other's kin if either died in the war. But McGrath and other biographers have concluded that something less wholesome was involved in the bond that developed between Lewis and Mrs. Moore after the war.

Lewis was eighteen when he first met Jane Moore; she, a handsome, married woman of forty-five. He hid the true nature of his relationship with Moore from his father and from the Oxford community he would call home for the next three and a half decades. And it was a weird love, indeed. Moore, it seems, played dual roles for him—at once his lover and the nurturing, if at times domineering, maternal figure he yearned for after his own mother's death.[24]

In January 1919, Lewis resumed his studies at Oxford. He did brilliantly as a student, earning first-class honors in classical languages, English, and what Americans would call the "great books" curriculum. But his young mind was divided against itself. There still fluttered in it inklings of the romantic sensibility that had enchanted his Irish childhood. At the same time, he was now ardently committed to what he called his "intellectual 'New Look'"—a hardheaded, and rather callow, materialism. "There was to be no more pessimism, no more self-pity, no flirtations with any idea of the supernatural, no romantic delusions," he wrote of his outlook during this period. What he needed was "good sense," and that meant "a retreat, almost a panic-stricken flight, from all that sort of romanticism which had hitherto been the chief concern of my life."[25]

This retreat from "romanticism" was almost a prerequisite of being an intellectual, including at Oxford. After World War I, the university faced enormous pressure to form practical men (and, increasingly, women) who could manage large public and private bureaucracies, and not just "clergymen, schoolmasters and professional men," as an editorial in *The Spectator* put it in 1922.[26] At this point, Lewis very much suffered from what we might call presentism: the unexamined bias that whatever is newest must also be truest or best. His own term for the condition was "chronological snobbery"—that is, "the uncritical acceptance of the intellectual climate common to our own age and the assumption that whatever has gone out of date is on that account discredited."[27]

What was new was best, and in the 1920s, that meant foremost a cynical spirit that called into doubt what little Joy sometimes flared up in his soul. He still recognized certain experiences—in nature, in literature—as beautiful or sublime or enchanting, to be sure. But under the press of the prevailing opinions, he came to conclude that even the highest subjective or spiritual aspirations were an illusion, often mere vehicles for baser desires. "Now what, I asked myself, were all my delectable mountains and western gardens but sheer fantasies?" Lewis wrote. "I decided I had done with all that. No more Avalon, no more Hesperides."[28]

Joy was, at most, an "aesthetic experience." It was "valuable," so far as that went.[29] But the moral or spiritual stirrings that came with Joy were suspect, and certainly not connected to any deeper reality or meaning. The romantic son of Ireland had traded his spirit-filled glens and meadows for the steely skepticism of the modern age.

JOY RECOVERED

But then Lewis changed his mind again—this time, for good. A fellow Oxford student named Owen Barfield acted as the catalyst. The pair met on campus and became fast friends, launching a four-decade-long dialogue carried out in the classroom, in the cozy pubs of Oxfordshire, and along the country trails they toured every year. Barfield's erudition awed Lewis ("Barfield has probably forgotten more than I ever knew," he wrote in his diary).[30]

Lewis's "chronological snobbery" was a special and frequent target of Barfield's critiques. The fact that any ancient idea—say, the immortality of the soul—had fallen out of favor, Barfield insisted, didn't suffice to discredit it. Lewis summarized his friend's position:

Was it ever refuted (and if so by whom, where, and how conclusively), or did it merely die away as fashions do? If the latter, this tells us nothing about its truth or falsehood. From seeing this, one passes to the realization that our own age is also "a period," and certainly has, like all periods, its own characteristic illusions. They are likeliest to lurk in those widespread assumptions which are so ingrained in the age that no one dares to attack or feels it necessary to defend them.[31]

Those afflicted with chronological snobbery could easily overlook or dismiss good ideas from the past *merely because they were from the past.* Lewis knew his Plato, and he revered Shakespeare. Did the fact that such seminal figures lacked knowledge of electromagnetism or the true nature of gravity invalidate their moral insights? Of course not. And why would the moral or aesthetic or spiritual opinions of a scientific age be any more secure than those of earlier times, if *every* age has its "characteristic illusions"? His own age had somehow convinced itself that the mere discovery of poison gas justified using it on human beings.

There was another, still deeper problem with Lewis's "New Look." If only those things "revealed by the senses" were truly knowable and believable, he realized, then his own materialist convictions rested on feet of clay. How could he be sure of the truth of the New Look, he wondered, if the only knowable reality is "the universe of the senses, aided by instruments and coordinated so as to form 'science' "?[32] The New Look itself was a philosophical claim or idea, after all, not something "out there" in the world and observable by the senses.

There were two ways out of this dilemma. One would have been to dig in his heels and insist that the New Look—and along with it *all* philosophical ideas, moral feelings, aesthetic judgments, and so on— were nothing but "behaviors," things people did in response to external stimuli, patterns of conduct reinforced by reward and punishment. That was the gist of the theory called behaviorism. As crudely reductive as it sounds, it had great purchase among many intellectuals of Lewis's time, because it promised to cut through all speculative reasoning, all romance and sensibility, all emotion and aesthetic experience—to present hard, experimentally proven *facts.*

But behaviorism suffered from the same shortcoming as the halfway house of the New Look. That is, it couldn't justify *itself*. Moreover, even granting its truth as a factual account of how people form judgments about beauty, morality, and so on, behaviorism couldn't tell Lewis whether those judgments were *any good*.

The pleasure I feel when I watch an artful performance of *A Midsummer Night's Dream* may well have roots in behavioral, evolutionary, and/or neurobiological phenomena. But science can't grasp—it can't measure—the subjective experience of beauty, even if it can graph the biological markers in hormonal surges. Why is *A Midsummer Night's Dream* considered a masterpiece? It is no answer at all to say that seeing it performed well causes certain synapses to fire in the brain.

For these reasons, Lewis came to see radical materialism as simply implausible. "I cannot force my thought into that shape," he wrote, "any more than I can scratch my ear with my big toe."[33]

So what was the other path out of his dilemma? It was to drop the New Look altogether and embrace an older worldview. This "Old Look"—my term, to be clear—perceived a "deeper order of things," as McGrath puts it, an all-encompassing truth or reason hidden behind the universe of bare facts.[34] Science could relate valuable information about it, to be sure, but this deeper order was much more than scientific facts. The order addressed itself to Lewis, if he would but listen, by other channels, as well: through art and the experience of beauty, through sentiments and premonitions, through myth, music, and epic poetry, through prophets and philosophers, through Scripture and liturgy. It spoke through Joy.

In a proper scheme of knowledge, Lewis came to believe, a narrowly scientific-technical way of knowing the world wouldn't lord it over these other ways of knowing, but live in concord with them. What might that look like?

"Only One Kind of *Hnau*"

When the spaceship lands on Malacandra, Weston and Devine waste no time in carrying out their evil objective: to deliver Ransom to the *sorns,* the planet's natives, for who knows what horrible purpose. After unpacking their ship, they compel Ransom at gunpoint to head toward a body of water. Across a vast distance filled with "dazzling blue soda-water, and acres of rose-red soapsuds," glistening against the planet's white-pinkish land, Ransom spots the *sorns:* "spindly and flimsy things, twice or three times the height of a man," "crazily thin and elongated in the leg," "top-heavily pouted in the chest," "stalky, flexible-looking distortions of earthly bipeds."[35]

There are six of them, and they are on the move—toward him.

At the mere sight of the *sorns,* Ransom defies his revolver-toting captors and flees. For a while, he wanders the Malacandrian wilderness desperately. But then his fortune improves. His skills as an expert in languages allow him to communicate with the Malacandrian natives. It turns out that his initial fight-or-flight instinct was completely misplaced; the Malacandrians are nothing like what he and his captors imagined.

There are three species, each inhabiting a different layer of the planet's surface. In the caves of the high mountains live the *sorns,* the thin and hugely tall humanoids, who excel at abstract thought and what might be called scientific rationality. The *hrossa* inhabit the rivers and valleys: seal-like creatures with shimmering black hair, adept at fishing and hunting—and epic poetry and mythmaking. Finally, in the hot depths dwell the *pfifltriggi,* frog- and insect-like, good with their hands, miners and builders and technicians. All three are what the Malacandrians call *hnau*—creatures possessed of rationality, sentience. Each *hnau* species has its own legitimate domain; none is entitled to dominate the others.

Ransom at first befriends the *hrossa,* the lovable seal-like species. Through them, he begins to unlock the secrets of Malacandrian society. At one point, he asks his *hrossa* hosts: Which of the two, the *hrossa* or the *sorns,* know or understand more about the world?

But the *hrossa* don't think in such terms. The *sorns,* they tell him, are "admittedly good at finding out things about the stars and understanding the darker utterances" of the planet's mysterious ruler. They know much about Malacandrian history. Yet the *sorns* are also "helpless in a boat and could not fish to save their lives, could hardly swim, could make no poetry, and even when the *hrossa* made it for them, could only understand the inferior sorts."[36]

Coming from a planet increasingly controlled by Weston types, Ransom takes this to mean that the *sorns* form the Malacandrian "intelligentsia" and "must be the real rulers, however it is disguised."[37] But that isn't, in fact, the case. The hyperintelligent, rationalistic *sorns* don't see themselves as being better or more essential than the *hrossa,* just as the *hrossa* don't look down their noses at the technically proficient, craft-making *pfifltriggi.* Each of these forms of knowledge has its place, revealing important things about the order that governs the cosmos. The scientific *sorns* don't try to "debunk" the knowledge contained in *hrossa* poetry, with its themes of valor, honor, and comradeship. And why would they? The knowledge conveyed by poetry isn't the kind that can be scientifically debunked—or proved, for that matter. (What would it even mean to do so?) And yet poetic knowledge *can be* true knowledge about the human—or in this case, alien—heart.

Ransom himself *feels* the truth of *hrossa* ideals when, midway through his Malacandrian journey, his fellow earthlings shoot one of his *hross* friends for no reason other than sheer human malice, aided by the technological know-how of twentieth-century Western civilization. Weston and Devine are trying to track down Ransom, and as soon as they find him mingling with the *hrossa*—*bang!* they take down Ransom's friend. A guilt-wracked Ransom draws the dying *hross*'s "round, seal-like head" to himself and offers an apology:

"It is through me that this has happened. It is the other [humans] who have hit you, the bent two that brought me to Malacandra. They can throw death at a distance with a thing they have made. I should have told you. We are all of a bent race. We have come here to bring evil on Malacandra. We are only half *hnau*...." His speech died away into the inarticulate. He did not know the words for "forgive," or "shame," or "fault," hardly the word for "sorry".... But the *hross* seemed to understand.[38]

Which species in this scene is the more upright and noble? The "simpler," seal-like alien that delights in friendship and hunting, song and poetry? Or the suspicious, arrogant terror from outer space—human beings—who would kill a sentient creature without justification? Can science justify the killing of innocent beings, merely because the technology that enables the killing works efficiently and is more "advanced" than its victim could understand?

Here, Lewis reveals his powers as a master allegorist: When science tries to claim an exclusive monopoly on knowledge, as Weston does when he dismisses all ancient morality as romantic rubbish, it acts barbarously. Barbarism, in this sense, isn't the mere opposite of civilization, but simply the refusal to communicate where communion is possible.

By this definition, the modern scientific outlook is a barbarous enterprise. It tears down traditional knowledge; it dismisses subjective ways of knowing; it rejects communion with the past, except, that is, on scientific-technical terms. Weston and Devine are thus quite literally barbarian invaders. They are highly educated, scientifically and technically proficient barbarians, to be sure, but barbarians all the same.

MALACANDRA IS AN allegory of knowledge. In his imaginary Mars, Lewis presents a touching and vivid picture of how different ways of knowing might coexist in harmony, without the browbeating of one by another, as too often happened in the real world of Lewis's time.

The author makes this critique more explicit later in *Out of the Silent Planet,* when Ransom comes to befriend the *sorns.* The aliens quiz the professor about his world (ours), and they are struck by the fact that "we had only one kind of *hnau:* They thought this must have far-reaching effects in the narrowing of our sympathies and even our thought."[39]

Weston's villainy illustrates the effects of this narrowing. He dreams of colonizing other planets and, if need be, eradicating their inhabitants to make room for advanced, scientific civilization. At a deeper, allegorical level, Weston stands for the misguided yearning to enshrine scientific knowledge or facts as the *only* kind of knowledge, to "colonize" realms that rightly belong to other ways of knowing.

The Malacandrian natives eventually arrest Weston and Devine and bring them before their ruler, an angel or spiritual creature they call Oyarsa. Ransom, too, is brought before Oyarsa, though he is accorded greater respect on account of the honorable way he has conducted himself while sojourning on Malacandra.

At first, Weston refuses to believe that Oyarsa even exists. The voice of the spirit addressing the gathering of Malacandrians, he thinks, must be the work of one of the *hrossa* playing ventriloquist ("common among savages," he tells Devine). Faced with the higher rationality of Oyarsa, and failing to unmask the "witchdoctor," Weston goes hysterical, now vainly offering shiny beads to appease the Malacandrians, now threatening them with genocide.[40]

Finally, he delivers a speech in his own defense. Lewis could have lifted Weston's words almost verbatim from the cold-blooded arguments made in the 1920s and '30s by the likes of Haldane and Darrow ("chloroform unfit children!"). But there is an amusing twist: Owing to Weston's infacility with the Malacandrian tongue, Ransom steps in to translate, with Lewis rendering the "translation" in English. The translation process unmasks, in hilarious fashion, just how ridiculous scientistic arrogance sounds under even the most elementary moral scrutiny. Weston tells Oyarsa:

I may seem a vulgar robber, but I bear on my shoulders the destiny of the human race. Your tribal life with its stone-age weapons and beehive huts, its primitive coracles and elementary social structure, has nothing to compare with our civilization—with our science, medicine and law, our armies, our architecture, our commerce, and our transport system which is rapidly annihilating space and time. Our right to supersede you is the right of the higher over the lower.[41]

Ransom translates this into "Malacandrian," which finally is nothing but the language of ordinary moral knowledge:

Among us, Oyarsa, there is a kind of *hnau* who will take other *hnaus'* food—and things, when they are not looking. He says he is not an ordinary one of that kind. He says what he does now will make very different things happen to those of our people who are not yet born. He says that, among you, *hnau* of one kindred all live together and the *hrossa* have spears like those we used a very long time ago and your huts are small and round and your boats small and light and like our old ones, and you have only one ruler. He says it is different with us. He says we know much. There is a thing happens in our world when the body of a living creature feels pains and becomes weak, and he says we sometimes know how to stop it. . . . He says we build very big and strong huts of stone and other things like the *pfifl-triggi*. And he says we exchange many things among ourselves and can carry heavy weights very quickly a long way.[42]

And so on.

Note that Weston begins by conceding there are types of conduct that are obviously wrong: theft, for example. Nevertheless, he insists, his own project of theft, murder, and conquest on an interplanetary scale is justified by the superiority of his civilization over that of the Malacandrians: "We," after all, have modern medicine, powerful weaponry and other technology, complex administrative structures, big buildings, science.

The colonialist, eugenic, and racial ideologies of the early twentieth century rested on just such arguments: that "advanced" civilizations had the right, by dint of their scientific advancement, to displace, subdue, and destroy "primitive" peoples and to exterminate the less intelligent. The "Malacandrians" are thus just stand-ins for the older moral tradition, with its thou shalts and thou shalt nots that bind everyone, whether or not a person has mastered the fundamental equations of physics. The contrary position—insisting that sheer accumulation of facts or technique can allow us to take moral shortcuts—doesn't make sense. It is as stupid as Weston's speech sounds when translated into "Malacandrian."

Weston, of course, believes that he is doing the right thing. But lacking a moral vocabulary, he can't quite articulate his reasons as a moral statement. If we were to drag one out of him, it might be this: that scientific civilization *ought* to persist, because it is good for the scientific enterprise to go on and for some humans to continue to enjoy its fruits. Sound familiar? We have returned, full circle, to the question that set us off on this journey to Malacandra.

More Than Raw Material

As I write, the world is battling a horrific respiratory virus that singles out for harm the elderly and the infirm. We must defeat it, and we will defeat it, through human solidarity and, yes, with scientific ingenuity. But afterward, the question would still remain: Why? Why are we prepared to shut down entire economies to save the most vulnerable? Why do we especially admire the doctors and nurses who risk their own lives to save those of others afflicted by the novel coronavirus? "Malacandrians" would have a moral answer to those questions. Do the proponents of the scientific outlook have such an answer?

The scientific outlook can't, and won't, bother with questions having to do with ultimate meaning, the stock-in-trade of faith and philosophy. And it insists that such questions don't belong to an inquiry into truth in the first place, since the answers don't take scientific form. Meaning and purpose, however, force us to consider nothing less than the value of being. Given the monopoly on knowledge they claim, proponents of the scientific outlook should be able to furnish an answer to our central question. Can they?

The stock answer, I suppose, is that our instinct to preserve our species is justification enough to do so. The problem is that animal instinct alone can't suffice to ratify the existence of a rational being—a *hnau*. "Because instinct says so" is a deeply unsatisfying answer for a *hnau* who defies instinct on a daily basis. No wonder many people today reject the instinctive answer and proclaim that human life *isn't* worth perpetuating, be they extreme climate-change activists, "antinatalists" like the South African philosopher David Benatar, or affluent classes across the West, growing ranks of whom are delaying having children, if they have them at all.

C. S. Lewis saw this coming. He argued that instinct, science's go-to answer to our central question, just isn't enough. For one thing, we have *many* instincts, and they "are at war."[43] The instinct to preserve our own lives battles with the instinct to protect our loved ones and communities. Which, Lewis asked, should we listen to?

> Each instinct, if you listen to it, will claim to be gratified at the expense of all the rest. By the very act of listening to one rather than to others we have already prejudged the case. If we did not bring to the examination of our instincts a knowledge of their comparative dignity we could never learn it from them. And that knowledge cannot itself be instinctive: the judge cannot be one of the parties judged; or, if he is, the decision is worthless.[44]

So much for the instinctive answer. Why, then, is there a duty to preserve the human species? Why is it good for us to go on?

Posing such questions, Lewis argued, immediately takes us out of the domain of science and technique and into the realm of that deeper order of truth he discovered at Oxford under his friend Barfield's influence. We, too, must be prepared to surrender our share of a "chronological snobbery" that has now prevailed for some four hundred years: It is a mistake to apply the scientific outlook, perfectly legitimate in its own domain, to the *whole of life*.

We all face serious philosophical, spiritual, and moral problems in the course of life: in moments of existential despair and of euphoric joy; when we are awestruck by the mere fact that we exist; or, more mundanely, when we come upon ethical forks in the road, forcing us to choose between the "easy" but unethical path and the one that is difficult but righteous. We can't leave it up to scientists to solve these problems for us.

Plenty of scientists are humble enough to accept science's limitations, of course. But the ideologues of scientism are a different matter. At best, they smuggle in their own ideals in response to such problems, even as they claim to have debunked all idealism. At worst, they invite us to despair (and immorality) by suggesting that the timeless problems of being human don't have right or wrong, true or false, answers—since neither the questions nor the potential answers can be kept contained in the world of sensible, measurable facts.

When one form of *hnau* negates all others, we finally risk negating ourselves as *fully* human beings: There is much about us, after all, that can't be plugged into scientific observations or mathematical equations—into "facts." As Lewis warned, "It is in man's power to treat himself as a mere 'natural object' and his own judgments of value as raw material for scientific manipulation to alter at will." But "if man chooses to treat himself as raw material, raw material he will be."[45] If we should treat human life itself as a bare fact or an experiment, much as science treats the objects of scientific inquiry—well, experiments can fail. Tampering with nature can yield hideous results. The yearning to "improve" the human race has too often led us to shameful acts of inhumanity against the most vulnerable.

Scientism, finally, alienates us from ourselves. Lewis knew the feeling all too well from his fashionable New Look phase—when he forced himself to deny the great truths that arose from within himself and from the world around him, merely because they couldn't be articulated as "facts." Once he abandoned the New Look, Joy gleamed once more: on the leafy, storied walking paths of Oxford, in the company of good friends, in his philosophical and literary work. He recovered, too, something of the peace shattered by his mother's death and the traumas that attended it. Gone was some of the fustiness that had characterized his materialist days, and he could approach even the wrinkles in his life—chief among them, the demands imposed by a declining and difficult Mrs. Moore—with a sober sense of moral duty. Joy and order, it seemed, went hand in hand.

Guided by the whispered promptings of Joy, C. S. Lewis also found his way back to a vibrant Christian faith in 1931, by which point he had been appointed a teacher at Magdalen College. He would go on to win global fame as a Christian apologist and as the author of some of the sanest, most humane books of the last century. He died at his beloved Oxford in 1963, aged sixty-four.

IS GOD REASONABLE?

———

If science can't supply a good reason for why we should go on, what can? For C. S. Lewis, the answer was faith: the will to believe that we are the visible handiwork of the invisible God.

Through eyes of faith, we can see ourselves as part of a divinely ordered scheme of creation—and happy is the part that *knows* it is part of a whole. There is no firmer defense against that shattering sense of cosmic loneliness and futility that has menaced men and women since time immemorial. Faith in God assures us that there is ultimate meaning in creation, even if we can't always discern it. At a minimum, it tells us that being is preferable to nonbeing, since our own being owes to the benevolent action of the divine.

But can we believe without betraying our minds? The prevailing attitude today is that we might choose to assent to God—but only by leaping across the demands of reason. The religious believer who prays for national deliverance from catastrophe, say, or who thanks God before every meal is thought to act against reason in doing so. The activity of the believer, in this view, has everything to do with *feelings,* such as guilt, gratitude, connectedness, yearning, awe, wonder, joy. These feelings, we are told, point us to God *over against* cold rationality. And if religious belief lacks a rational basis, then no wonder believers would act irrationally.

Many believers go along with such an account, renouncing any claim to reason as the price of admission into faith. We see this, for example, in the suburban Baton Rouge pastor who defiantly continued to hold services at the height of the COVID-19 crisis, telling his congregants, very few of them wearing protective masks, "I've just got to get to Jesus. . . . Come on America, let's get back to Jesus."[1] A more repulsively stupid example came from my native Iran, where in February 2020 two men filmed themselves *licking* Shiite shrines in the holy city of Qom, as if to dare the virus to infect them and possibly others (Iranian authorities later arrested the pair).[2]

"That's just irrational," you might be tempted to say. Yet some religious communities are *happy* to insist that faith was never supposed to be rational. Human reason, like everything else about human beings, is untrustworthy, fallible, broken. Meanwhile, God has revealed himself to us through his prophets, inspired texts, and actions in history. Our responsibility is not to think, but to believe and render worship—even if that latter means imperiling our own and others' lives amid a pandemic.

Most faithful don't go so far, but many are nevertheless quick to scorn rationality when it comes to their relations with God. No less influential a figure than Martin Luther infamously called reason "the devil's whore."[3] While Luther himself was a suppler philosopher than such rhetoric might suggest, his thundering disdain for reason continues to reverberate among many Christians. Their posture mirrors the view of religious faith promoted by the real-world Westons of our first chapter: Faith is an unreasonable act, and so, therefore, must be its object. But is that correct? *Or is God reasonable?*

FROM THE BREADCRUMB PATH TO THE ROYAL ROAD

Before we can decide if God is reasonable, we need to consider a story about reason itself. This story might surprise you, if you, like me, were reared on a narrative that sharply divides the history of Western thought into three distinct phases: a classical period that saw reason flowering in ancient Greece; a long era called "the Dark Ages," when the Catholic Church locked up reason in one of its dungeons; and finally, something called a "Renaissance" followed by an "Age of

Enlightenment," which scattered the darknesses of the Dark Ages and set reason free.

As we shall see, this narrative is almost exactly the opposite of the truth.

Many ancient peoples wondered about the causes behind things. But the Greeks elevated such reasoning to a concerted intellectual discipline. A Greek thinker, Pythagoras of Samos, gave that discipline a name, philosophy (literally, "love of wisdom"), two and a half millennia ago. To philosophize, to love and to seek wisdom, meant to pierce the veil of myth that shrouded the pagan world, to find truth by means of rational inquiry—reason.

The Greeks encountered a world with an endless array of things in it—things, moreover, that appeared to be in constant flux: from the motion of the heavenly bodies, to the regular cycle of the seasons, to the shifts that took place in the human soul, its tendency to rise to virtue or descend to vice and corruption. The philosophers sought the fundamental principle or deepest origin of reality that could unite all this variety and account for all this change.

Studying the natural world, they made remarkable discoveries (the roundness of the earth, the predictability of eclipses, etc.), even if they fell far short of modern scientific standards and got many things wrong. These physical investigations led the earliest philosophers to essentially materialist conclusions not unlike those that prevail today: They identified various fundamental elements—fire, water, air, bodily humors—as the ultimate cause of things.

That is, until Socrates (c. 469–399 B.C.) arrived on the scene. The historical Socrates didn't leave behind any written works; the Socrates we know was largely a literary creation of his greatest student, Plato (c. 429–347 B.C.). For Plato's Socrates, treating physical elements or particles as ultimate causes couldn't satisfy a rational mind—indeed, it often yielded absurd explanations. In the dialogue *Phaedo,* for example, Socrates recounts his own intellectual journey for his disciples while sitting in prison, awaiting execution at the tail end of his life. He tells them that he began by examining the work of his philosophical predecessors but ultimately came to reject their approach. These other philosophers, he charges, didn't use the "mind at all" but ascribed causation to "air and ether and waters and a lot of other strange things."[4]

How, for example, would one of these pre-Socratics explain why Socrates was imprisoned? "He'd say," Socrates mockingly tells his friends,

> first of all, that the reason I'm sitting here, is that my body is made up of bones and sinews, and whereas the bones are solid and separated from each other by joints, the sinews are such as to tense up and relax and surround the bones along with flesh and skin that envelops them. So when the bones are being moved about in their joints, the relaxing and tensing of the sinews makes me somehow able to move my limbs, and for this reason I'm sitting here with my limbs bent.[5]

None of this, of course, had anything to do with the *true* cause. Socrates was in captivity awaiting execution because his fellow Athenians had convicted him of impiety and of corrupting the youth. Though he could have run from the law, he "thought it was more just and finer to accept whatever sentence the state ordained."[6] Socrates's bones were a necessary precondition to his taking a certain course of action, but the latter couldn't have been reduced to the former.[7]

If particles and bodily humors couldn't get at the true cause of things, then philosophy had to look elsewhere—to seek transcendent, rather than immanent, causes for change. This Socratic shift heralded a revolution in human thought: It would lead Plato and his most illustrious student, Aristotle (384–322 B.C.), to conclude that there must be some unchangeable being in whose absolute being all others participate (Plato), or some unchanged cause that is the ultimate cause of all other change (Aristotle).

Which is a roundabout way of saying that one strand of Greek thought reached the God of classical theism by the light of naked reason.

AS THE GREEKS outgrew their city-states and formed larger kingdoms, and then expanded massively into an empire in the fourth century B.C., their philosophy proved both challenging and enticing to the peoples they conquered.

Now, among the nations the Greeks subdued was one people, the Jews, who professed faith in a singular, universal God. A God who claimed sovereignty not just over any one place but over all of creation, the heavens, and the earth. A God who laughed at his rival deities as mere local, manmade idols, impotent compared to himself (cf. Ps 115). A God who identified himself as the very ground of being, who said his name was "I AM" (Ex 3:14).[8] Moreover, accident or providence (take your pick) had readied the Jewish religion for an encounter with Greek philosophy. Even before the Hellenistic conquest, the Babylonian exile had already forced the Jews to articulate the universalistic aspects of their faith in the midst of a hostile culture.[9]

Greek philosophy sought after a first cause, the unchanging source of all change in the cosmos; the Jews worshipped a God proclaimed to be all those things. The Greeks were intrigued, especially as Greek translations of the Jewish holy book began circulating in the Hellenistic world in the three centuries before the advent of Christ. A courtship of sorts was afoot between Greek philosophy and Jewish revelation, though like so many courtships, it wasn't without its heartbreaks, not least for the Jews, the conquered party.

Even so, the courtship continued to deepen, especially with the dawn of Christianity. In Christian scriptures, composed in Greek, the same God of the Jews revealed himself even more explicitly as that which the Greek sages had always desired. The opening verse of the Gospel of Saint John couldn't have but astonished the Greek world with its philosophical overtones: "In the beginning was the *Logos,* and the *Logos* was with God, and the *Logos* was God" (1:1).

The Greek *Logos* in this verse is usually rendered in English as "the

Word," but to a Greek speaker, it also would have meant "reason." "In the beginning was reason, and reason was with God, and reason was God." *Reason was God.* Socrates and his heirs had courted a God who satisfied reason, a reasonable God.[10] Now the courtship had finally been consummated in a marriage. Yet it would take more than a millennium for this marriage of faith and reason to produce its greatest defender and intellectual heir.

NOT ALL EARLY Christians were inclined to answer philosophy's call in charity. Some utterly contemned philosophy. They argued that since God had fully revealed himself, first on Mount Sinai and then in an even more intimate way as the incarnate God of the Cross, all philosophy was vanity, at best pointless, and at worst likely to confuse and mislead the faithful.

They remembered Saint Paul's warning to "see to it that no one makes a prey of you by philosophy and empty deceit, according to human tradition, according to the elemental spirits of the universe, and not according to Christ" (Col 2:8). Elsewhere, the apostle had declared that the "foolishness of God is wiser than men" (I Cor 1:25). Taking their cue from these and other passages, ignoring context and contrary messages that pointed to reason as a pathway to God, the anti-philosophy hard-liners dismissed human reason wholesale.

The second-century Church Father Tertullian, for example, raged against philosophy as "the rash interpreter of the nature and dispensation of God." He traced all heresy to early Christians' misguided attempts to reach truth by means of the "world's wisdom." Salvation lies on a hilltop on the outskirts of Jerusalem called Calvary, Tertullian thundered, and "what indeed has Athens to do with Jerusalem? What concord is there between the Academy and the Church, what between heretics and Christians? . . . Away with all attempts to produce a mottled Christianity of Stoic, Platonic and dialectic composition!"[11]

This anti-philosophical strand of faith persisted as antiquity gave way to the Middle Ages. In the twelfth century, for example, Saint

Bernard of Clairvaux, the hugely influential French monk-theologian, urged his students to walk with the confidence of the psalmist, who sings: "I have more understanding than all my teachers" (119:99). And "wherefore, O my brother, dost thou make such a boast?" Bernard asked. "The reasonings of Plato and the subtleties of Aristotle? 'God forbid!,' thou answerest. 'It is because I have sought thy commandments, O Lord.'" A poem from the thirteenth century similarly gloated that the Lord greets "only a pure and simple mind," while "far behind lags the world's philosophy."¹²

Not exactly an attitude befitting a religion whose God is reason itself (cf. Jn 1:1). As the eminent twentieth-century historian of philosophy Étienne Gilson has written, "Had the Middle Ages produced men of this type only, the period would fully deserve the title of Dark Ages."¹³

But the Church in antiquity and then the Middle Ages didn't, in fact, produce thinkers of "this type only." There were others who saw philosophy and faith as friends, and among their ranks were some of the Church's greatest scholars and thinkers, above all, Augustine of Hippo, whom we will meet in a later chapter. To these pro-philosophy believers, it was clear that even before disclosing himself in revelation, God had dropped clues in his creation, like breadcrumbs sown in a dark forest. The greatest of the Greek philosophers had followed this breadcrumb path by rational inquiry and found something of God. Human reason, then, was no contemptible vanity. On the contrary, the kind of rational understanding sought by the Greeks was much to be desired.

But with the benefit of revelation, the breadcrumb path had become a royal road to wisdom that lay wide open to all humanity, not just a brilliant, philosophically trained few. The philosophical quest would go on as before, but now the *starting point* was faith, and its task was to understand revelation by means of reason.

This way of relating reason and revelation opened a new space for philosophy in religious life. But it also raised a new question: How were believers supposed to blend faith and reason, especially when it came to the biblical accounts of miracles and other mysteries that surpassed rational understanding?[14] This was *the* philosophical problem of the Middle Ages. Many thinkers wrestled with it, but only one truly bested it. Yet during his youth, his quietness and introversion initially made his peers think him dense. They even nicknamed him the Dumb Ox.

THE LIGHT OF THE DARK AGES

The life of Thomas Aquinas is the stuff of legends. A scion of Italian nobility, he was probably born in 1224 or 1225 at his father's castle at Roccasecca, in southern Italy.[15] The county of Aquino, from which Thomas got his last name, was a seat of family power. Thomas's family expected him to enter the nearby monastery at Monte Cassino and eventually assume the abbacy—a prestigious and likely profitable position.

On May 3, 1231, Thomas's father offered the young boy, age five or six, to the Monte Cassino monks along with a stash of gold "for the remission of his sins" (it was typical for noble families to give alms to the monasteries where they pledged their children as trainees).[16] After a decade or so of basic studies, Thomas decamped to Naples for higher learning. It was there that the teenaged Thomas came into contact with the newly founded Order of Preachers.

The Dominicans, as they were known (after their founder, Saint Dominic), promoted intense intellectual formation and study. Thomas joined the order at age nineteen, dashing his family's dreams of securing the Monte Cassino abbacy. To change his mind, the family kidnapped Thomas and placed him under house arrest, during which time he committed the entire Bible to memory and chased away a prostitute hired by his brothers to seduce him out of his Dominican vocation.

After a year, his family yielded to his persistence, and Thomas was free to study in Paris and at the Dominicans' new college in Cologne. There, he stood out for being both very taciturn and very wide in girth; a contemporary described him as "very fat," while his first bi-ographer reported that he was "large in body."[17] Combined, the two qualities earned him his famous bovine nickname. Eventually, how-ever, a colossal intelligence burst through the young man's colossal frame, leading his teacher and mentor, the German Dominican Al-bertus Magnus, to prophesy: "We call him the Dumb Ox, but he will make resound in his doctrine such a bellowing that it will echo throughout the entire world."[18]

Once Thomas Aquinas finished his studies, the order sent him to teach at the University of Paris, then the beating heart of Christian intellectual life. We might pause here to note the sheer cosmopolitan-ism of Thomas's environment: From an early age, he was immersed in universities and other institutions of high learning that spanned Europe, overcoming myriad local prejudices thanks to a shared faith (Catholic) and language (Latin).

This academic network existed to prepare priests to carry out the Church's mission. Priests had to understand what exactly they were doing when they heard confessions, say, or celebrated the Mass. And they had to master a body of orthodox doctrine that would allow them to root out heresy among their flocks and persuade unbelievers. All this "medieval" activity required intense reasoning, even from those Christians who rejected philosophy by name.

By the time Thomas arrived in Paris, however, the old synthesis between faith and reason faced a new challenge, posed by Muslim scholars whom war and conquest had brought into contact with Christians. Though they believed in a very different sort of God, many Muslim thinkers also grappled with the relationship between faith and reason as they discovered it in Greek philosophy. One such thinker in particular, Ibn Rushd, put forward an unalloyed rational-ism that proved perilously tempting to Aquinas's peers.

The jurist Ibn Rushd (1126–1198), often referred to by his Latinized name, Averroes, spent most of his life in Muslim Spain. His life's proj-ect, as Gilson tells us, was to show Muslims that "some sort of agree-ment between religious faith and philosophical reason was not an absolute impossibility," provided faith "keeps to its own place" and philosophy "is intelligent enough to realize the specific function of religion."[19] Fine. But how?

Well, the Quran itself instructs believers to seek natural wisdom, the domain of philosophy. "Reflect, you [who] have vision," the Quran commands Muslims (59:2). In other words, apply reason to the world and to the events unfolding around you. Elsewhere, the Muslim holy book praises those who "give thought to the creation of the heaven and the earth" (3:191). Thus, as Averroes put it, in a tight syllogism in one of his treatises, "if the theological study of the world is philosophy, and if the [Islamic] Law commands such study, then the Law commands philosophy."[20]

If God positively commanded philosophical reason, it fell to Muslim thinkers to adopt the best reasoning available, and that meant Greek philosophy. But if Greek philosophy was so important to God, and if it was indeed possible to discover God by means of philosophical reasoning, why then did the Almighty reveal himself to Muhammad and the prophets who came before him? Why indeed bother with miracles and holy books when all truth could be found in contemplating Aristotle's books?

Averroes's shocking answer was that God had to reveal himself through preachers and miracles because most men and women couldn't handle philosophy. If all people were philosophers, perhaps revelation wouldn't have been necessary. For Averroes, the Quran was "miraculous" only insofar as it taught lesser minds what higher minds could understand independently.[21]

Averroes's ideas gained a wide following among Christian thinkers in Aquinas's time; there even emerged a school of Latin Averroists. These thinkers were in a tough bind, for they were churchmen and taught at universities controlled by the Roman church. In these settings, it was impermissible to claim, after Averroes, that unalloyed reason was superior to revelation, and none ever said so explicitly.

A more discomfiting feature of Latin Averroism was that it required its adherents to uphold diametrically opposed ideas at the same time: As men of the cloth, they preached that every person is endowed with a unique intellect, known and loved individually by God, whereas Averroist philosophy deduced that all humankind shares one collective mind. As Christians, the Latin Averroists believed that the universe had a beginning in time, whereas philosophy held the universe to be eternal. And so on.

In each of these cases, the Latin Averroists considered their chosen position to be the absolutely necessary outcome of natural reason. But God's revelation was also unimpeachable. In the philosophy faculty, two plus two was four; among the theologians, two plus two could equal five. They assented genuinely to theology but also viewed philosophy's objections as insurmountable by human reason.

Okay, but so what? Why would any of this matter to the ordinary medieval man or woman? Isn't all this just the kind of abstract speculation that made medieval philosophy so tedious and irrelevant to ordinary life? Actually, no. At stake was nothing less than how—or even whether—we as individuals could fit into the world.

The so-called double-truth theory of the Averroists—two plus two makes four in philosophy but five in theology—ripped reason away from our search for ultimate meaning. Taken to its logical conclusion, it suggested that reason and faith could never share the keys to the household of reality, but had to rotate in and out like the unfriendly owners of a timeshare condo. When faith stopped by, reason had to pack its bags and take its leave, and vice versa. Either God was unreasonable, or reason was bereft of God.

Averroism had tangled the medieval mind in quite the knot. Then along came Aquinas to cut the knot with the scissors of common sense.

One Truth and Only One

Aquinas could be called *the* philosopher of common sense. I don't mean that he followed mere convention or conventional wisdom, but rather that his writing rested on a principle every good teacher knows: You begin with what students know before rising to things they don't.

For all the difficulty of his writings, Aquinas always began by considering the world as ordinary men and women experienced it before moving to abstract reasoning and judgments; he was foremost a realist.

Thus, he solved the two-truths dilemma by comparing, on one hand, how people learned about things or events in the observable world—the growth of crops, the flight of birds—and, on the other, how they assented to religious teachings. And he noticed that the two forms of assent were distinct. Seeing and believing weren't, in fact, the same thing. Out of this simple insight, Aquinas fashioned one of the most elegant and path-breaking ideas in the philosophy of religion.

"It is impossible," he wrote in his masterwork, the *Summa theologiae,* "that one and the same thing should be believed and seen by the same person. Hence it is equally impossible for one and the same thing to be an object of science and of belief for the same person."[22] You either grasp something on your own—or I tell you that you should believe something, and you can choose to go along or not, depending on how much credence you lend my authority in the matter.

The distinction is present in many mundane situations. Consider the example (offered by Gilson) of a lecturer referring his students to a certain obscure passage in Aristotle's writings. "If you look up X passage," he might tell them, "you will find Y written there." Assuming the students don't pull out their smartphones to double-check the lecturer's claim instantaneously, they can choose to believe him or not, depending on how much they trust his authority. While they are sitting in his classroom, the lecturer's claim about the passage in Aristotle is an object of faith for the students. Afterward, of course, they will be free to check the passage in question, at which point the claim becomes an object of science. In both instances, the lecturer's claim is either true or not true. If the claim is false, then it really is false, and the fact that it is an object of faith for the students while they are in the classroom doesn't magically make it true.

There is only *one truth*.

Something might be an object of faith for a mortal (the Trinity, for example, whose existence is only hinted at in the Bible) but observed directly by another class of rational creatures (the angels, we are told, see God face-to-face).[23] There is no rational argument in this life that could prove that the godhead contains three persons, Father, Son, and Holy Spirit. The Trinity can be known only by faith. And that's okay. We take all sorts of knowledge on faith in our daily lives; that is, we believe things on the authority of the person who reveals them to us, from meteorologists' predictions about the weather to doctors' diagnoses of bodily ailments. God, of course, is the most trustworthy of revealers. So it isn't crazy to believe in the Trinity on his authority. Far from it. It just means we can't rationally grasp or prove the Trinity and other truths of faith.

Note that Aquinas's position is not at all the same as that of the Averroists, who doubted by philosophy what they professed by faith. For Aquinas, faith and reason might take different paths and often go in search of answers to different kinds of questions. But God, as the master of reality, is the source of both faith *and* reason, and both paths ultimately point back to one reality, one truth, which can't contradict itself. The fact that reason seems to contradict some aspects of revelation isn't justification enough to throw out one or the other— but an invitation to cultivate faith and reason to the point where they could enrich each other.

Aquinas's argument about the unity of truth, as we saw, was based on a simple insight into how ordinary people understood the world. And it ultimately vindicated such people, serving what the English writer G. K. Chesterton called a "decidedly democratic and popular" impulse. The argument reflected Aquinas's abiding faith, as Chesterton put it, that such people "would ultimately listen to reason" and could thus be rationally persuaded of at least some moral and spiritual truths.[24] At the same time, Aquinas paid due respect to the limits of rational argument when it came to the deepest mysteries of faith, before which the learned and intelligent were ultimately as helpless as the illiterate and simple-minded.

What Everyone Understands to Be God

Even by the grinding standards of today's elite lawyers and management consultants, Aquinas's work habits boggle the mind. One contemporary recounted:

> Every day, Friar Thomas celebrated Mass early in the morning. . . . Another priest immediately followed him, who celebrated Mass in turn. After having heard [the second Mass, Thomas] took off his [priestly] vestments and immediately gave his course. That done, he began writing and dictating to several secretaries. After that, he ate, returned to his room, where he attended to divine things until rest time. After rest, he began again to write, and it was thus that he ordered his whole life to God.[25]

Aquinas remained active well into the twilit hours. While his assistant, Reginald, slept, the master continued to write, pray, or think out loud; on at least one occasion, Aquinas awakened Reginald to dictate a commentary (on the Book of Isaiah).[26]

He exerted himself so out of a blistering love for Jesus, the *Logos* who took flesh and continued to nourish his disciples from his own Eucharistic body following his death, resurrection, and ascension into heaven. According to one eyewitness, Aquinas rendered this judgment of his own life near its end: "I have written and taught much about this very holy body, and about the other sacraments in the faith of Christ, and about the Holy Roman Church, to whose correction I expose and submit everything I have written."[27]

Aquinas believed this one church to be the exclusive ark of human salvation, and so naturally he wished to see as many people as possible board it. But he also knew that plenty of people didn't accept the Christian faith's basic precepts, let alone the Catholic Church's cosmic claims for herself. What were Christians to do about people who rejected that authority? Was there no way to persuade unbelievers, or to find common ground between believers of different religious traditions?

If God and the things of God were utterly beyond the grasp of human rationality, then the grim answer to these questions would have to have been no. But Aquinas didn't think that to be the case. While he insisted that the divine mysteries couldn't be rationally proved, and that bad arguments in favor of them risked hindering the witness of Christians, religious belief for him was emphatically more than a leap of faith. It *was* possible to find out some things about God by naked reason. Scripture said as much:

> For the wrath of God is revealed from heaven against all ungodliness and wickedness of men, who by their wickedness suppress the truth. For *what can be known about God is plain to them,* because *God has shown it to them.* Ever since the creation of the world, *his invisible nature, namely, his eternal power and deity, has been clearly perceived in the things that have been made.* (Rom 1:18–20; emphasis added)

The wonder that fills us when we contemplate creation—stars and galaxies, oceans and mountain ranges, the ordinary miracle of a newborn baby—tells us something. It points to God. C. S. Lewis might have related that sense of wonder to what he called his Joy, that ineffable and often fleeting awareness of some deeper truth or order behind everyday reality. And what Saint Paul is talking about in the passage above surely encompasses those kinds of *feelings*. But for Aquinas, the kind of contemplation urged by Saint Paul entailed more than Joy, more than mere feelings: It also involved *rational* contemplation, the kind a thinker like Aristotle engaged in.

Making use of Aristotelian concepts, Aquinas argued that the philosopher, unaided by revelation and without appealing to feelings, could prove God's existence. Aquinas's five proofs—or Five Ways, as he called them—remain as formidable today as they were nearly eight hundred years ago. From ordinary factual observations and deductions, each of the Five Ways establishes the existence of a necessary being, on which hangs quite literally the existence of everything else. Without this ultimate, necessary being, as Aquinas demonstrated, we couldn't explain any of the changes or orderly causation we observe around us. *Poof!* would go the whole universe the instant this necessary being is removed. This being, as Aquinas famously concluded each of his proofs, is just "what everyone understands to be God."[28]

Covering the Five Ways at a worthwhile level of detail would fill up a whole book. We can't be detained that long here; the best I can do is to point you to the contemporary Thomist philosopher Edward Feser's *Aquinas: A Beginner's Guide,* an introductory text that is marvelously accessible yet deep and rigorous. What matters for our purposes is to appreciate just how high the stakes in Aquinas's project were.

For starters, the Five Ways, and the Thomistic edifice as a whole, attest to philosophy's enduring power to answer the deepest yearning of the heart: to know that we are part of an orderly whole, the creation of a being whose existence explains why everything happens in the world. As coldly rationalistic as the Five Ways might appear at first glance, their ultimate import couldn't be more warmly hopeful: We are wanted. We belong. We are here for a reason. We are loved.

Second, and relatedly, inherent in Aquinas's proofs is the assurance that this being, this God, is *good,* as all major religions insist he is. In the Thomistic scheme, goodness and being are really the same thing: The most perfect thing is that which is perfectly actual, as opposed to having its being depend upon some other cause. The God whose existence the Five Ways prove is the supreme being from which everything else derives being. Therefore, he is also goodness itself.

Thomistic thought, moreover, is an unabashed celebration of reason and a vigorous defense of its prerogatives. If our minds can learn of God's existence by hewing to the well-tested syllogisms of Aristotle, it follows that right reason has a share of the sacredness of the Almighty. This is good news for philosophy, because it suggests that reason can penetrate into the most fundamental structures of reality.

And it is good news for religion, since it implies that acting reasonably is a divine imperative. The God who allows us to know him by reason is a reasonable God; those who believe in him must, therefore, aspire to the same thing in the way they deal with other human beings.

Thomas Aquinas gave ample proof of this reasonableness in his own life as a religious controversialist. He was deeply, fanatically Catholic, yet his commitment to reasonableness meant that his was a gracious and generous fanaticism. Although he wasn't entirely above the prejudices of his time, Aquinas did, for example, hold up the Jews as an exemplar to Christians for keeping the Sabbath holy.[29] He often sat writing and dictating with a copy of the *Guide for the Perplexed,* the work by the Jewish philosopher Moses Maimonides (1138–1204), sitting open in front of him.[30] His passionate dialogues with Islamic thinkers like Averroes and Avicenna (Ibn Sina, c. 970–1037), not to mention his debts to the pagan Aristotle, are well known.[31]

If God left an imprint of rationality in every mind, and if human reasoning is analogous to the divine *Logos,* then the Christian philosopher must be prepared, Aquinas thought, to seek and to accept truth wherever it may lie, including among representatives of rival religions and worldviews. Aquinas put this belief into practice when arguing with his contemporaries. As witnesses and biographers ancient and modern attest, he was charitable, patient, ever prepared to argue on his adversary's ground and to allow him to make his best case (before proceeding to demolish it). This spirit—of confident reasoning, of generous fanaticism—is very far from the one usually evoked in our minds by the word "medieval," yet it was the authentic spirit of Thomas Aquinas. His "dumbness"—that gentle, introspective quality that so struck his classmates—was thus not a mere accident of his character. It was a mark of his faith in the God who is reason itself.

THE REVENGE OF THE ANTI-PHILOSOPHERS

Aquinas never finished the *Summa theologiae.* On December 6, 1273, he went into a mystical trance while saying Mass, after which he told his companions, "I cannot do any more. Everything I have written seems to me as straw compared to what I have seen."[32] A few weeks later, while riding a donkey from Italy to France to participate in a church council, he hit his head against a tree branch, an injury from which he never recovered. He died on March 7, 1274.

Half a century later, the Church canonized him, but not before the Parisian bishops condemned some of his teachings as heretical and launched a posthumous doctrinal inquiry against him—proof that the anti-philosophical streak was far from vanquished. Indeed, while the Catholic Church eventually adopted Aquinas's system for harmonizing faith and reason as its own, the opponents of that harmony continued to gather strength in the centuries to come.

The new opponents arose, first, from within the Church. The Scottish theologian John Duns Scotus (c. 1266–1308) insisted that most of the things Aquinas had proved about God using naked reason couldn't be philosophically proved. God, in Scotus's view, was capricious and largely veiled from human reason. A strange, unreasonable deity.

The English friar William of Ockham (c. 1287–1347) went even further, holding that not even God's existence could be proved philosophically—but only known by faith.[33] Ockham's doctrine, known as nominalism, took an extremely stingy view of human understanding. The things we observe in the world, he believed, are simply too different from one another to allow for any kind of essential classification or generalization. Lost was that sense of rational kinship with God and with other human beings that the marriage of Greek philosophy and Judeo-Christian faith had nurtured.

Two centuries later came Martin Luther (1483–1546) and the Reformation. Luther viscerally hated philosophy, even if he was prepared to grant it some space in practical matters like government.[34] In a 1520 treatise, he fulminated against the prevalence of Greek reason in Catholic universities: "What else are the universities," he asked, "than what the Book of Maccabees calls *gymnasia epheborum et graecae gloriae*"—that is, places where the youth are inculcated in (pagan)

Greek ways? Jerusalem had to be defended once more against Athens—against the pernicious influence of the "blind, heathen teacher Aristotle," whose books "should be completely discarded," since "nothing can be learned from them either about nature or the Spirit."[35]

If men and women couldn't reason with confidence about being itself—if they couldn't see how the good, intelligible, causally ordered world around them gave proof of the God who is being, goodness, and reason itself—then reason and revelation would have to go their separate ways. We are the children of this cruel divorce, caught between the horns of scientistic Westons and cranky Louisiana pastors.

We have been sold a bad bill of goods. Modern philosophy, with its tendency to judge everything by the standard of its own ideas and claims to greatness, has conditioned us to see the rejection of everything medieval as a victory of reason over obscurantism. But that narrative is mostly self-serving mythology, as we have seen. It wasn't the case that with the rise of the Enlightenment, philosophical reason eclipsed irrational faith. Rather, an illiberal conception of reason's powers came to eclipse reason as Aquinas understood it: a reason that could get at the very mind of God.

But this needn't be a permanent eclipse. We can go back behind intellectual mistakes, even epochal ones. We can retrace our steps and recover reason in its full, rich, *medieval* sense. For in the beginning was reason, and reason was with God, and reason was God. And God is the same yesterday and today and forever (cf. Jn 1:1; Heb 13:18).

WHY WOULD GOD WANT YOU
TO TAKE A DAY OFF?

———

In March 2019, North Dakota governor Doug Burgum signed a bill abolishing his state's Sunday-trading ban. In the past, business owners faced up to a month in jail and a $1,500 fine for keeping their doors open on Sunday mornings. Businesses complied, as they had done going back to the nineteenth century. But by August that year, America's last statewide blue law had gone the way of the rotary phone and the airplane smoking section.

During the twentieth century, North Dakota had twice gone to the U.S. Supreme Court to defend the constitutionality of the ban—and prevailed. But the chamber of commerce lobbied tirelessly for repeal, and the Republican-led legislature finally wearied of the whole debate. Supporters of the ban insisted that the law wasn't about "imposing times of worship" but fostering "rest and relaxation" for "families and communities."[1] Their pleas fell on deaf ears.

"I think the majority of [the] state wants to make decisions for themselves," the repeal bill's main sponsor, GOP state representative Shannon Roers Jones, said. Plus, the tax commissioner, Ryan Rauschenberger, was enthusiastic about the potential uptick in revenues. "We've always believed more hours and more opportunities leads people to spending more," he told the Associated Press. "More hours in which to shop will mean more shopping will occur."[2]

More choice. More consumption. More growth. More revenues. More, more, more. Who but a few scoldy God-botherers could complain about this latest triumph of freedom over the antiquated rules that once constrained our use of time?

Well, for one, mom-and-pop shops, some of whom admitted they weren't prepared to staff the extra hours to compete with the big-box, corporate outlets that pushed hardest for repeal. Then, too, as one North Dakotan observer pointed out at the time, the burden of the corporations' new staffing needs would undoubtedly fall on "those conscripted into hourly wage jobs: the young, the impoverished, single mothers, and all those who struggle."[3]

Blue laws are vestiges of the nation's withered Puritan heritage. It would be one thing if American life were still organized around Puritan precepts. But as it is, the share of Americans who don't identify with any religion—the "nones"—continues to grow, and those hourly wage workers are the most likely to be unchurched. And while the ban's defenders may have tried to play down the religious basis of blue laws to win the public and legal debate, let's be honest: These laws are meant to protect *divinely ordained* rest—Sabbath.

We Americans hustle. We are encouraged to chase lives of action and purpose, and we do. For white-collar professionals, the advent of smart devices means we can freely mingle work and play. The gig economy, meanwhile, has further blurred the line between the two. Divinely ordained rest has no meaning for us. It doesn't fit into the rhythm of our lives. It feels like an imposition—it *is* an imposition.

So the question is: *Why would we need the God we barely worship to carve out a time of rest for us?*

In Defense of Time

On Friday afternoons, Rabbi Abraham Joshua Heschel's apartment on Manhattan's Upper West Side hummed with activity. The rabbi would rush home from work an hour or two earlier than on other days to assist his wife with the preparations. Under Jewish law, all servile tasks had to be completed before sundown: the kettle boiled, the oven turned on, the chicken soup and Cornish hen cooked (or maybe a little overcooked).

Then, twenty minutes before dusk, it was time. All unfinished tasks left unfinished, the family gathered in the dining room to bless and light the candles. Another Sabbath had arrived "like a caress," Heschel wrote, "wiping away fear, sorrow and somber memories."[4] At the table, the rabbi would begin by reciting Psalm 23 ("The Lord is my shepherd . . ."), followed by the Sabbath verses of Genesis (2:1–3):

> Thus, the heavens and the earth were finished, and all the host of them. And on the seventh day, God finished his work which he had done, and he rested on the seventh day from his work which he had done. So God blessed the seventh day and hallowed it, because on it, God rested from all his work which he had done in creation.

Next came the *kiddush,* the blessing over the wine, which Heschel had learned to recite in Hebrew when he was barely older than a toddler:

> Blessed are you, Lord our God, king of the universe, who has hallowed us with his commandments, has desired us and has given us, in love and goodwill, his holy Sabbath as a heritage, in remembrance of the work of creation; the first of the holy festivals, commemorating the Exodus from Egypt. For you have chosen us and sanctified us from among all the nations and with love and goodwill given us your holy Sabbath as a heritage. Blessed are you Lord, who hallows the Sabbath. Amen.[5]

As Heschel's daughter, Susannah, has recounted, her parents' friends, mostly Jewish refugee academics from Europe like the rabbi himself, often joined them at the Sabbath table. "Invariably, they talked about German scholars they had known: Jews who had fled to the U.S. or Israel, others who had perished," she writes in the introduction to her father's book *The Sabbath.* Yet on the Sabbath, "they did not discuss the murder process of the Holocaust, nor did they use that word in those days."[6]

Nor did the rabbi, one of midcentury America's foremost Jewish intellectuals, read on the Sabbath the books of politics and philosophy whose study occupied his time during the rest of the week. Now was the time for Hebrew scriptures and religious texts, which he annotated with bits of napkin and paper clips. Handwriting was forbidden by the rules of the Sabbath, which meant that in this bargain of divinely ordained rest, he also had to give up his beloved writerly craft.

But it was a bargain he treasured—indeed, lived for.

"The Sabbath is not for the sake of the weekdays," Heschel wrote. "The weekdays are for the sake of Sabbath. It is not an interlude but the climax of living."[7] The Sabbath came with its own sublime earthly delights, of course: conversations about God in the company of beloved students; naptime and walks in Riverside Park; afternoon high tea, sometimes with his wife's *Herrentorte,* an Old World concoction of bread, fish and egg salads, and cream cheese; chamber music; and, during summers in a rented house in Los Angeles, long, languid hours by the pool. Yet he took pleasure in these things for the sake of something more.

Heschel's postwar writing on the Sabbath, and his personal practice of its requirements, stood out sharply against a backdrop of rapid assimilation among American Jews, many of whom were "embarrassed by public expressions of Jewishness," as Susannah Heschel has observed. "Even among rabbis and Jewish leaders, a rejection of Jewish mysticism, Hasidism, and even of theology and spirituality was common. It was as if they desired a religionless Judaism—a Judaism without God, faith, or belief." The Sabbath, in particular, was a liability, because it "interfered with jobs, socializing, shopping, and simply being American."[8]

American liberty—the liberty to work as much as you want (the more the better), to socialize when, where, and how you want, to shop till you drop—couldn't be put on pause for ancient ritual. Yet for Heschel, this brand of liberty was missing something profound. It barred entry to an entire dimension of existence: namely, time, whose inexorable passage reminds us that everything is contingent, everything passes away—everything, that is, except God, the eternal, necessary being.

Heschel wrote about "the realm of time" in relation to "the realm of space." Modern civilization is all about conquering space: winning territory in geopolitical contests, building ingenious contraptions and monuments to this ingenuity, growing and prospering economically. It seeks relentlessly to convert time, priced like any other commodity, into achievements in space. But "the danger begins," Heschel worried, "when in gaining power in the realm of space we forfeit all aspirations in the realm of time." In that realm, "the goal is not to have but to be, not to own but to give, not to control but to share, not to subdue but to be in accord."[9]

The Sabbath, Heschel thought, is the guarantor of our "inner liberty," while restless, Sabbath-less societies could too often and too easily descend into tyranny and outright barbarism.[10] The rabbi had learned this from bitter firsthand experience.

ABRAHAM JOSHUA HESCHEL was born in 1907 in Warsaw. Ruled by czarist Russia, the Polish city was a site of spiritual and intellectual ferment, where the main Jewish crosscurrents of the era converged—and clashed. There was Heschel's own Hasidic community, which combined mysticism with strict observance of Jewish law. Then there were the *Mitnagdim* ("opponents"), traditionalists who, though equally assiduous about the law, looked askance at the Hasidic "exaggerations of prayer and ecstasy," as Heschel's biographer, Edward Kaplan, has written.[11] Finally, there were the various offshoots of the Jewish Enlightenment: socialists, Zionists, liberals, feminists.

Heschel was a prince of sorts, heir to Polish and Lithuanian Hasidic dynasties on his father's and mother's sides, respectively. He grew up in a loving but poor and regimented environment, designed to mold him into a *rebbe,* or rabbi, like his father and illustrious forebears. From an early age, he spent long days learning by heart the Torah, the Jewish prayer book, the canon of Jewish law, the foundational medieval commentaries on the Bible—rote work at which

Heschel excelled, thanks to a photographic memory and a clever mind. By the age when most children today begin to read their first novels, Heschel had devoured nearly all the volumes in his father's library and boasted that he could probably write better ones.

That early display of pride earned his father's rebuke. Still, even as a boy, "Heschel was treated like a rebbe, with deference," notes Kaplan. "Expecting wise answers to their questions, people rose to greet him when he entered a room. Some even brought him *kvitlakh* (petitions), joking that if he became a rebbe, all the other rebbes would lose their followers."[12]

This wasn't just a matter of precocity. There was a real holiness to the boy, a radical piety born of competing Hasidic impulses that vied for his soul: an ecstatic spiritual optimism in tension with an austere moral vision that harshly judged human nature. The one gave "me wings," he would later write, the other "encircled me with chains."[13]

Only the Sabbath could reconcile the two antagonistic impulses. The celebration of God's rest opened a holy dimension to its observers—"a dimension," Heschel wrote years later, "in which the human is at home with the divine."[14] The Sabbath made men and women aware of the moral griminess of daily life, thus validating the righteous judgments of God's law. But it also gave them a taste of that other, redeemed dimension, thus vindicating the Hasid's fundamental optimism.

As childhood gave way to young manhood, Heschel began to harbor as-yet inchoate secular ambitions. His father had died at age forty-three, when Heschel was only ten years old—a loss so traumatic that he barely spoke of it for the rest of his life. His maternal uncle took the boy under his wings, though he also put Heschel in the care of a cruel tutor who at every turn tried to break his student's self-confidence.

In response, "the young man took charge of his own discipline," Kaplan reports, and "sought out books that could transform him."[15] Though ordained a rabbi at age sixteen, Heschel began absorbing secular knowledge at a Polish government-run high school: mathematics, science, literature, history.[16] Solidifying his independence, his mother around this time rebuffed an offer from Heschel's uncle to have the young rabbi marry his prettiest daughter. Consciously or not, she was steering her son away from a well-trodden Hasidic path. Instead, under the growing influence of a religiously observant but worldly family friend, Heschel swam ever deeper into nontraditional currents. His intellectual vocation was beginning to take shape: He would apply the timeless truths of traditional faith to Western modernity using the language of modern philosophy and literature—but without permitting the modern to overwhelm the traditional.

Even as he shaved off his sidelocks and put on modern suits, Heschel never lost his faith or his fidelity to the commandments. He believed that there exists a living, personal God, who had entered history and revealed himself to Israel at the Sinai, whose commandments held for all time and who continued to address humanity through prophetic channels. Heschel's openness to Western philosophy and his secular erudition couldn't shake this faith.

Nor, for that matter, could the Nazi Holocaust.

"From What Time May One Recite the Shema?"

In the fall of 1927, Heschel made his way to Berlin, where he entered the top-flight philosophy program at the Friedrich Wilhelm University. Golden-age Weimar was in full swing: This was the Berlin of Fritz Lang movies and German-expressionist paintings, boozy jazz nights and plunging necklines, wild opulence and an even wilder business cycle. The prospect of total ruin loomed over the whole scene like a volcano over a valley.

Heschel for the most part kept his nose in his studies and in Jewish milieus. At the time, the so-called critical-historical method dominated his chosen fields, theology and the philosophy of religion. It was an invention of mainly Protestant scholars who treated the Bible not as living, inspired Scripture, but as an ancient artifact to be decoded with the techniques of modern literary criticism and historical analysis.

Approaching the Bible in this way yielded some smart insights. Practitioners could show, for example, how biblical narratives employed certain structures and devices common to Middle Eastern literature and civilizations. Yet the method's ultimate effect was to sever biblical scholarship from divine truth. If God, the protagonist of the biblical story, couldn't be known by "reason" (limited, of course, to human sensory experience and mental categories), better then to "demythologize" the text and expose the cultural and civilizational forces that lay behind it. The scholars Heschel encountered wouldn't have asked: *What does this text tell us about God or morality?* But rather: *What do these claims about God and morality tell us about the culture that produced the text?* Heschel rejected these premises. For him, biblical faith wasn't just a sensory phenomenon; the Hebrew Bible was more than a mere artifact.

To his professors, Heschel recounted later, "religion was a feeling. To me, religion included the insights of the Torah, which is a vision of man from the point of view of God. They spoke of God from the point of view of man."[17] Or, as he declared more starkly in a letter to a friend at the time: "There is a God in the world."[18]

Holding fast to such faith among the critical-historicists of Weimar, and trying to articulate it in their language and categories, proved spiritually and psychologically taxing. As he told a group of American rabbis decades later, "I went through moments of profound bitterness. I felt very much alone with my own problems and anxieties. I walked alone in the evenings through the magnificent streets. . . . I admired the solidity of its architecture, the overwhelming drive and power of a dynamic civilization"—that is, the marks of a space-bound, space-dominating order.[19]

But one night in the early 1930s, Heschel had a breakthrough. "Suddenly, I noticed the sun had gone down, evening had arrived." He had forgotten about time. He should have been preparing for the evening prayer. *"From what time may one recite the Shema in the evening?* I had forgotten God—I had forgotten Sinai—I had forgotten that sunset is my business."[20]

The sunset reminded Heschel of his "task" as a believer and a faithful Jew: namely, *"to restore the world to the kingship of the Lord."*[21] It also affirmed his antagonistic posture—toward the critical-historicists, toward secular Weimar and the whole "pagan" spirit of Germany in the early twentieth century.[22] Fired up by this reawakening, Kaplan tells us, Heschel would go on to write a dissertation on the Hebrew prophets that reversed "the secular-humanistic projects of his time": The goal of a philosophy of religion, Heschel thought, shouldn't be to understand "God" as an idea or symbol, still less as a disturbance in the human mind—but to understand human beings as God's project and as partakers in the divine "pathos."[23]

This God-centric, eternity-centric understanding, he argued, was the only sure guarantee of human dignity and social justice. Without an absolute standard that reflected the will of a supreme being, men and women could countenance and rationalize any evil in their dealings with one another; everything could be relativized. And it wasn't enough merely to contemplate this supreme being. Rather, the God-centric vision had to be nurtured in a life of prayer and ritual—that is to say, in the dimension of time. In the Sabbath.

"Happy Holiday, Pure-Bred Germans!"

On January 30, 1933, President Paul von Hindenburg administered the oath of office to Adolf Hitler. Within weeks, the newly appointed chancellor of the German Republic and his Nazi Party seized dictatorial power and went on to suspend legal guarantees of equal rights. At the top of their list of undesirables, inferior races, and public enemies were the Jews.

At that time, Heschel was desperately looking for a publisher for his now-finished dissertation, a requirement for receiving his doctorate. Unable to find one in Germany, he hoped he might have better luck back home in Poland, and he obtained the necessary travel documents on March 31. The following day, Nazi stormtroopers and thugs launched their infamous anti-Semitic boycott, "Germany's first large-scale anti-Jewish attack."[24] Jewish merchants were required to post yellow stars on their storefronts, and Brownshirts stood outside, warning "Aryans" to take their business elsewhere.

The boycott took place on a Saturday—on the Sabbath.

The timing wasn't lost on Heschel. Now back in Warsaw, he published an anonymous Yiddish-language poem pouring scorn on the Nazis: "On Sabbath day / At ten o'clock, a filthy-brown mass of people / Sat on shoulders, on doorsteps, on thresholds. . . . / *Gut yontif* [happy holiday], pure-bred Germans!"[25]

He returned to Berlin by mid-decade. In a pair of essays published as the city geared up to host the 1936 Olympics, he warned of an unfolding calamity, a sign that "the world has fallen away from God," and he called on his fellow Jews to observe a fortnight of repentance and solemn self-examination, starting on Rosh Hashanah.[26] Resistance began with conversion and recollection.

The Jews had ancient models to follow. There was, for instance, the second-century mystic Rabbi Shimeon. Shimeon belonged to the generation of Jews who had risen up with Bar Kochba, who launched a rebellion against Roman occupation following the destruction of the Second Temple. The Romans crushed the rebellion and, with it, Jewish hopes of rebuilding the Temple. But while they may have lost their sanctuary in space, they couldn't lose their sanctuary in time, the Sabbath. With many Jews buckling under the compulsion to blend in and hallow a foreign power, Shimeon reminded Israel of its covenantal obligation to hallow God's day of rest. Wrote Heschel: "At a time when, in Rome, the deification of the emperor was an official doctrine, Rabbi Shimeon extolled the most abstract of things: time."[27]

And who was Hitler but the latest pagan emperor demanding blasphemous deification? Heschel blamed the disaster on the moral confusion that characterized Germany and, indeed, the whole of Europe in the decades leading up to Hitler's rise. The Continent "could not survive if all ethical systems were deemed to be equally valid."[28] Yet the era's reigning schools of thought had promoted just such relativism. They undermined moral absolutes by suggesting that the old rules were merely the product of historical circumstances and/or irrelevant to determining whether a given law or legal regime is valid. If every system were as valid as any other, Heschel asked, why not Hitler's?

Against such thinking, Kaplan tells us, Heschel held fast to "the theocentric view of the Hebrew prophets," in which God stands as the "living source of an absolute standard" of right and wrong.[29] The Jews of Europe had no army and no friendly foreign power to protect them against the enormities of this new, would-be emperor. But a Jewish intellectual *could* remind his brethren of their perennial duty, the same one Shimeon had invoked some eighteen centuries earlier: to hallow the divine source of the moral law, including through the traditional piety of the Sabbath, in the face of a profane regime.

Heschel received his doctorate in 1935, a year before his attention-grabbing Olympics essays appeared. Miraculously, the pair of Nazi academics who ran his university waived the requirement that doctoral candidates print and circulate at least two hundred bound copies of their dissertations. (Heschel did later check this box with the help of a Polish academic publisher.) His academic work and his popular writings were beginning to attract admiration in Jewish intellectual circles in Germany and abroad. Yet he had no job prospects, while the Shoah's noose continued to tighten around the necks of European Jewry.

Three years later, Heschel's brother-in-law in Vienna began to face repeated brutality from Nazi thugs. Every day, Kaplan reports, they would enter his home, march him outside, and force him to clean a swastika painted on the street, all while Austrian mobs leered and pointed and laughed.[30] Heschel faced his own humiliations. In October 1938, the Gestapo expelled him to Poland along with some seventy thousand other Polish Jews living in Germany. This reunited him with his Polish kin, but it also left him vulnerable to the genocidal threat that would soon descend upon Polish Jewry. It was a time of misery and creative fecundity (the two often coincide in the lives of intellectuals). Heschel the man was penniless and anxious, but Heschel the thinker had found his prophetic calling.[31] His booming prophetic voice, and the growing prominence that attended it, saved him.

Though Heschel didn't know it at the time, his scholarship had brought him to the attention of Julian Morgenstern, the president of Hebrew Union College in Cincinnati, Ohio. Morgenstern had resolved to save Heschel along with a number of other imperiled Jewish scholars. By the spring of 1939, Morgenstern was working with the U.S. State Department in Washington toward that end.

The cruel workings of American immigration policy, however, meant that Heschel didn't arrive in the New World until March 1940—and couldn't save his Warsaw kin. His mother died of a heart attack when Nazi troops stormed her apartment in the Warsaw Ghetto. One sister perished under Nazi bombing, while two others were murdered in German death camps—two of the six million Jews immolated in "the fire of an altar to Satan," as he famously wrote.[32]

HESCHEL IS TODAY best remembered for his 1960s activism in the United States: He marched arm-in-arm with Martin Luther King Jr. and was the only Jew to eulogize King at the civil-rights leader's funeral. He also emerged as Vatican II's leading Jewish interlocutor, helping shape the council's interfaith declaration, *Nostra Aetate,* which definitively clarified that Jews didn't bear collective guilt for Jesus's death. He spent his final years fiercely opposing the Vietnam War.

Yet it would be a category mistake to class Heschel among those religious thinkers who reduce the teachings of the Bible to a vague and loose progressive ethic. On the contrary, Heschel was a loud, even irascible critic of such readings. He railed against those who would "minimize prayer" and turn houses of worship into "community centers." He likewise rejected the treatment of the biblical God and of biblical prayer as "symbols" of social action.[33] In opposition to such trends, Heschel spoke of a God who really exists, who discloses himself to men and women, and who demands a response, foremost, in piety.

Heschel's lifelong hatred of injustice—be it the unspeakable mass murder of the Holocaust or the discomfiting sight of a black man polishing a white man's shoes, the first thing he saw after arriving in New York Harbor—was an outpouring of this piety.

Before Heschel ever denounced the racial and class injustices that disfigured the land that gave him refuge, he denounced the commercialized and technocratic way of life that denied time to the Sabbath. Indeed, he believed that the two deplorable phenomena were bound up with each other. The cycle had to be broken, and only the Sabbath had the power to do that.

This was the hard-won and urgent moral logic that spurred Heschel to rush home for the ritual leisure of Friday evenings: meditating on old books, praying with friends and family members, and breaking bread with them. What his industrious fellow Americans might have mistaken for "wasted time" was, in fact, an absolutely necessary act of *abandonment,* without which inner liberty was impossible.

In biblical logic, holiness always requires abandonment. Something must be handed over to God, surrendered, even given up for destruction. This logic of sacrifice is at work in an especially tangible way in the Sabbath. Heschel explained this in some of the most poetic biblical exegesis ever put to paper:

He who wants to enter the holiness of the day must first lay down the profanity of clattering commerce, of being yoked to toil. He must go away from the screech of dissonant days, from the nervousness and fury of acquisitiveness and the betrayal in embezzling his own life. He must say farewell to manual work and learn to understand that the world has already been created and will survive without the help of man.[34]

Such submission feels inconvenient; it seems like an imposition. It interferes with industry and online shopping and tax revenues. All true—but divinely ordained rest is also a durable source of human freedom and dignity.

Consider the Exodus account of Israel's liberation from slavery under Pharaoh. In the popular telling of Exodus, God frees the Jews from the Egyptian yoke so that they may have their own homeland. But as numerous Jewish and Christian sages have noted through the ages,[35] that is *not,* in fact, God's main ask from Pharaoh. God doesn't tell Pharaoh via Moses, "Let my people go, so they may have their own country in the Promised Land." What he *does* command is: "Let my people go, so they may serve me in the wilderness" (Ex 7:16; cf. Ex 8:1, 9:1, 9:13, 10:3). And what does the Almighty command Israelites to do once they have made it to Sinai, while they are yet awaiting their political liberation?

> Remember the Sabbath day, to keep it holy. Six days you shall labor and do all your work; but the seventh day is a Sabbath to the Lord your God; in it, you shall not do any work, you, or your son, or your daughter, your manservant, or your maidservant, or your cattle, or the sojourner who is within your gates; for in six days the Lord made heaven and earth, the sea and all that is in them, and rested the seventh day; therefore, the Lord blessed the Sabbath day and hallowed it. (Ex 20:8–11)

The Sabbath, then, is deeply linked with the biblical vision of human freedom and serves as its precondition. As Heschel wrote:

> To set apart one day a week for freedom, a day on which we would not use the instruments which have been so easily turned into weapons of destruction, a day for being with ourselves, a day for detachment from the vulgar, of independence of external obligations, a day on which we stop worshipping the idols

of technical civilization, a day on which we use no money, a day of armistice in the economic struggle with our fellow men and the forces of nature—is there any institution that holds out a greater hope for man's progress than the Sabbath?[36]

It is difficult to imagine just how revolutionary the Sabbath vision must have appeared in the ancient world, where the vast multitudes of people were slaves and nearly all derived their identities from the servile work they did: a world where *who* you were was inseparable from *whom* you served and *what* you did for that master. Into such a world, there appeared a religion that told slaves they had an identity separate from their labor, that their *non-work* was sacred. Even more, they were called to respect and hallow the *non-work* of others.

For all our advancement, we moderns still need the Sabbath vision. Political freedom isn't enough. For Heschel, a civilization might be politically free, as America indeed was, and its citizens could still remain unfree in their souls:

> Nothing is as hard to suppress as the will to be a slave to one's own pettiness. Gallantly, ceaselessly, quietly, man must fight for inner liberty. Inner liberty depends upon being exempt from domination of things as well as from domination of people. There are many who have acquired a high degree of political and social liberty, but only very few are not enslaved to things. This is our constant problem—how to live with people and remain free, how to live with things and remain independent.[37]

Traditional civilizations—Jewish, Christian, and Muslim—appreciated the bond between Sabbath restrictions and human freedom, even as they designated different days to be holy. They saw that by freeing men and women one day a week, so they might rest and refresh themselves in the image of God's own celebration of creation, society could reaffirm that people had a dignity and worth apart from whatever they produce through their work.

Yet across the West today, the drive toward maximal market liberty has squeezed out the liberty of the Sabbath. We have banished the Sabbath in the name of "choice." And some choice we have: Working-class people are denied even a half-day of rest together, and we are puzzled by astronomical divorce rates, abysmally low rates of family formation, alienation and drug abuse, harried lives, and missed human connections. We have cashiered the Sabbath for algorithmic human-resources scheduling: computer code designed to minimize labor costs and maximize efficiency, regardless of the impact on families and communities.

Sure enough, the Sabbath's cultural and political defeat correlates with advances in productivity and gross domestic product. Yet even for the "winners" in this scenario, ours is a world without a break: for upscale professionals, nonstop barrages of emails to be answered and sleepless nights spent by the ghostly blue glow of the smartphone; for downscale workers, meanwhile, the Sabbath's defeat means missed baseball games, lunches wolfed down on impossibly short breaks, and bladders relieved in bottles in the vast warehouses of endless consumer choice.

In our day, as in Heschel's, a world without the Sabbath is a world without soul.

RABBI ABRAHAM JOSHUA Heschel celebrated his final Sabbath on Friday, December 22, 1972. As usual, the dinner was attended by friends, who read aloud from the Yiddish poems the rabbi had written while forging his biblical thought in the crucible of the Holocaust. The next morning, he didn't wake up. His daughter notes: "In Jewish tradition, dying in one's sleep is called a kiss of God, and dying on the Sabbath is a gift that is merited by piety."[38]

CAN YOU BE SPIRITUAL
WITHOUT BEING RELIGIOUS?

———

Divinely ordained rest has a decidedly different character from time spent bingeing on Netflix and Grubhub. The Jewish Sabbath, as we saw, comes with meticulous rules governing the preparation of food, the prayers to be said, the readings to be read, the kinds of activities permitted or prohibited. Such rules aren't limited to one faith, of course; rules have governed human encounters with the sacred for millennia, even as people have disagreed about the content of those rules and the nature of the sacred itself. The Greeks and the Trojans, as Homer took pains to inform his readers, worshipped their different deities at specific altars, in specific locations, with specific animal sacrifices. Muslims pray in the direction of Mecca and not any other. Catholics cross themselves with the right hand, not the left. And on and on.[1]

But many moderns set themselves apart in this respect. Even if they concur with the likes of Abraham Joshua Heschel on the need to make room in life for the eternal, for higher and spiritual things, a growing number of them don't see the point of *religious* ritual—or religion as such. This loss of religious sensitivity, centuries in the making, has accelerated lately. As *Vox* has reported, one in five Americans now identify as "spiritual but not religious." These Americans are generally younger, better-educated, and more politically liberal than traditional religious believers. Speaking to pollsters, they tend to describe their spirituality as a sense of feeling connected to something "much larger" than themselves or of being drawn toward a "higher purpose."[2]

The exact meaning of these clichés varies depending on the individual. An Arizona puppet artist told *Vox* that he finds a kind of "ceremonial" spirituality in his puppetry shows. A New York actress said: "I cleanse with Dead Sea salt baths and other herbal healing baths. I love nature and herbs, they are the magic healers of the earth and connect us to the spiritual." A woman employed by a yoga studio explained that "the practices I consider spiritual"—mainly yoga and meditation—"are the things I do to care for myself in a deep way, to calm myself when I'm distressed, to create meaning out of the experiences of my life." But she said she steers clear of anything that hints of "uniformity of practice and belief," because "that gets a bit culty."[3]

These statements express a widespread modern idea: that religion locks people into rites inherited from the past, when the spiritual realm is, or should be, accessible to anyone, anywhere, without the need for priests, sacraments, and altars. But is that correct? Were the premoderns just superstitious and narrow-minded to think that the sacred had to be mediated by ritual? Perhaps a better, more comprehensive way to pose our fourth question is: *Is it possible to be spiritual without being religious?*

The Solemn, Cosmic Game

My son's current obsession is the solar system, which he discovered in a small book his mother bought him not too long ago. Each thick page showcases one of the eight planets—sorry, Pluto!—accompanied by a little squib of astronomical information that is hopelessly beyond a toddler's comprehension. He can, however, list the names of the planets from memory, from Mercury to Neptune and back.

When I take him to our local park, Max invariably wants to play "rocket ship," a game we invented together that involves "traveling" from the Earth to the other planets via the playground climber. It goes something like this: First, the two of us make our way to a little bench under a little enclosed area in the climber. This is our "cockpit." Once we are settled into it, I ask Max, "Which planet should we fly to?" "Mewcuwy" is, of course, our first destination. To get there, Max has to turn various wheels and doodads attached to the climber. And he does this in a certain precise order, climbing over and through the whole apparatus before returning to the little bench. That done, we "buckle in," and the countdown begins: "Ten, nine, eight, sewen, six. . . ." And liftoff! Once we "land," Max explores the planet—by sliding down the slide into the sandbox below. Then it starts over. He climbs back onto the little bench, he names the next planet ("Wenus"), and off we go again.

Max can play this game for hours on end without tiring of it, but his father can only go so long. Sometimes, I try to take little short-cuts, to minimize the time between each trip down the slide. Can I somehow persuade my boy that he needn't press every doodad and turn every wheel? But no. Every arbitrary rule has to be followed to the letter; each step has to be taken just *this* way and not another way.

To watch Max play is to see his ritualistic nature at work. And that's no accident: The parallels between play and religious ritual are well-established in scholarship.[4] In both, objects and actions stand in for things other than themselves. For Max, the bench becomes a cock-pit and the slide a passageway to an entirely different world. Likewise, in religious rituals, many of the objects, actions, and even architec-tural elements stand for things other than themselves: The domes in a Muslim mosque, for example, symbolically represent the vaults of heaven; the fifth cup of wine ("Elijah's cup") at the Passover seder table is left undrunk in anticipation of messianic redemption.

Both children's games and the ritual "game" are played primarily for their own sake. Max plays the rocket game not seeking anything other than enjoyment within the rule-bound activity (even if his mother and I also relish the fact that it leaves him ready for a nap af-terward). Likewise, ritual worship aims to allow us to just *be* in the presence of the divine. Whatever personal or utilitarian purposes we bring to it are secondary (though these secondary uses are vital to the right functioning of traditional societies, as we will presently see).

Ritual is far from limited to religion. We humans do all sorts of things that have no functional or utilitarian value in themselves but that help us communicate symbolically. We shake hands when we first meet each other (or at least, we did before the coronavirus outbreak). We ask each other "how are you?" without usually expecting a detailed response. We dress up in costumes for carnivals and other special occasions. We seal our marriages by exchanging rings. And on and on. We are wired, as it were, for ritual.

A ritual, per a well-known definition, is a "culturally constructed system of symbolic communication" involving patterned or sequenced words and actions, characterized by formality, rigidity, and repetition.[5] Religion just combines such rituals with beliefs about the ultimate meaning of existence. Together, ritual and belief regulate access to what is normally set apart, inaccessible, even forbidden—that is, the sacred.[6]

Something very special happens when men and women temporarily leave behind profane everyday reality to play the solemn, cosmic game of ritual. For one hugely influential husband-and-wife pair of British anthropologists, the attempt to scientifically understand what that *something* was awakened them to their own longing for ritual—and traditional religion's singular power to build true community.

THE CURSE OF THE MATRIKIN

"Suggest you change to Ndembu tribe northwestern province much malaria yellow fever plenty of ritual."[7] It was the telegram that would transform Victor and Edith Turner's lives and revolutionize the way we understand religious ritual's role in human societies.

The year was 1951, and Victor Turner was studying as an anthropology postdoctoral fellow at Manchester University in England. The telegram came from his director, Max Gluckman, soon after the Turners arrived in Zambia for fieldwork. "Vic," as friends and colleagues called him, had originally planned to study tribal hierarchies and "chieftainship politics"[8] among Central Africa's Mambwe tribe. But Gluckman knew that his star student's heart lay elsewhere, in tribal ritual.

The subject had fascinated Vic ever since he had read *Coming of Age in Samoa*, Margaret Mead's landmark 1928 study of puberty rites among the Pacific people of Ta'ū island.[9] With Gluckman's blessing, the Turners were now poised to spend two and a half years among another isolated people, the Ndembu. In time, Vic and "Edie" would come to closely identify with the tribe, and the Ndembu would force the couple to rethink their own spirituality.

Victor Witter Turner was born in 1920 in Glasgow. His parents divorced when he was eleven, and his mother moved with her son to England's southern coast. For Turner, losing touch with his father proved a lasting wound. Years later, he would insist that his academic employers shoulder the cost of having his own family join him on fieldwork ("the absence of a father is no good for kids"[10]).

As a boy, Turner managed to find a father figure in a local Anglican priest, who immersed him in spiritual literature. They read the great Christian mystics—Francis of Assisi, Teresa of Avila, John of the Cross—and Muslim ones such as Rumi and al-Ghazali, plus a smattering of Hindu and Buddhist spirituality. But then he lost this substitute father, too, when he was about twelve. The "padre," as Vic called the priest, complained of an illness one day. Later, at three in the morning, Vic suddenly awoke and "saw a big oval light at the end of my bed," as he later recounted. "This light was like nothing I had ever seen, it was warm, full of love, it was alive, *mild*. I looked and looked. I knew everything was all right." The following day, Vic learned that the padre had died—at around three in the morning.[11]

This budding spirituality wouldn't outlast Vic's childhood, however. As a teenager, he joined the Young Communist League and threw himself into the leftist scene at University College London, where he enrolled as a comparative-literature major. When World War II broke out, he declared himself a conscientious objector and was assigned to a bomb-clearing squad. His heady admixture of ideals—leftist, pacifist, "skeptical," and even "pagan"—would prove irresistible to his future wife and lifelong intellectual partner.[12]

Edith Davis was born in 1921 in Ely, England, to a large and devoutly Anglican family. By her own admission, she was a rebellious, "bitchy daughter." She was intoxicated at a young age by the radical anti-Christianity of the German philosopher Friedrich Nietzsche. She also embraced Marxism, mainly because it was a worldview "wrung clean of religion."[13] None too pleased with this, her parents stopped paying for her education, leaving her without even a high-school diploma.

Vic met Edie in 1942 and reported to a friend that he had found her "vivacious and buxom, full of ideas, energetically expressed, with all the intellectual's contempt for the intellectuals."[14] Six months later, the two wed in a thoroughly and deliberately secular ceremony, and they then moved into a gypsy caravan. A son was born before war's end; a second son and a daughter soon followed. Amid the demands of career and parenting, the couple took part in a Marxist reading group and hawked copies of *The Daily Worker*.

It was after the war that the Turners discovered *Coming of Age in Samoa* at a public library or bookshop. Mead's book, along with the work of the legendary British anthropologist Alfred Radcliffe-Brown, inspired Vic to switch majors and declare: "I'm going to be an anthropologist!"[15] He was thrilled, Edie later recalled, by the thought of living hand-to-mouth in remote places, far preferable to "writing papers on books that discussed [other] books"—what a career in comparative literature would have involved.[16] How much more romantic to picture themselves settled on a farm, embedded in some aboriginal community on an unexplored island.[17]

As a budding intellectual, moreover, Vic was drawn to the "neat social system[s] among indigenous islanders," which seemed to exist "like an organism within its own social structural laws."[18] Ritual, of course, was central to the operation of those "social structural laws" and to defining and upholding the individual's roles and responsibilities within them. For instance, many tribal peoples marked the passage from childhood to adulthood with highly elaborate ceremonies, whereas in the modern West, childhood often merged imperceptibly into adulthood, leaving it to each individual to figure out what it meant to "come of age." What could the similarities and differences tell us about society—and social change—in our world, so far removed from that of indigenous islanders?

On a trip to London, Gluckman discovered Vic's talents and recruited him to his department in Manchester. The school would fund Vic's fieldwork, which was a good thing, since the couple couldn't count on any financial support from Edie's family. Her mother had cut Edie out of her will over her apostasy from the Church of England, and the rupture between the young dropout and her mother was near-total. As the biographer Timothy Larsen notes, Edie sought "unconditional love" from her mother but rarely received it.[19] It was fortuitous, then, that she and Vic would soon find themselves among the Ndembu, a people for whom the mother-daughter bond was paramount—and who had a peculiar cure for troublesome maternal spirits.

THE NDEMBU ARE a people of central southern Africa, who ranged across modern Zambia, Zaire, and Angola before European colonizers carved new borders across their domains. Zambia, where the Turners encountered them, was then a British colony known as Northern Rhodesia. There, the Ndembu lived off the land, combining hoe-farming with hunting. Though they didn't generally domesticate animals, they were experts at woodcarving and the plastic arts, and they possessed an "elaborate development of ritual symbolism," as Vic would write years later in his seminal 1969 text, *The Ritual Process*.[20]

Many of the Turners' scholarly predecessors dismissed African tribal ritual as unintelligible, the mumbo jumbo of a "simpler" people. The Turners' time among the Ndembu convinced them that such attitudes couldn't be further from the truth. "In matters of religion as of art," Vic found, "there are no 'simpler' peoples, only some peoples with simpler technologies than our own. Man's imaginative and emotional life is always and everywhere rich and complex." Nor, he believed, was the modern, Western "cognitive structure" any different from, or superior to, the tribal one.[21]

Happily, Vic found, "the Ndembu were not at all resentful of a stranger's interest in their ritual system and were perfectly prepared to admit to its performances anyone who treated their beliefs with respect."[22] From the beginning, the Turners tried to counteract the racial hierarchies baked into colonial rule: They did their utmost to live like their African hosts and never used terms like "boy" to address black assistants.[23] To win trust, the couple also distributed medication and treated snakebites with serum.[24]

Although it was Vic who wrote most of the books and won the early academic accolades, the Turners' work was a joint intellectual enterprise. Edie observed and participated in the rites her husband would write about. She took extensive notes. And back home in Britain, he kept her in the loop on all the lectures he attended and the books he read. The conclusions that made them famous were all the products of a husband-and-wife mind meld, a fact that Vic never failed to acknowledge.

One of the Ndembu rites the Turners witnessed was the *Isoma*, used to treat women suffering from infertility or repeated miscarriages. The Ndembu believed that such conditions resulted when a woman neglected the spirits of her matrikin, typically her mother or her mother's mother, who then schemed with other spiritual forces to frustrate the woman's procreative powers.

Ndembu society was matrilineal, meaning ancestral descent (and therefore power and property) flowed from the mother's side. But marriage forced women to leave behind their home villages and devote themselves to their husbands and children. This naturally created tensions within families that affected the wider community. In the tribe's language, Lunda, a woman unable to bear children was said to be "caught in *Isoma*," a word that derives from *ku-somoka*, meaning both "to slip out of place" and "to leave one's group."[25]

The aims of the *Isoma* ritual, Vic surmised, were the "restoration of the right relation between matriliny and marriage; the reconstruction of conjugal relations between wife and husband; and making the woman, and hence the marriage and the lineage, fruitful." More fundamentally, the shamans sought to effect a "reconciliation between visible and invisible parties," between women now living and those gone before, with ritual serving as the medium between the two.[26]

The encounter took place in a consecrated outdoor space, arranged with special objects, plants, and animals, each serving as a symbolic referent for something beyond itself. These ritual objects and elements were collectively called *chijikijilu,* which means both "landmark" and "to blaze" (as in "to blaze a trail"). The *chijikijilu* represented a trail blazed into the world of the "mysterious," the Turners discovered, and back into the known and structured world of everyday tribal life.[27]

Vic and Edie watched, with not a little initial puzzlement, as the shamans dug a pair of holes in the ground through the entrance to a rat or antbear (aardvark) burrow. They would then collect various medicines, classified as "hot" and "cold": These included leaves from the Zambian *mulendi* tree, known for a slipperiness that seemed to physically manifest the woman's condition ("slipping out"), and others that represented fecundity, virility, and health. The shamans heated the hot medicine "on a fire that is kindled just outside" the one hole, while pouring the cold medicine into a broken gourd, placed next to the other hole.[28] The two holes dug into the ground, the Turners gathered, symbolized the grave but also human procreativity.

The central action of the *Isoma* ritual involved the afflicted woman and her husband—in the nude except for narrow waist-cloths—walking from one hole to the other. That is, they passed from life to death and back again, from the cold realm of the ancestor spirits demanding appeasement to the moist and hot birth canal. At some point, the woman was handed a white hen, whose purpose only became clear after some time.

At each stage, the shamans sprinkled the couple with medicines, twenty times in total, while ritual performers sang songs and swayed to a dance that "mimes the contractions of an abortive labor."[29] Finally, the husband and wife took their place in a newly built hut, where they waited until the white hen laid its first egg. Once the egg—new life—arrived, the *Isoma* was complete. The drums went silent, and the community of the living and the dead was once more at peace.

Going "Betwixt and Between"

Observing Ndembu rites led Vic and Edie Turner to conclude that religious ritual is indispensable to building authentic community, resolving otherwise intractable conflicts, and upholding the humanity of the weakest members of society.

To make sense of the *Isoma* and other Ndembu rituals, the Turners began with the rite-of-passage theories posed by the Dutch-German anthropologist Arnold van Gennep (1873–1957). In van Gennep's famous scheme, every such rite involves three distinct stages. First, there is a separation, when the ritual subjects—in the case of the *Isoma,* the woman "patient" and her husband—are separated from the social structure.

Next comes the liminal stage (from *limen,* or "margin" or "threshold" in Latin), when the ritual subjects become somehow ambiguous, indeterminate, even outcast. For example, in the *Isoma* ritual's liminal stage, the man and woman no longer occupy their essential roles as husband and wife in Ndembu society. Instead, they assume the aspects of newly born children and the dead, emerging from the womb and descending into the grave—and back out again. Finally, there is a reaggregation, when the ritual subjects return to the social structure.[30] Sometimes, they reemerge in a changed state or condition, as in the case of a boy who has undergone a puberty rite and returned as a full-fledged man. In other cases, the subjects are merely restored to a prior condition, as in the "healed" *Isoma* woman, once more at peace with her newly appeased matrikin.

The Turners centered their analysis of ritual on the liminal stage, when the subject sheds the symbols that normally identify his or her position in society. During rites of initiation into adulthood, for example, males become liminal. They are isolated from the community and often forced to endure extreme hardship. While in seclusion, they are neither boys nor men but rather something in between these stable, familiar categories. As Vic explained, liminal beings

> are neither here nor there; they are betwixt and between the positions assigned and arrayed by law, custom, convention, and ceremonial. . . . Thus, liminality is frequently likened to death, to being in the womb, to invisibility, to darkness, to bisexuality, to the wilderness, and to an eclipse of the sun or the moon.[31]

All liminal entities, Vic observed, "have this common characteristic: They are persons or principles that (1) fall in the interstices of social structure, (2) are on its margins, or (3) occupy its lowest rungs."[32] In the *Isoma* ritual, as we saw, the "patient and her husband . . . had some of these attributes—passivity, humility, near-nakedness."[33] The going-under of the couple, their submission and passivity, seemed to exorcise and heal hidden hostilities among the Ndembu.[34]

But how?

Ritual liminality fosters what Turner called *communitas*, Latin for "community." *Communitas* is different from the structured hierarchies we inhabit most of our lives. It is the primordial human community, before manmade sedimentation along lines of rank or class sets in. When we "go liminal," the ritual reminds us that the high and mighty have their status only in relation to the low, and "he who is high must experience what it is like to be low."[35] (Or, in the case of the *Isoma*, living women are reminded of their debts to women past.)

Communitas thus unites the strong and the weak. Take the rite of initiation for tribal chiefs. Among the Ndembu, the mythic figure who bestowed chieftainship was associated with the land itself and the people who tilled it—those who weren't politically or militarily strong but who nevertheless possessed a kind of sacral power. The Ndembu saw this figure, known as the Kafwana, as symbolically feminine in relation to the chieftain-to-be.

Before he assumed power, the chief had to undergo ritual liminality at the Kafwana's direction. Among other things, he had to absorb a barrage of insults and criticisms from the other villagers; once installed, he didn't dare hold these ritual humiliations against the people who had dished them out during the liminal stage. In this way, religious ritual taught the chieftain that he was foremost the people's servant.

By humbling themselves in ritual liminality and dispensing with their normal privileges, the participants recall that there exists what Turner called "humankindness," that is, "a generic bond between men."[36] That bond derives from *communitas*. Without it, the hierarchical community has no qualms about excluding, and even destroying, those who, through no fault of their own, don't fit into its structures of rank and class.

Instead of doing that, however, many traditional societies treat such members with extra privilege: twins, for example, or those with intellectual disabilities. They don't fit into the tribe's ordinary hierarchies, but for that very reason they are well cared for and considered the responsibility of the community at large. The presence of such people makes visible the *communitas* underlying everyday society, with all its petty rivalries and clamorous pretensions. Ritual, in this telling, humanizes societies. Far from locking people into the past, it allows them to confront present and future challenges. It does this by humbling the mighty and uplifting the low, by airing out what can't be expressed under normal conditions, and by evoking the communion that transcends power structures and inequalities.

"You Have Killed the Lord!"

One rite in particular highlighted the universality of these concepts in such a profound way that it impelled the Turners to change their own

beliefs. It was the secret rite no outsider was supposed to witness. Vic
and Edie got to watch and even participate, because the elders feared
that soon it "would be forgotten by the young people" under the
press of modernization and urban migration.[37] Better to have their
traditional ways recorded somewhere, even if that somewhere was
books written by this oddball white couple. My summary below is a
necessarily abridged version of a monthlong process Vic recounted
and analyzed in clinical detail in several books and extensive articles.
Many more ritual elements—food, beer, vegetation, tribal medicines,
and the like—were involved than I have room to detail.

The Ndembu seldom performed the *Chihamba* rite; it was reserved
for when serious disaster struck an individual or group, generally as a
result of some failure to honor ancestor spirits or to maintain right
relations with living relatives.[38] Such grave misfortune called for the
supreme sacrifice of the Ndembu religion, the victim being an African bush-god called Kavula.

Who was Kavula? Native informants described him as the "grandfather (*nkaka*) of all people." Like any grandfather, he cared for his
progeny, the Ndembu, and healed their afflictions, even as he also
disciplined them on matters moral (he forbade mistress-taking and
other conduct that bred strife, for example). Kavula was more than
just any old ancestor spirit, however. He was said to be closer to the
African High God, but whereas the High God was "above," Kavula
was "in the ground"—a god or nature spirit who entered the history
and affairs of his people.[39]

In the course of *Chihamba,* the Ndembu's ritual "doctors" or adepts initiated the "candidates" or "patients" into the cult of Kavula.[40]
On the occasion the Turners observed it, there were twenty-seven in
all—the English couple included as honorary candidates.[41] Among
these candidates was a pair of "principal patients," both females suffering ailments.[42] Others were novices keen to be initiated. Still others
were roped into it against their will.

This was all unpleasant, and it was *meant to be so,* as a ritual with
penitential aims: Male adepts beat the candidates with branches, fe-

male adepts taunted them, and Vic and the others found themselves frog-marched, harried and humiliated, to the hut of one of the principal patients. There, they were forced to stand facing the wall, while adepts quizzed them about Kavula and mocked them if they got the answers wrong. Vic noted that the mocking elicited laughter from the group, "but rather uneasily, as though they were frightened at the same time."[43]

The human atmosphere was cloudy and tense. At several points, storms broke out, as adepts had heated arguments over the proper liturgical steps.[44] Eventually, the candidates were taken to a makeshift bush structure that symbolized Kavula's dwelling, but they weren't allowed to see the "tabernacle" of the god, as Vic called it.[45] Instead, the adepts huddled them back to the hut and back again to Kavula's tabernacle, approaching a little closer each time.

Finally, after some four dozen such trips, the candidates came face-to-face with Kavula—or rather, a representation of him made of an upside-down meal mortar (the head) and tree saplings, the whole thing covered by a blanket "rendered dazzling white by consecrated cassava flour." Then each candidate struck the god's head with a special rattle, sending the figure trembling (one of the adepts controlled the gimcrack contraption with a string). Afterward, the adepts told the candidates: "You have killed the Lord!"[46]

The candidates temporarily left the hut, while the adepts sprinkled a red rooster's blood over Kavula's head. Upon returning, the candidates were informed that what they saw was the "blood of Kavula." After some more quizzing and ritual jeering, the candidates were "told that they are 'innocent'" and at that point could leave the ritual site. The following day, adepts now dressed as Kavula, with the deity's signature cross painted on their arms, symbolically "beheaded" the candidates.[47] They had gone under with Kavula and now shared in his death.

"Finally," Vic recounted, "a personal shrine is constructed for each newly initiated adept, one ingredient of which is a white root representing Kavula. Around it are planted seeds or cuttings of the main

food crops cultivated by the Ndembu." Then a taboo period com-
menced, during which various foods and ordinary social and sexual
relations were prohibited for the candidates. Only once the newly
seeded plants grew about knee-high were the candidates released
from the taboos that formerly bound them. Having gone under with
the self-sacrificing god, the candidates were restored to a newly consecrated life.[48]

The ritual the Turners had witnessed was elaborate, obscure, now
sad, now humorous, now terrifying—and strangely familiar: A god
submits willingly to humiliation and death, thus redeeming his mortal fellows. The vessel that was rejected becomes the foundation of a
new, fertile *communitas*. Where had the Turners heard all this before?

THE ECHO OF THE DRUMS

Modern anthropology comes with a decidedly godless outlook. Some
influential early scholars recognized the paramount role religious
ritual plays in human societies, but they sought to explain—or rather,
explain away—that role in purely secular, materialist terms. It didn't
help that they often did their theorizing while ensconced in ivory
towers, far removed from the people and places they wrote about in
supercilious, colonialist terms.[49] Some scholars lost their own faith in
the bargain of anthropological knowledge. Having uncovered the all-
too-human forces at work in tribal ritual, they could never look at
their own religious traditions in quite the same way. To demystify the
one was to demystify the other.

Not so with the Turners. In May 1958, four years after returning
from the second of their two stints in Zambia, the couple and their
children entered into full communion with the Catholic Church. The
decision rocked their tight-knit academic clique. Manchester anthropologists were uniformly secular; many were card-carrying Com-
munists, the Turners included. In that milieu, Edie later recalled,
becoming Catholic "was probably the worst thing we could have
done."[50]

Reproaches flew. Gluckman insisted that his department be united by a single analytic frame. Skeptical anthropology and Rome's hocus-pocus couldn't possibly coexist under the same roof. The Turners found themselves shunned, and Vic resolved to get out, eventually landing a job at Cornell University in Ithaca, New York. (His and Edie's Communist Party membership, renounced post-conversion, was no small obstacle when it came to obtaining U.S. visas, though they did eventually manage to migrate.)

What made them do it? In a word, Africa.

As Vic recounted in 1975, the couple didn't remain "immune to the symbolic powers" they saw at work in Ndembu ritual. They couldn't explain away the rites as mere "disguises" for social or psychological needs. Religious ritual was its own thing, with its own independent logic. "Religion," Vic concluded, "is not merely a toy of the [human] race's childhood, to be discarded" on the road to "scientific and technological development." Rather, ritual and religion "are really at the heart of the human matter."[51]

Edie was rather more direct: "After we came back home, with the drums still echoing in our heads and making us long for Africa, both of us suddenly joined the Catholic Church, a religion full of ritual."[52]

The Turners began by trying out various Christian services. One Sunday, they would attend a Quaker gathering, the following Sunday, a Unitarian service, and so on. Yet they heard the mystical drums reverberating most deeply in, of all places, a working-class Catholic parish in Stockport, England.

The celebrant was a young Irish priest, not exactly a master theologian or liturgical virtuoso. Yet Vic recalled feeling "in the texture" of the priest's "performance something of the same deep contact with the human condition tinged with transcendence that I had experienced in Central Africa."[53] The similarities were too many, and too astonishing, to ignore.

Start with the formal parallels. Both the Christian liturgy and the African ritual assembled centuries of ritual practice and belief within a complex network of symbols. The Ndembu hadn't invented rites like the *Isoma* and the *Chihamba* in a single day, drafting by commit-tee; likewise, the traditional Christian liturgy of the Eucharist had risen organically across millennia into an intricate cathedral of sym-bolic action.

Both, moreover, involved all of the senses and multiple media: not just preached words but also song and music and bodily movement and even taste (the consecrated bread and wine, the chalice of tribal "medicines"). In this way, both sets of rituals engaged the whole per-son, the ritual specialist/priest as well as the village/congregation.

Then, too, both combined what anthropologists call *canonical* and *indexical* messages. Indexical messages relate what ritual participants are going through in the present moment, as individuals and a com-munity. Canonical messages, meanwhile, transmit enduring beliefs about the ultimate meaning of existence.[54] Thus, for example, the *Isoma* ritual brings together the patient's sorrow over infertility (in-dexical) with timeless messages about cycles of life and death (ca-nonical). The same process is at work in, say, the penitential rite of the Mass, which the Turners would have heard murmured in Stock-port ("I confess to Almighty God, to Blessed Mary ever virgin, to Blessed Michael the Archangel . . ."). The public expression of pen-ance is canonical, yet each worshipper brings to it her own regrets over sin. As the liturgy scholar Uwe Michael Lang has written, "where such sentiments and thoughts are genuine, an integration if not fu-sion of canonical and indexical messages has been achieved."[55]

Vic saw just such an integration in the performance of the *Isoma*—and again among the Stockport parishioners. For the latter, the Mass "gave magisterial form to their pure, immediate insights." The lit-urgy fused "past inspiration," embodied in rigidly rule-bound, sym-bolic action and words, with the "present experience, person by person, of bereavement and other sufferings, the whole adding up to a divine-human meaning beyond any individual's experience."[56]

The thematic parallels were more striking still, especially those between the sacrifice of the *Chihamba* deity and that of Jesus Christ. Kavula, Vic wrote, "is a single deity who allows himself to be slain by many people." In turn, the sacrificers "are themselves sacrificed, while the 'white spirit' of Kavula becomes the principle of growth." At one point in the ritual, the participants even shared a meal of white beans, the white symbolizing Kavula. The Ndembu ate the body of the self-sacrificing god in what they considered a "love feast."[57]

What, the Turners wondered, was the Kavula myth but a natural echo of the Christ story? And what was the *Chihamba* rite but an isolated tribe's murky vision of the God-Man who enters human history; who, though mighty and invulnerable, takes on the vulnerability and liminality of men and women; who finally submits to their rattle-blows in a redemptive sacrifice? What was the primitive *communitas* but the longing for the marriage supper of the lamb (cf. Rev 19:9)?

The Ndembu tribesmen and the Stockport parishioners shared identical longings and worked through them via remarkably similar rituals. Were a pair of anthropologists, however erudite and sophisticated, really all that different from these "simple" men and women?

THE TURNERS THREW themselves into the sacramental and moral life of the Roman church. Among other things, they stopped using contraception. They had three more children—though one, a girl they named Lucy, had Down syndrome and died when only a few months old. Not surprisingly, perhaps, Vic later emerged as a champion of the Traditional Latin Mass and a critic of the liturgical changes wrought by Vatican II, which he felt diminished the ritual aspects of worship.

The question might be asked, though: Why didn't the Turners convert to the Ndembu religion? The answer is that an outsider could never become a Ndembu "believer." The tribe's ritual system, after all, doesn't address itself to humankind at large but only to a few thousand isolated people bound by thick ties of blood. (As she grew older, however, Edie did increasingly adopt a syncretic religious practice that incorporated Catholicism with shamanism and the like.)

For Vic, the Ndembu system amounted to what theologians call natural revelation, that is, the inklings unevangelized peoples can gather on their own about the divine and about salvation. Christianity, by contrast, was a product of divine revelation and thus held a salvific message for all.

Even so, the Turners maintained an abiding respect for what Vic called the world's other "vital" religions.[58] They insisted that the "simple" Ndembu were more in touch with their humanity than were Westerners who dismissed religious ritual as cultish and backward. "It is a mistake to think that the archaic is fossilized or surpassed," Vic once wrote. "The archaic can be as contemporary as nuclear physics."[59]

Which brings us to our contemporaries. In the light of the Turners' discoveries, it should be clear that the trouble with "spiritual but not religious" practice isn't a lack of ritual—but that it fails *as spirituality*. Dead Sea salt baths, homemade liturgies, severe diets, meditation and mindfulness (in their faddish, corporate-friendly forms), and other activities of the kind are ritualistic, in a sense: They entail repetitive action, some of the same "play" involved in liturgy, not to mention devotion and even austere self-denial.

But the rites of the "spiritual but not religious" are essentially *privatized*. Though they act ritually, adherents don't bind themselves to a shared account of ultimate meaning or a network of symbols handed down over generations. Those today who claim to believe but reject ritual, or who create their own privatized rites shorn of belief and ultimate meaning, are missing crucial elements of what makes ritual spirituality possible and worthwhile.

By their very nature, privatized rituals can neither endure, nor take us out of ourselves, nor bind us to our community or humankind at large. The contrast here is especially sharp: No single individual could invent the *Chihamba* rite or the Mass or Muslim public prayer. But a human-resources manager in Los Angeles or Paris *could* create her own privatized "rite": forty-five minutes of spinning, thirty minutes of hot yoga, followed by some cold-pressed juice. No doubt such a "rite" imparts all sorts of wholesome benefits. But it lacks existential seriousness. The proof is this: There is no shirking ritual for a traditional believer, lest she upset her own relations to the cosmic order, whereas the spiritual-but-not-religious manager can skip her privatized rite under the pressure of a work deadline and feel, at worst, bummed out. How shaky is the spirituality? As shaky as the religion that supports it.

Privatized rites are perfectly suited to thoroughly privatized societies like ours. But then is it any wonder that one in ten Baby Boomers is aging without any family members around?[60] Or that one in five millennials has no friends?[61] That racial and class antagonism are at a fever pitch, fueling the rise of angry identity politics and backlash movements? Where can the isolated and privatized modern subject begin to access true liminality and *communitas,* to appreciate the humankindness of his fellows? Where can we participate in a visible principle of unity and fellowship that transcends social and political divisions? Could it be that our angry online politics, with their ritual shaming and confession, simulate some aspects of traditional liturgies—only without the authentic redemption and community-building of the genuine articles?[62]

I'm not suggesting that if we only had more religious ritual, we could heal various antagonisms or fix all of our social problems. Many are the product of unjust political arrangements; they call for political action, not ancient rites. Then again, there might be a reason why our society is seemingly designed to prevent people from living liturgical lives—why so many of us are too harried, distracted, and isolated to play the cosmic game of ritual. Ritual, after all, can inspire countercultural action. When we glimpse the *communitas* lying beyond everyday structures, we are possessed by a blessed vision of what structural society *could* or *should* look like: a place where the mighty chieftain submits to the lowly Kafwana, where the omnipotent Son of God consents to be humiliated, where "the wolf shall dwell with the lamb, and the leopard shall lie down with the kid, and the calf and the lion and the fatling together, and a little child shall lead them" (Is 11:6). Ritual can serve as a basis for social critique and supply a blueprint for change.

Modern society can't return to the African bush, and the Turners never suggested we should. But we mustn't ignore what the bush can tell us about our human nature, our societies, and what we have lost in the bargain of "advancement."

AFTER STINTS AT Cornell and the University of Chicago, Vic held his final professorship at the University of Virginia in Charlottesville, where he died from a heart attack on December 18, 1983. His requiem Mass included selections from the Book of Ezekiel, Saint Paul's First Epistle to the Corinthians ("Love never ends . . ."), and Saint Matthew's Gospel. Afterward, the biographer Larsen notes, "there was a gathering at the Turners' home," where Vic's friends "mourned in traditional African ways such as ritual dance. Some students had even made a Ndembu funeral mask."[63]

Thanks to a special University of Virginia graduate program for older women, Edie eventually obtained the academic degree her angry matrikin had denied her. She carried on the couple's intellectual project and continued to win renown as a researcher and thinker in her own right. She died in 2016. We might, if we wish, imagine the Turners reunited now in the heavenly *communitas,* with the drums of Africa still echoing in their midst.

DOES GOD RESPECT YOU?

————

The Iran I left behind was a republic of indignities. It was an oil-rich land, yet poverty was widespread, even if the worst of it spared my own bohemian family. We weren't exactly prosperous; the Islamic Revolution and the war with Iraq that followed it had devastated the Iranian middle class. But we were middle class all the same, and everywhere around us were people wallowing in unfathomable depths of dispossession that turned our relative affluence into a source of shame.

I will never forget the day my father took me and the son of our live-in housekeeper, Habib, to a Western-style steakhouse. Normally, the son stayed with his mother and siblings at their farm in the Kurdish region while his father worked in the capital during the winter months. But on one such stint, Habib brought his son along with him. Being an only child, I was delighted to have a playmate roughly my own age for an extended period.

I had insisted on eating at the steakhouse as a treat, only to find myself embarrassed and squirming as this Kurdish boy struggled to decode the menu, to address the haughty waiter, to pin down the meat with his fork, and so on. I could feel the cutting glances of the other patrons. Mostly, I was ashamed of myself: Had there not lurked in the back of my mind an unseemly desire to show off? This was my first brush with inequality's tendency to degrade the souls of the "haves."

Then there were the indignities that bore the name of God. The Islamist regime that sailed to power on the waves of a popular uprising in 1979 empowered a new vanguard. Its members formed a distinct class of professional ideologues, security apparatchiks, and vice inspectors, and the rest of us were made to understand that the country now belonged to them, to these fanatical partisans of Allah and the supreme leader.

My family wanted out. But would the Islamic Republic permit us to leave? Would this stern bureaucrat stamp this document and that submachine-gun-toting border guard wave us through that barrier? When we did finally get out, it felt to me as if we had escaped from the clutches of God himself.

But America, the republic of rights, had its own indignities, even if they couldn't be compared in scale and brutality with the ones that afflicted my native land. There was poverty here, too, and as fresh-off-the-boat migrants, my family now found itself on the other side of the have/have-not divide. Our Mormon neighbors in northern Utah could be almost unbearably friendly. But they were also clannish, judgmental, and quick to withdraw the welcome mat once they figured there was no hope of converting us to their peculiar religion.

To feel excluded or humiliated is an all-too-common part of life, no matter where one lives. For the poor and marginalized of the earth, however, that feeling is relentless and near-permanent. Which is why so many of the dispossessed turn to religious faith. Miserable and trampled upon in this world, unable to secure the rights and dignity proper to them as human beings, they seek succor from a heavenly king ruling a just world beyond.

Or so runs one highly influential line of thinking, summed up in Karl Marx's famous dictum that religion is the "sigh of the oppressed creature" and "the opium of the people." The German arch-materialist considered the abolition of religion an essential precondition of the true happiness of the oppressed. So long as they held on to their misty "illusions," he argued, the oppressed could never overcome "a condition that requires illusions" in the first place.[1]

Marxist regimes in the twentieth century tried, and failed, to abolish religion. Even so, Marx's charge against faith retains great purchase in our time. Given the abuses carried out in the name of God in places like my native Iran, many people today view faith not only as an opiate, but as an ideological ally of injustice, lending (supposedly) supernatural legitimacy to all-too-natural domination. To survive, the dispossessed must assert their dignity, foremost by political action. Can the God who demands obeisance as "Lord" and "Master" be of any help to them in this task? Then, too, people who suffer daily humiliation need someone to show them a modicum of respect, even politeness. Can a heavenly king offer that?

In other words, *does God respect us?*

"What Are *You* Doing Here?"

Our fifth question consumed the life of Howard Thurman, one of America's great, if sadly forgotten, mystics and a major influence behind the civil-rights movement. For Thurman, divine concern for the dispossessed was a specifically *Christian* problem, a quandary he had to resolve as a believer in the crucified God—and as a black man living under an American regime that abused the Cross in its attempt to legitimate racism.

He came face-to-face with the problem while traveling in British Ceylon (now Sri Lanka). The year was 1935. Thurman, then a pastor and teacher at Howard University, was leading a delegation of African American Christians to evangelize in South Asia and to uplift fellow believers in the region. The sponsors had billed the trip as a "pilgrimage of friendship" crossing national, religious, and racial divides. Naturally, Thurman's audiences wanted to hear about the condition of black Americans.[2] He obliged, speaking as frankly as he could without upsetting the sponsors.

Following one talk at the Ceylon Law College, the chairman of the law club asked Thurman for a private chat. The fellow must have been unusually blunt, for he almost immediately gave his American guest a piece of his mind. "What are you doing here?" he asked. "I know what the newspapers say about a pilgrimage of friendship and the rest, but that is not my question. What are *you* doing here?"[3] By "*you*," he meant Thurman as a black American Christian.

Not waiting for an answer, he then leveled a searing indictment of Thurman's faith. "More than three hundred years ago," he told Thurman,

> your forefathers were taken from the western coast of Africa as slaves. The people who dealt in the slave traffic were Christians. One of your famous Christian hymn writers, Sir John Newton, made his money from the sale of slaves to the New World. He is the man who wrote "How Sweet the Name of Jesus Sounds" and "Amazing Grace"—there may be others, but these are the only ones I know. The name of one of the famous British slave vessels was *Jesus*. The men who bought the slaves were Christians. Christian ministers, quoting the Christian apostle Paul, gave the sanction of religion to the system of slavery.[4]

If *that* is Christianity, the law-club chairman suggested, what business did Thurman have bringing its message to South Asia, where the masses seethed with anger at British colonial rule and its racial hierarchies? Wouldn't Thurman have been better off staying home, working to improve his own people's legal and material conditions in a "Christian nation in which you are segregated, lynched, and burned"? He concluded: "I am a Hindu. I do not understand. Here you are in my country, standing deep within the Christian faith and tradition. I do not wish to seem rude to you. But, sir, I think you are a traitor to all the darker peoples of the earth. I am wondering what you, an intelligent man, can say in defense of your position."[5]

How was Thurman supposed to answer this challenge to his most deeply held beliefs?

INDIGNITY UNTO DEATH

Howard Thurman didn't need a Sri Lankan to open his eyes to the wickedness of American racism. He was born in 1899 in Daytona Beach, Florida, then a resort town of about five thousand souls. The ocean air and teal-blue horizons must have filled his days with a sense of possibility. But this was a mirage, for an intricate system of written laws and unwritten custom narrowly circumscribed the lives of black people in Daytona.

And not just their lives, but even their deaths. As Thurman recounted in his autobiography, when he was eight, his father, a railroad-track worker, came down with pneumonia. No hospitals served black people in the area, and Saul Solomon Thurman died in a matter of days. Jim Crow laws also meant that the town's sole, white undertaker couldn't embalm the body, lest the black race contaminate the white in the realm of the dead. The child had to help as his family bathed his father's body for burial.[6]

Thurman's father wasn't a churchgoing man and may not even have been a believer. Under the precepts of their Baptist community, this meant he had died "out of Christ" and couldn't be given a church funeral. Thurman's grandmother berated the ministers to get the rule waived, but even then, no minister would preach. A traveling evangelist agreed to give the sermon, a fire-and-brimstone jeremiad who consigned the departed to eternal damnation.[7]

To make ends meet in the months that followed, Thurman's now-single mother had to spend long hours away from home, working as a cook for wealthy white families (she did eventually remarry). It fell to Thurman's grandmother to raise the boy and his sisters, and what a grandmother she was. Known as Lady Nancy for the gravitas she seemed to carry in the ruffles of her elegant black dresses, she had been a slave before the Civil War. Lady Nancy rarely spoke of her captivity, Thurman later recalled, "except occasionally in poignant memory of a moment, the sharing of which would speak to the condition of her grandchildren."[8]

That condition was precarious at the beginning of the twentieth century. Slavery had been abolished decades earlier, yet the three "hounds of hell" (in Thurman's later telling) stalked the community: fear, hypocrisy, and hatred.[9]

"Lynchings, burnings, unspeakable cruelties were the fundamentals of existence for black people," Thurman wrote. "Our physical lives were of little value. Any encounter with a white person was inherently dangerous and frequently fatal."[10] Racial terror extended even to worship: Whites were free to attend services at black churches, yet a black Christian stepping into a white church risked a beating or worse.

A twisted theology lent a veneer of legitimacy to such outrages. In the Jim Crow South, Thurman recalled, religion was "made a defender and guarantor" of racist "presumptions." In the era's iconography, for example, God was "imaged as an elderly, benign white man." Meanwhile, "the imps, the messengers of the devil" were black; the phrase "black as an imp," commonly used in the South in those days, subtly associated African Americans with the evil one.[11]

Bad theology has consequences. White children learned to see blacks as less than human. The daughter of a family that employed Thurman would jab him with a hairpin, and when he cried out, she would say: "Oh, Howard, that didn't hurt you. You can't feel!" Thurman recalled: "Our manhood, and that of our fathers, was denied on all levels by white society, a fact expressed insidiously in the way black men were addressed." The honorific "Mister" never attached to an African American man's name, no matter how old or distinguished he was. "No," Thurman wrote. "To the end of his days, he had to absorb the indignity of being called 'boy,' or 'nigger,' or 'uncle.'"[12] Years later, when Thurman was a theology student and junior minister in the North, the daughter of a white family that hosted him for dinner kept using the N-word at the table; it turned out she was addressing the family dog while blissfully indifferent to Thurman's dignity.

What could sustain a child's inner integrity in such an environment? What kind of force could cut through the muggy, all-pervasive atmosphere of racial degradation? For Thurman, the answer was education—the moral education he received from his grandmother and the black Baptist community, as well as the formal schooling he fought tooth and nail to obtain, over and against the racist fiction of "separate but equal."

Lady Nancy, who bore the literal scars of slavery, acted as "the receptacle for the little frustrations and hurts" Thurman brought her. She also proved a loving but stern moral monitor. When Thurman successfully fought off a bully for several blocks down the street, Lady Nancy wasn't impressed. "No one ever wins a fight," she told him. "But I beat him!" he protested. "Yes," she replied, "but look at yourself."[13]

While his father's wretched death and funeral gave Thurman an early (and unfortunate) distaste for organized Christianity, his grandmother painted a different picture of the Christ event—one that directly addressed the plight of African Americans under Jim Crow.

During his grandmother's captivity, the plantation owner would regularly bring in white ministers to preach to the men and women he kept in bondage. These ministers never failed to emphasize Paul's words in Ephesians: "Slaves, be obedient to those who are your earthly masters" (6:5), while skipping all the verses that utterly condemn unjust masters, such as a later verse in the same epistle, which instructs masters to "forbear threatening" subordinates, "knowing that he who is both their master and yours is in heaven, and that there is no partiality with him" (6:9). Likewise, Paul's words in Philemon—urging a well-to-do Christian to receive a former slave of his "no longer as a slave, but more than a slave, as a beloved brother" (1:16)—weren't preached.

Sometimes, however, the owner would allow a black minister from a nearby plantation to preach. This black minister, himself a slave, staged a one-man passion play, beginning with Jesus's agony in the garden and through his crucifixion and resurrection. It must have been quite the performance, for by the end the slave-minister would be utterly drained, and "his congregation would be uplifted with courage." Such plays had been familiar enough to generations of slaves in the South. But this particular minister always ended the performance with an extra message, a secret doxology, if you will: "You are not slaves!" he would whisper. "You are God's children!"[14]

Lady Nancy would often recount this for Thurman and his siblings. When she "got to that part of her story," he recalled, "there would be a slight stiffening in her spine as we sucked in our breath. When she had finished, our spirits were restored."[15] Decades later, when Thurman had to answer secular anticolonial activists' charge that God was an ally of bondage, his grandmother's story of the slave-minister would stiffen his own spine.

THURMAN JOINED THE Baptist church at the age of twelve. The ministers initially rejected him on a technicality (at one point in the interview, he had told them that he *wanted* to be a Christian, when he should have declared that he was already one). Lady Nancy rebuked the ministers. "He is a Christian and was one long before he came to you," she said. "Maybe you did not understand his words, but shame on you if you didn't understand his heart."[16]

In the event, Thurman joined the other twelve-year-olds as they walked in procession from the local church to the Halifax River while the older ladies sang, "Oh mourner, don't you want to go, / Let's go down to Jordan, Hallelujah."[17] (Note how the lyrics accompanying this rite identify the going-under of the baptized with mourning and death, thus signaling their liminality; the Turners would have smiled, had they heard of it.)

Afterward, the ministers assigned Thurman to an adult couple, who would serve as his sponsors and catechists in the church. Soon, they would drill him in the patterns of sin, responsibility, and redemption that formed the warp and weft of a serious Christian life. Not long after his baptism, Thurman was fishing from a boat in the Halifax when a strong wind blew and it began to rain. Rowing back to shore against the tide, he fumbled the oar, fell back, and hit his head against the seat. The pain inspired "a spectacular series of profanities." Then he remembered that just a few days earlier, he had been born again in Christ in those very same waters. "I cried all afternoon." His sponsor, when Thurman confessed his cursing, was unsparing: "Let that be an object lesson to you. Satan is always waiting to tempt you to make you turn your back on the Lord."[18]

Thurman found an uncommon freedom in these boundaries— and a new sense of confidence. If he were truly less than human, as white society told him, then his actions would carry no moral weight; he would be irresponsible. But he *was* responsible, and when he fell out of line, his sponsors were there to tell him so. Thus, "whatever I did with my life *mattered*."[19]

The adults in Thurman's life took note of his moral seriousness— and his smarts. His facility with language and book-learning hinted that he was destined for higher things. But what could they do? "Separate but equal" was the law of the land, and Daytona Beach made no provision for educating black children beyond the seventh grade. When Thurman reached that point, his academic prowess did shame the authorities into creating an eighth grade. But beyond that, he would have to try his luck with one of several Christian schools that catered to blacks.

Fortunately, the Florida Baptist Academy in Jacksonville admitted him, and a cousin there offered him lodging in exchange for chores. On the day of departure, however, the train agent refused to let Thurman bring his suitcase on board because of a missing handle. He only had a dollar to his name after buying his ticket, not enough to cover the cost of shipping the case to Jacksonville.

"I sat down on the steps of the railway station and cried my heart out," he recalled in his memoir. Then he looked up and saw through his tears a pair of heavy boots. They belonged to a black man in workman's clothes.

The stranger calmly lit a cigarette and asked Thurman why he was crying. When Thurman told him, he replied: "If you're going to get out of this damn town to get an education, the least I can do is help you."[20] The man paid the cost of shipping the suitcase—and disappeared. Thurman never saw him again. Some six decades later, he dedicated his autobiography in gratitude to his working-class benefactor.

THURMAN GRADUATED AS the valedictorian of his high-school class and was admitted to Morehouse College in Atlanta with a full scholarship. A trio of Baptist ministers, one of them a former slave, had founded Morehouse shortly after the Civil War out of a sense of obligation to educate newly liberated slaves. There, Thurman found a wholesome community that counteracted the disrespect daily endured by black men, and that instilled in them military-style discipline and a deep sense of duty to black America—to the "many, many others who had not been fortunate enough to go to college," as Thurman wrote.[21]

One way to fulfill this duty was simply by taking full advantage of the school's academic opportunities. Thurman did this by, among other things, reading quite literally every book on the shelves of Morehouse's admittedly modest library, most of them religious texts donated by retired white ministers. Another way to live the Morehouse ethic was by teaching Sunday school at local churches in Atlanta, a requirement that gave Thurman his first real taste of ministry.

He acquired a new political consciousness that was concerned, naturally, with the ugly imprints left by racial indignity on the African American spirit. These stirrings led to his first dabbling in political action. At one point, Morehouse's president, John Hope, invited Thurman to a meeting with Southern white liberals. At issue was a proposal to alter the segregated seating arrangement in the city auditorium. From now on, the white "reformers" suggested, rather than having whites sit in the front and blacks in the back, the line of segregation should run vertically, so blacks would be on one side and the whites on the other. That white liberals considered this a step toward racial justice so appalled Thurman that he walked out.

Hope followed him. "I know how you feel about what is going on in there," he told Thurman.[22] But no matter how offensive the liberals' proposed "reform" was, prudence required blacks in that moment to accept whatever white allies they could find. Hope's clear-eyed resoluteness would color Thurman's own approach in years to come.

If Southern liberals had their shortcomings, the North didn't exactly overflow with racial justice, either. As he completed his undergraduate studies, Thurman resolved to become a minister, to "provide religious education for my people" and put into action his early insight into the link between moral growth and racial liberation.[23] He had set his heart on Newton Theological Seminary outside Boston. Yet the seminary told him that while his application was indeed impressive, admitting an African American was out of the question. His second choice, Rochester Theological Seminary in upstate New York, accepted no more than two black applicants a year—a fact the school condescendingly underscored in a letter informing Thurman that he had been admitted.

The change from balmy Atlanta to the long winters of Rochester was overwhelming, but not just on account of the weather. For the first time ever, he found himself in an all-white environment. In terms of raw ability, he was no worse off than his fellow graduate students. But these sons of white ministers had spent their whole lives in the company of abstract ideas—a comfort that gave them an initial leg up over the slave's grandson.

Thurman compensated as he always had—by drilling down. He plowed through books and courses on Greek and Latin, philosophy and theology, Scripture and ethics and homiletics. In short order, he became the most prominent student in his class. He would go on to prestigious chaplaincies and professorships in Washington, San Francisco, and Boston, winning renown as he preached on the spiritual dimension of the emerging civil-rights struggle. Morehouse's grueling training regimen in oratory came in especially handy, as Thurman mastered a preaching style all his own. His pulpit voice oscillated between soft, intimate murmurs and thundering crescendos at just the right points; he was a spellbinder.

With growing renown came tougher resistance from racist whites.

The Ku Klux Klan was in those days quite active in the Northeast, though it directed much of its venom at Jews and Catholics. Still, one Klansman followed Thurman as he went on a sermon tour addressing the race question before mostly white audiences. The message: *We are watching you*. The attempted intimidation only made Thurman bolder. In his second year at RTS, he and two white students moved in together, smashing the seminary's taboo against interracial housing.

By the 1930s, Thurman's life project was clear to him. It was to spiritually diagnose the "disordered world"[24] of segregated America, and then chart a spiritual and ethical path out of that disorder. He found the building blocks for this project in the life of Jesus Christ—in whose suffering his enslaved forebears had discovered their own infinite worth.

A RELIGION OF THE POOR

When the Hindu nationalist in Sri Lanka pressed him to defend his Christian faith, Thurman had already worked out his answer, though it would take him several more years to articulate it fully, in his classic 1949 book, *Jesus and the Disinherited*. The crux was that the form of Christianity used to justify racial oppression had little if anything to do with the authentic faith, what Thurman called "the religion of Jesus."[25]

The religion of Jesus, Thurman contended, is a religion of the poor. It is an outpouring of divine solicitude for all "those who stand, at a moment in history, with their backs against the wall." Too often, Christians had exchanged this religion's liberatory calling for the "security and respectability" that came with being "on the side of the strong against the weak."[26] Institutional Christianity, especially in the American South, had tamed the radical Christ.

It was this trading of a royal birthright for a mess of worldly pottage that accounted for white Protestant churches' complicity in slavery and Jim Crow. It also accounted for the failure of missionary

Christianity to speak out against the domination of the earth's dispossessed by imperial powers. "The most important religious quest of modern life," Thurman thus concluded, was to recover a Christianity that stood with those with their backs against the wall.[27]

At times, Thurman painted with too broad a brush. He convicted almost the whole of institutional Christianity of twisting the original faith into a spiritual alibi for the "ruthless use of power applied to weak and defenseless peoples."[28] But that claim is ahistorical, belied by the countless, well-documented ways that the early Church humanized the Roman Empire—and later, by unequivocal papal denunciations of indigenous slavery in the New World, starting with Pope Paul III's 1537 edict *Sublimis Deus*.[29]

Still, it is hard to blame Thurman. Decades after the fact, the tactless sermon at his father's funeral, and the ministers' pastoral betrayal of his family in their moment of grief, struck him as an expression of the essential malevolence of the institutional church.[30] Plus, as we have seen, many churches, Catholic ones too often included, *were* deeply complicit with racism and colonial oppression. The conclusion he drew was that all hierarchy and dogma as such betray Jesus. He didn't consider the possibility that the *right* hierarchy is precisely what could guard the radicalism of Jesus against tampering by selfish men.

This not-so-minor quibble aside, Thurman had profound insights into Christianity's meaning for the people "with their backs against the wall." Those insights remain powerfully relevant today, when many dismiss religion's centrality to the quest for justice—and many "orthodox" Christians reinforce the impression by holding fast to an essentially depoliticized spirituality. The man on the Cross, Thurman insisted, couldn't possibly be indifferent to political indignity.

Why? Reading the New Testament closely, Thurman made three basic observations about Jesus of Nazareth.

First, "Jesus was a Jew."[31] In Thurman's telling, anyone wishing to understand the political import of the Christ event, and its meaning for the dispossessed especially, must grapple with Jesus's Jewishness.

God doesn't do things accidentally. Having handed down an absolute ethical ideal at Sinai to *this* people, and not another, the God of the Bible then took flesh as one of them—a people who had already faced the sharp end of slavery, exile, and foreign occupation. That had to mean something.

Second, Thurman noted, "Jesus was a *poor* Jew."[32] Beginning with the circumstances of his birth, Jesus identified himself with people on the social and economic margins. "There was no place for them at the inn" (Lk 2:7). When the Creator of the universe became man, he wasn't among the comfortable; he was in a manger, adored by shepherds and farm animals. And when it came time for Mary to present her newborn at the Temple in Jerusalem, as Mosaic law commanded, she brought two young pigeons for the sacrifice (cf. Lk 2:22–24). The relevant regulation in Leviticus normally required the mother of a newborn to bring a lamb and a dove; the two doves were an exception for women who couldn't afford the lamb (cf. 12:6–8). This, Thurman pointed out, shows that "the mother of Jesus was one whose means" were modest.[33]

As Jesus grew up and began his public ministry, he followed the pattern of an indigent, traveling from town to town in the company of outcasts, living hand to mouth: "Foxes have holes, and birds of the air have nests, but the Son of man has nowhere to lay his head" (Mt 8:20; cf. Lk 9:58). It is irrelevant whether he could have afforded more worldly comfort but forwent it for the sake of his mission. What matters, Thurman insisted, is simply that his poverty put Jesus in the same camp as the vast majority of people, the masses, then as now.

And as with his Jewishness, Jesus's poverty couldn't have been a mere accident:

If we dare take the position that in Jesus there was at work some radical destiny, it would be safe to say that in his poverty he was more truly Son of man than he would have been if the incident of family or birth had made him a rich son of Israel.[34]

This poverty ensured that Christianity would be a mass religion; after all, its founder eagerly joined the throngs of ordinary people, despite his royal birthright. His first miracle took place at a wedding, a communal event (cf. Jn 2:1–11). Again and again, we find Jesus feeding the poor. This feeding has a theological significance but also a political one: It suggests a religion sensitive to the miseries, and everyday joys, of the poor and the excluded.

Third and finally, Thurman observed, Jesus couldn't have been indifferent to the political realities of his time. He was "a member of a minority group in the midst of a larger dominant and controlling group," meaning Rome and the wider Greco-Roman civilization that encompassed Israel. For many Jews, the occupation of their homeland was cause for shame and anger. Some took up arms in rebellion, including perhaps two of Jesus's twelve apostles, as some scholars speculate.[35] The Zealots' uprising against Rome was in the air Jesus breathed, much as, say, the 9/11 attacks and their aftermath were inescapable for anyone who came of age at the turn of the third millennium.

From this, Thurman concluded: "It is utterly fantastical to assume that Jesus grew to manhood untouched by the surging currents of the common life that made up the climate of Palestine. Not only must he have been aware of them; that he was affected by them is a most natural observation."[36] Would, for example, the sight of a Roman centurion insulting a Jewish woman in the street have affected Jesus? How could it not have? He was a man and a member of a political community.

GOD IN OUR SHOES

Nothing about Jesus's identity was random: a poor Jew whose life was touched by the political realities facing his people. In this trio of historical facts, Thurman found the answer to his Hindu interlocutor's challenge. The gross distortions of a racist Christianity in the American South notwithstanding, Thurman insisted, the God of the Bible could put himself in the shoes of "the negro in American life."[37] Indeed, God had already worn those shoes.

Jesus had wrestled with the same hounds of hell that trailed poor black people in Daytona—that is, fear, deception, and hatred. The fear that any random encounter with a white person could lead to a lynching. The little deceptions and hypocrisies that the oppressed adopted as coping mechanisms. The burning hatred of the oppressor. Yet as God without sin, Jesus didn't succumb to the hounds. Rather, he taught men and women how to defang them.

How? By pointing to the only enduring source of self-respect— that is, the realization that "God is mindful of the individual."[38]

This was the idea first planted in his soul by his mother and grandmother when Thurman was a boy—the seedlings of a black spirituality that had blossomed into a mighty tree, well-cultivated by life experience and theological reflection. "Nothing will happen to us, Howard," Thurman's mother used to tell him when he felt anxious as a boy. "God will take care of us."[39] It was the conviction, too, that rang in the words of Lady Nancy's slave-minister ("You are not slaves!").

Around the world and across history, Thurman wrote, "the socially disadvantaged man is constantly given a negative answer to the most important questions," namely: "Who am I? What am I?"[40] The answers, for African Americans under Jim Crow, came in the form of racial epithets, separate water fountains, and substandard schools. Against that barrage of negativity, Thurman argued, the only enduring shield is the eternal.

Manmade social hierarchies, like all manmade things, will one day wither and die. But the eternal, infinite God doesn't, and he has told men and women that they are made in his own image (cf. Gen 1:27). More than that, God has taken human flesh and assured us that he is mindful of each individual human being: "Are not two sparrows sold for a penny? And not one of them will fall to the ground without your Father's will. . . . Fear not, therefore; you are of more value than many sparrows" (Mt 10:29, 31).

When the oppressed keep this realization at the forefront of their minds, Thurman suggested, the three hounds lose the chase.

Fear vanishes, since the oppressed know that "to fear a man," no matter how powerful, "is a basic denial of the very integrity" of their lives. To fear the oppressor is to break communion with the infinite God who took flesh as a poor Jew. Thus, the religion of Jesus "lifts mere man to a place of preeminence that belongs to God and God alone."[41]

Deception, too, is rendered useless in the face of Jesus's overwhelming sincerity. In Christianity, Thurman noted, "the climax of history is interpreted as a time when the inner significance of men's deeds would be revealed to them."[42] At the end of the age, God reveals the secrets of every heart and judges men and women according to whether they honored him in the poor: "For I was hungry, and you gave me food, I was thirsty, and you gave me drink, I was a stranger, and you welcomed me, I was naked, and you clothed me, I was sick, and you visited me, I was in prison, and you came to me" (Mt 25:35–36).

Therefore, Thurman concluded, "sincerity in human relations is equal to, and the same as, sincerity to God." Suddenly, the "advantage due to the accident of birth or position is reduced to zero. . . . A man is a man, no more, no less."[43] I am no better than the Kurdish boy I tried to show off to in Tehran. The white girl who humiliated Thurman, jabbing him with a pin and reminding him that he wasn't supposed to feel pain, upset not only the right relation between people but between people and God.

Hate, finally, is decisively rejected. Hatred's effects "seem positive and dynamic" while they last, Thurman observed. "But at last, it turns to ash, for it guarantees a final isolation from one's fellows" and "blinds the individual to all values of worth, even as they apply to himself."[44] Which is why

Jesus rejected hatred. It was not because he lacked the vitality or the strength. It was not because he lacked the incentive. Jesus rejected hatred because he saw that hatred meant death to the mind, death to the spirit, death to communion with his Father. He affirmed life; and hatred was the great denial.[45]

Fear, hypocrisy, and hate are powerless before the Christ event—before the infinite Lord who bears the indignity of the finite, so that the finite might be raised to his infinite lordship.

Thurman's insight was as old as Christian political thought. And it remains pertinent in our time, when many of those who stamp their feet over threats to human dignity scorn God, while those who have faith often don't recognize a *religious* duty to enact justice at the collective, political level: Secularists sneer at the prayers of believers in response to rampant school shootings and racialized police brutality, while too many believers fail to link their prayers to political action in defense of the human dignity they profess in pious words.

Where, Thurman would have asked our secularists, does human dignity come from? If men and women don't share a divine paternity, can they ever truly be brothers and sisters to each other? If there is nothing special about the origin and destiny of the human person, why *shouldn't* societies tolerate new forms of domination equally as, if not more, horrible than those that marked Thurman's century? By the same token, he skewered a brand of religious faith content to offer thoughts and prayers—and nothing more—to those standing "with their backs against the wall": service-industry workers unable to make ends meet on unjust wages; the shut-away and forgotten elderly; disabled lives treated as unworthy of life; the black man struggling to breathe under a sadistic police officer's knee.

COULD DIVINELY INSPIRED courage, sincerity, and love conquer a regime of racial hatred armed with guns, truncheons, and fire hoses? American history turned the Sri Lankan interlocutor's question to Howard Thurman into a practical challenge.

Thurman wasn't, by nature, an activist. He was a preacher, a writer and an intellectual, a spiritual adviser. Yet he did occasionally engage in direct action. One notable instance came in the early 1950s, while

Thurman was serving as co-pastor of the Fellowship Church in San Francisco. Strolling by one of the city's chicest department stores, he spotted a vitrine featuring a black woman with her children, "the stereotypical Black Mammy and Pickaninnies," as he later recalled; he "was shocked and angered."[46] Here was a public display designed to appeal to white shoppers—and utterly indifferent to the humiliation it dealt to blacks. How was he to respond?

The following Sunday, Thurman urged his racially mixed, progressive congregation to go see the "'interesting' window display" for themselves. He neither told them what to expect "nor why I wanted them to see it."[47] Come noontime Monday, the racist display was gone. Presumably, many or most of Thurman's congregants had gone and had a calm word with the manager. And that was enough to alert the manager that *this* community wouldn't tolerate the humiliation of one group of people for commercial purposes.

"There can never be a substitute for taking personal responsibility for social change," Thurman wrote. In this case, "personal" meant individuals, but it also meant the church as a corporate person, a "beachhead in our society" that helped the "solitary" individual overcome the fear that could otherwise stifle action against racism.[48] This model of nonviolent, God-imbued activism, so central to the civil-rights movement, was arguably Thurman's most tangible contribution to the cause. He lived long enough to see his spiritual program bear fruit in the activism of the likes of Martin Luther King Jr. and Rosa Parks and in the collapse of de jure racial apartheid in the United States in the 1960s.

For the most part, he was happy to leave thinking about "techniques and strategy" to other figures in the movement, King being chief among them. Thurman, who was of an older generation, had overlapped with King's father at Morehouse. When Thurman taught at Boston University, he came to know "Martin" himself, then a theology doctoral student. They watched the World Series together at the Thurmans' house and discussed King's career; mostly the friendship was "informal." Only once did they have a long, "serious" talk about the civil-rights movement, and that was in 1958 at Harlem Hospital, where King was recovering after being stabbed by a mentally unstable woman. Thurman urged King to extend his period of convalescence by two weeks, "to rest his body and mind with healing detachment." As for the "progress, success or failure of the movement itself," the two men didn't touch on the topic at any depth.[49]

And perhaps they didn't need to, because they were on the same page—quite literally. As he traveled across the land preaching against racial injustice, King carried a well-thumbed copy of *Jesus and the Disinherited* in his briefcase.[50]

QUESTION SIX

DOES GOD NEED POLITICS?

———

The previous chapter considered God's promise to the excluded and dispossessed, those more likely to be ruled than to rule. By recognizing God's special care for them, Howard Thurman believed, such people can discover their spiritual dignity, the sturdiest basis for self-confidence and positive political action. But if human dignity has divine origins, then a society that wants to fully honor it must also honor the divine.

We thus come to perhaps the biggest question that diverts modernity from the great stream of traditional thought. Moderns, from celebrated philosophers to ordinary people across the political spectrum, are certain that religion and politics don't, and shouldn't, mix. Since we can't agree on the highest end or ultimate meaning of human life, their thinking runs, politics must be "neutral" ground, where citizens can vie over questions of "secular" public policy without God's sticking his nose into how much taxes the wealthy pay, how we treat immigrants and refugees, how we organize health care, and so on. Spiritual concerns thus belong to a private sphere: Each citizen can hold fast to her own private account of ultimate meaning—including, crucially, the belief that life has no meaning at all.

This position would have been unintelligible to the premodern West. Neither the Judeo-Christian nor the Greco-Roman traditions made such a sharp distinction between "religion" and "politics." Yet nowadays, even most Christians think such a split is not only possible but even desirable: After all, didn't Jesus instruct his followers to "ren-

der to Caesar the things that are Caesar's, and to God the things that
are God's" (Mk 12:17)? Before he was executed, didn't he tell Pilate,
"My kingship is not of this world" (Jn 18:36)? In this view, the kingdom of heaven is tainted when it mingles with earthly kingdoms.
What need has God of Caesar's sword? *Does God need politics?*

"If Rome Can Perish"

During the autumn of A.D. 410, Africa's Mediterranean shore was witness to a sorry sight: thousands of men and women of every social
class—nobles and their servants, lawmakers, priests, artisans, and
others—disembarking vessels that had carried them across the water
from Italy. The younger ones trembled with worry over what the future might hold, while the elderly were too dazed to worry, for their
whole world had collapsed in an astonishingly short span. What they
had endured still seemed to flicker in the eyes of these new arrivals.

They were escapees from the barbarian invasion of Rome. On
August 24, 410, Alaric, the Visigoth chieftain, broke through the last
defensive barriers following a two-year siege that had starved the Romans and reduced them to cannibalism. The invasion was a catastrophe on a scale that we today can hardly fathom. Though the capital
of the Western Roman Empire had by then been transferred to
Ravenna, Rome was still the center of gravity of the whole Latin
West, home to many senators, religious eminences, and members of
the nobility. One survivor recalled what he had seen:

> Rome, the mistress of the world, shivered, crushed with fear, at
> the sound of the blaring trumpets and the howling of the
> Goths. Where, then, was the nobility? Where were the certain
> and distinct ranks of dignity? Everyone was mingled together
> and shaken with fear; every household had its grief and an all-
> pervading terror gripped us. Slave and noble were one. The
> same spectre of death stalked before us all.[1]

Rome, as the eminent historian of Late Antiquity Peter Brown has written, "was the symbol of a whole civilization; it was as if an army had been allowed to sack Westminster Abbey or the Louvre."[2] For survivors, the sense of psychological insecurity was somehow worse than the physical destruction. Brown quotes Saint Jerome, the great Latin biblical scholar and translator, who spoke for the whole civilized world when he wondered, "If Rome can perish, what can be safe?"[3]

It could have been much worse, actually. Alaric and his men for years had inhabited the peripheries of the empire.[4] They weren't complete foreigners, nor were they utter heathens but Christians of a sort: followers of a heretical sect that saw Jesus as a creation of God the Father, rather than a coequal person of the Trinity. For this reason, the barbarians spared at least some churches and those who took sanctuary inside.[5] Plus, as it would soon become clear, the barbarians were "no more than ambitious blackmailers" who only wanted a piece of the power pie.[6] They demanded pensions (somewhat hilariously) and high positions in the Roman administration. One could negotiate with such people.

Still, the sack of Rome *was* a sack, and the Visigoths inflicted on the Romans the full range of atrocities evoked by the words "barbarian invasion": pillage, torture, rape, massacre. As if suffering these things weren't enough, the survivors who escaped to Africa had to contend with a further indignity. Having spent their lives in the Eternal City, amid the din of elevated Latin oratory wafting from the Forum, they now found themselves in a relative backwater.

Carthage, the capital of Roman Africa, remained a lively, dynamic city. Yet the region as a whole had lost much of its pagan splendor. As Brown writes, "The mighty amphitheaters had already begun to crumble" as a result of the recent turmoil.[7] In other cases, the pagan temples, shrines, and other monuments had been defaced, repurposed, or destroyed entirely. Three generations had passed since the Constantinian conversion, and the religion of Jesus was now the official religion. The emperors regularly handed down diktats to suppress paganism and other rivals to the Christian faith.

The locals stood out from the refugees. The African Romans, hardened farmers for the most part, were uncultured, even if a few were fabulously wealthy. Many spoke a Punic dialect that must have grated on the ears of men educated at Rome's great schools of rhetoric. And just beyond the olive groves that encircled the cities and towns lay inhospitable mountain ranges, their sun-scorched heights trodden by seminomadic tribes and their animals; farther beyond, the absolute desert.

What had happened? How had the distinguished Romans fallen so low? For some pagans among the refugees, the wellspring of their misery bore a Jewish name: Jesus.

The men in these small but influential circles had never taken to the Christian religion. As conservatives in this sense, they now gathered in salons to wax nostalgic about the polytheist past, with its "dear, old religion," captured in the epic poetry of Virgil (70–19 B.C.).[8] It was there, and not in some Judean holy book, that the Romans were supposed to learn their glorious history and their true religious obligations.[9] If only Rome had hewed to older ways, they argued, things might have turned out differently. For clearly, this would-be Jewish king put to death by a Roman governor had failed to keep Rome safe. "Therefore," as the theologian Edmund Waldstein summarizes the conservatives' thinking, "a return to the gods of their ancestors was necessary."[10]

This neo-pagan upsurge, and the sentiments it carried, posed a dire threat to Christianity's political position. For while the laws upheld the Christian faith, the conservatives could still draw on pagan support networks stretched throughout the empire, particularly among academe and some aristocrats. From the Church's perspective, says Brown, the danger was that the conservatives might use their power to "harden a prestigious tradition"—Grandpa's religion!—"against the spread of Christianity" just when the masses were reeling from the sack of Rome.[11]

Who in Roman Africa could answer these charges against the one God? As it happened, the region was home to one supremely influential Christian sage. He was a man deeply rooted in African soil but who earlier in life had won entrée to the most cultivated circles of Italian society. He knew his way around the Bible—but also the works of Cicero, Sallust, Varro, and other pagan sages. And he had climbed the summit of Latin oratory, the art the neo-pagans revered most highly.

This man was Augustine, the Catholic bishop of Hippo. By the time the refugees arrived, Augustine was nearly sixty years old and in failing health. Putting down the neo-pagans would form the *magnum opus et arduum*, "the great and arduous work," of his twilight years.[12]

A Restless Heart

It's impossible to do full justice to the life of the author of *The Confessions,* inarguably the greatest spiritual autobiography ever written. But we must sketch an outline.

He was born in A.D. 354 in Thagaste, a small town 170 miles from Carthage, in present-day Algeria. His parents were poor. His father, Patricius, was a hard man, a pagan given to strong drink, who put all his hopes in the education of his son. Patricius knew that "a classical education was one of the only passports to success" for men of his class, as Brown tells us.[13] Augustine's mother, Monica, was a Catholic Christian, a woman of prayer and copious tears, who tirelessly beseeched the Almighty for the conversion of her abusive husband and that of her son. Augustine would later address God in *The Confessions:* "Within my mother's heart, you had already established your temple and laid the foundations of your dwelling-place."[14]

His own heart and loins, however, stirred with temptation. Few who read *The Confessions* will forget Augustine's account of joining a gang of kleptomaniac teens as they stole pears from some poor local farmer. It wasn't the pears he wanted, for "I had plenty of pears." No, "I feasted only on wickedness that was the fruit of my theft," he explained. Likewise, any former teen will recognize himself in the future saint's admission that he took on a bad-boy persona merely to impress his peers: "When my actions were not enough to put me on a level with hardened delinquents, I would pretend to have done things I had not."[15]

Augustine's father did little to restrain the youth's wildness. So long as his son remained on the path to a remunerative career as an orator and lawyer, the old man was content. In this sense, the pagan Patricius's indifference wouldn't be so out of place in our age: Only think of all the young meritocrats today whose parents don't bat an eyelid at any moral deformity so long as Junior checks the right résumé boxes and masters the patois of the professional-managerial class.

In the event, Augustine did excel at his studies and soon found himself working as a teacher of rhetoric. But while his academic and professional successes placated his father, they didn't suffice to make Monica a happy mother. To her natural worries for his physical well-being, Augustine added anxiety over the state of his soul. For while studying at the university in Carthage, he joined a cult called the Manichaeans and had a son with a concubine. His conversion deeply offended Monica's orthodox Christian sensibilities and even led her to bar him from the family home for a time.

It all began when he read the *Hortensius,* a book by Cicero (106–43 B.C.) now largely lost to us. "If the souls which we have are eternal and divine," the Roman philosopher-statesman had argued, "we must conclude, that the more we let them have their head in their natural activity, that is, in reasoning and in the quest for knowledge, . . . the easier it will be for them to ascend and return to heaven."[16] For Cicero, as for many pagan sages, philosophy's final aim was spiritual: to free the soul to soar to its true home—the realm of eternal wisdom. Wisdom was the way and the end.

As a student, Augustine thought he had found such liberating wisdom in the teachings of the Persian guru Mani (A.D. 216–274). Manichaeism had spread from Mani's native land all the way to the Latin

West and all the way to China in the opposite direction. It described a world starkly divided between two kingdoms, light and darkness. The kingdom of light was the domain of spirit, of noble truth. The kingdom of darkness was the realm of the fleshly and impure.

The divine spark was bound, quite against its will, to human bodies that throbbed with impure desires and did disgusting things like bleed, defecate, and ejaculate. Light was trapped in darkness, and the whole universe was a battleground in the war between the two. The Manichaean thus, as Brown has written, radically externalized "inner, spiritual conflict": Evil was something *bodily* that had nothing to do with the true self—or its moral choices.[17]

Augustine learned that the religion involved all sorts of physical austerities, especially for those in its higher echelons: no meat, no alcohol, no procreation. At the same time, a central feature was the "elaborate avoidance of any intimate sense of guilt."[18] The rupture between Augustine's body and spirit meant the latter was untainted by his sins, no matter how deplorable. (Keep these ideas in mind; we will treat them in greater depth in a later chapter on the body.)

It comforted Augustine to think that, "for all his intense ambition, his disquieting involvement with his concubine, the pervasive sense of guilt that came so often to cloud his relations with his mother, at least the good part of him remained throughout, unsoiled."[19] But the restless seeker still longed for answers to many burning questions. Fear not, his Manichaean handlers assured the brilliant convert, Faustus will answer them all.[20]

Faustus was a Manichaean divine renowned for his debating skills. When he addressed the Carthaginian throngs, his apparent brilliance at first wowed Augustine, and "I praised and extolled him like the rest and perhaps more."[21] But when he got up close to Faustus and pressed him on his views, Augustine found an ill-read man out of his depth. It was one thing to be a clever debater, able to win over crowds with laugh lines and pseudo-profundities, quite another to possess true wisdom.

The bigger problem was that Manichaean religion failed to console Augustine in the face of his own temptations—and failings. Why couldn't he stay away from the gladiatorial fights, even as he sensed that watching such brutality degraded his character? How could he overcome his propensity for other acts that, while pleasurable for a moment, left him soul-sore? These questions gnawed at him, but even so, he stayed a Manichaean for a few more years. Meanwhile, he felt drawn to the bustle and dynamism of the imperial center—to Italy. In 383, he crossed the Mediterranean to work as a teacher of rhetoric, taking jobs first in Rome and then in Milan.

His departure for Italy occasioned another one of those immortal scenes in *The Confessions:* that of Monica following "me to the edge of the sea, holding on to me violently, so as either to call me back or to set out with me." To rid himself of his mother, Augustine told her that she could accompany him on the boat the following day, only to set out alone in the middle of the night; "she stayed behind, praying and weeping."[22] In fact, Monica wasn't prepared to give up. A year later, she would sail to Italy to win back her son for God.

IN MILAN, AUGUSTINE found the serious intellectual milieu he had been looking for. This milieu consisted of two, often-overlapping circles. One was Christian, dominated by Ambrose, the Milanese bishop. (Ambrose was the churchman whom Monica implored to convert her son once she arrived in Italy.) The other circle belonged to the Neo-Platonists, gentleman-scholars who promoted a revival of Plato's thought.

At a basic level, Brown notes, the two camps shared "a single horizon of ideas." The Neo-Platonists lamented how the soul inevitably "loses touch with its deepest activity"—the contemplation of wisdom—amid the distractions of the physical world. Earthly life was one long procession of illusions, with each layer dragging the soul further away from the absolute, immutable form of the world, from the capital "O" One. Yet remembering its former, unfallen state, the soul constantly longed to return to it, a striving most familiar to the Christian mind.[23]

A chasm, narrow but deep, divided the two sets of ideas, however. Neo-Platonists thought the individual could "work out his own salvation by his own power alone," through his "unaided, rational ascent" to wisdom.[24] A Christian bishop like Ambrose would have agreed that the soul was meant for reunion with the eternal and unchangeable, for God. But he would have put no stock in the individual will. Self-salvation was a fool's errand. Rather, salvation was to be found in God's grace and the grace-dispensing body he had established on earth, the Church.

Augustine tried the individualist route for a time. While pursuing his worldly affairs as a handsomely paid and respected teacher of rhetoric in Milan, he dabbled in Scripture and delighted in the company of Christian friends. They told him he was meant for God, and he saw the truth of that. But he couldn't will himself into purity and salvation. Even when he removed himself from the proximity of temptation, the force of habit was too strong. His memory recalled the shape of a woman's body, the taste of her lips, the ecstasy of some long-ago drunken revelry. Memory and habit tripped him up, so that he would cry out to God in agony: "Grant me chastity and continence, but please, not yet."[25]

That is, until his final conversion. In the year 386, Augustine, thirty-one years old and having achieved career and financial security, had moved in with like-minded friends devoted to spiritual enlightenment.

Late that summer, the group received an African acquaintance, Ponticianus, who told them about the life of the Egyptian monk, Anthony of the Desert (c. 251–356). Anthony was a simple man, probably an illiterate, who had climbed stupendous mountains of chastity, self-denial, and asceticism. He lived for decades as a hermit in the wilderness, devoting himself to prayer and contemplation and resisting many demonic temptations, according to his popular biography. The more Augustine heard about such spiritual achievements, he wrote, "the more I loathed and execrated myself in comparison with them." Eleven years had passed since Cicero's *Hortensius* inspired him to seek wisdom. Yet Augustine had spent his twenties in "misery," following a confused cult, a slave to his appetites.[26]

What had he done with a decade? What had he done with his soul?

Agitated, Augustine retreated to the garden. He wept. He prayed. He cursed himself. "And behold, suddenly I heard a voice from the house next door; the sound, as it might be, of a boy or a girl, repeating in a singsong voice a refrain unknown to me: 'Pick it up and read it, pick it up and read it.' "[27] He raced back to the sitting room, opened his copy of Saint Paul's epistles at random and read the first verse that caught his eye: "Not in riotousness and drunkenness, not in lewdness and wantonness, not in strife and rivalry; but put on the Lord Jesus Christ and make no provision for the flesh and its lusts" (Rom 13:13–14).[28]

God had sought out the seeker: "No sooner had I finished the sentence than it was as if the light of steadfast trust poured into my heart, and all the shadows of hesitation fled away."[29]

Augustine realized that he couldn't save himself. As a creature, he was a composite of soul and flesh. The higher, undying part of him sought communion with God. But the lower parts, his corruptible flesh and defective will, undermined the soul at every step. That much, he had known before his flight to the garden. Then the Pauline words smacked him like a gust of hurricane wind: The only medium between God, the supreme spiritual being, and a creature composed of spirit and flesh was *faith*—faith, specifically, in the incarnate God, the God who became man.

As he put it decades later in a more mature theological reflection, since flesh derails the soul on the path to knowing and loving God,

God's Son, assuming humanity without destroying his divinity, established and founded this faith, that there might be a way for man to man's God through a God-man. For this is the mediator between God and men, the man Christ Jesus. . . . Now the only way that is infallibly secured against all mistakes is when the very same person is at once God and man, God our end, man our way.[30]

The point was to go *through* flesh, rather than around it—to allow wisdom-made-flesh to elevate corruptible flesh to the level of wisdom. Soon, he would seek baptism in the Church, quit his job, and eventually return to his native soil. Back in Africa, he entered the Christian priesthood and was later appointed bishop of Hippo.

A Tale of Two Cities

Augustine dedicated the rest of his life, until his death in 430, to thinking for and with the church he now helped lead. As a bishop in Roman Africa, he reacted to events both local and in the wider world, resolving numerous dilemmas, big and small, posed by the dramas of the day: How was the Church to deal with fanatic sectarians who refused to recognize any but their own bishops and churches? Was it appropriate to appeal to Roman authorities to coerce these and other heretics? If so, by what means? More mundanely, how was he to root out debauchery among his own flock—without, crucially, closing his gates to the throngs of ordinary sinners and ending up with a church too "pure" to encompass a whole civilization?

The overarching problem had to do with God and politics. To wit, did government have a role in promoting faith? And did such faith work to the benefit or detriment of civil life? The immediate challenge arose, as we saw, from the neo-pagan conservatives. Before the rise of Christianity, they argued, Rome had gathered great wealth and vast dominions. Their pagan forefathers were admirable men, who had subdued their passions to their reason in pursuit of a grand vision. Had they not built a magnificent commonwealth (*res publica*)? And hadn't the Christian conversion now sunk that commonwealth into chaos?

Augustine could see members of his own demoralized flock succumbing to the dark allure of such questions. They were cursed, he sighed in a letter, with "a constitution so weak that the pressure of a comparatively light affliction" could make them go wobbly, let alone the awful "tribulation" of a barbarian invasion.[31] More alarming still: What if the Roman elite succumbed to the same thoughts, too? Might the combined force of mass and elite demoralization shake Christianity's still-fledgling status in the empire?

In mounting his defense against the neo-pagans, Augustine leveled a withering critique against the Roman past. By failing to honor the one God, he countered, the Romans had failed to realize their own vision of the *res publica*.

BEGINNING WITH THE Greek city-states, "the worship of the gods was deeply interwoven with social and political life," Waldstein tells us. Each city had its patron deities, who bound citizens to one another and to the political order. "Important religious rites were performed by the rulers themselves to ensure the security, peace, and prosperity of the city."[32] Thus, "patriotism was piety, and exile excommunication."[33]

This didn't change with the advent of philosophy. The classical philosophers, too, considered belief and worship central to political community. To Plato and, especially, his student Aristotle, it was clear that politics ordered all other human activities. Hence, the aim of the political life wasn't to protect maximal individual autonomy but to discern and promote the common good of the whole community. Common goods are those that only the community can secure, and they aren't diminished by being shared. Peace and justice, for example, only *increase* the more people partake of them.

Now, what rulers believe about the final end or ultimate purpose of human life necessarily shapes their view of the common good. If they believe that the ultimate end of life is for everyone to hoard as much wealth as he can, they will order politics in a certain way. If, however, they believe that the point is to grow in virtue, not least charity, they will order politics differently. Therefore, "for Aristotle as for much of classical philosophy, the end of life was a public matter," and "religion had to be fully integrated into politics."[34]

Roman thought more or less adopted Greek ideas when it came to faith in public life. As Waldstein reminds us, the Latin word *religio* "meant reverence not only toward the gods, but also toward human superiors."[35] *Religio* was necessary for the maintenance and expansion of the *res publica,* which Romans believed they had been charged by destiny to spread to the ends of the earth, to every rational being.[36]

Cicero, the same author who had set off the teenaged Augustine on his quest for wisdom, had defined the *res publica* as simply the "property of a people. But a people is not any collection of human beings brought together in any sort of way." Rather, a *true* people is "an assemblage" of individuals "associated with respect to justice and a partnership for the common good."[37] A true people shared an account of justice and pursued the common good of all.

Were the pagan Romans a people by the crisp definition of their own master statesman and orator? Were Roman politics *true* politics, their civil life *true* civil life? Augustine didn't think so. To rebuke his compatriots' pride, he recast the entirety of human history as a tale of two cities: the earthly city, which sought its highest good in this world, and the city of God, which sought it in the next. This was his great and arduous work following the Visigoth sack of Rome. He titled the massive tome *The City of God.*

AUGUSTINE BEGAN BY describing the city of God as the community of believers, living "by faith in this fleeting course of time," traveling "as a stranger in the midst of the ungodly." The earthly city, meanwhile, is home to "those who prefer their own gods."[38] It is any earthly city whose foundation is "the love of self, even to the point of contempt for God."[39]

Rome was the earthly city *par excellence* in his time, and part of Augustine's task was to prove that it had been just as violent, in fact more so, before the adoption of Christianity as the official religion. This was easy work for Augustine, who knew the Roman past as well as he knew the wrinkles on his own face. The pre-Christian era, he showed, was no golden age of peace, the neo-pagans' sweet nostalgia notwithstanding. Rather, it was disfigured by horrendous violence— beginning with Romulus's murder of his twin, Remus, at the city's mythic founding.

But Augustine's deeper project was to show that the Roman *res publica* didn't add up to a true commonwealth, because its inhabitants didn't, in fact, share a full and sound account of justice (one of the two requirements set out by Cicero). If justice meant giving each his due, then pagan Rome fell far short of it. Its laws, after all, failed to encourage and even impeded the fundamental human desire to know and love God: During the first three centuries after the advent of Christ, it had crushed his followers and driven them underground.

The impulse that the Neo-Platonists identified at the level of the individual soul—the longing to return to the One unchanging and unchangeable supreme being—was blocked at the collective level. Simply put, Rome didn't give God *his* due, and therefore its justice wasn't *true* justice. As Augustine put it in a crucial passage in *The City of God*,

> where there is not this righteousness whereby the one supreme God rules the obedient city according to His grace . . . and whereby, in all the citizens of this obedient city, the soul conse- quently rules the body, . . . there is not an assemblage associated by a common acknowledgment of right, and by a community of interests [the Ciceronian definition of a people]. But if there is not this, there is not a people, if our definition be true, and therefore there is no republic [*res publica*].[40]

Elsewhere in the book, Augustine did seem to offer a more minimal definition of peoplehood, as "an assemblage of reasonable beings bound together by a common agreement as to the objects of their love." The higher the objects of love, he suggested, the more superior the people and, therefore, the *res publica*. Nevertheless, in the same passage, Augustine was quick to reemphasize that a city that doesn't give God his due "is void of *true justice*."[41]

Romans told themselves comforting stories about how they were spreading rational rule to the ends of the earth. Virgil, whom the neo-pagans so honored, sang of "bring[ing] all the world beneath [Roman] laws."[42] As the modern classics scholar Eve Adler noted, this imperial ideology called for a "universal peace" that only Rome could bring about by subduing the many nations under one—itself.[43]

Augustine exposed the *libido dominandi*, "lust for domination," that lurked behind these lofty pretensions. "Tear off the disguise of wild delusion," the bishop of Hippo wrote, "and look at the naked deeds: weigh them naked, judge them naked." Far too often, the Romans had launched unjust wars of conquest on such pretexts. And as their own greatest historians had recorded, the real-world consequences were parricide and fratricide in civil wars and wars between neighboring states: "plains . . . filled with the carcasses," "a profane spectacle both to those alive at the time and to their posterity."[44]

The bishop of Hippo laid the blame for this state of affairs at the feet of the gods who bestrode the Roman spiritual landscape. These, he said, were more akin to demons: lustful and capricious, irrational and chaotic. The pagan deities, the same ones who had supposedly charged the Romans with building "universal peace," perversely delighted in the scenes of human carnage, much like spectators at the gladiator arenas. Sometimes the gods joined in, quarreling among themselves and mixing it up with the humans.

In Augustine's telling, the capriciousness and cruelty of these gods reflected not divinity but the lusts and confusions of their adherents. The perversity was, in turn, mirrored in the various Roman worship rites, "with stupid and monstrous idols, with human victims, with putting a wreath on the male organ, with the wages of unchastity, with the cutting of limbs, with emasculation, with the consecration of effeminates, with impure and obscene plays."[45] Given *whom* the Romans worshipped, it was no wonder Roman politics exploded with periodic bouts of bloodletting between brother and brother. Nor is it hard to see why the Romans lusted after domination of other nations, even if they draped this lust in "rule-of-law" rhetoric.

At a more personal level, Augustine the African had seen firsthand the shortcomings of pagan peoplehood—and later tried to correct them as a Christian bishop.

Take almsgiving. Wealthy Romans liked to throw massive, decadent feasts on certain pagan holidays, their idea of redistributive justice. But to Augustine's mind, the feast-giving amounted to a pseudo-virtue rather than true charity, for the real purpose was to cement "ties of mutual obligation" among "friends, clients and allies," as Brown explains. You threw big parties to show off to other local bigs, not to help the poor as a moral obligation in itself. For Augustine, true almsgiving had to be anonymous and indiscriminate—"a judicious transfer of capital from this unsafe world to the next."[46]

There were other evils: the rites offered by some farmers to pagan demons in the hope that food shortages might drive up prices; the miserable state of serf-like tenant laborers, which only deteriorated once they achieved a measure of independence from their lords, the latter now freed from any obligation of care to their former charges; the overtaxation of crop yields by the administration in Rome for consumption by the imperial troops; and so on.[47]

A *kind* of virtue was at work in some of these cases—industriousness, martial hardness, and so on. But as Waldstein puts it, Rome's "civic life was turned into a mockery" by the "fundamental injustice" of not giving God his due at the level of the community.[48] By failing to order society to the true highest good of human life—well-being in the next world, communion with the source of all goodness—the Romans deformed even their virtues into vices. High and important as they are, even virtues swell with pride without reference to the most high.

As a Manichaean, Augustine had struggled to rightly relate his body to his soul without God's help. Likewise, says Waldstein, "if the souls of Romans did not serve God, then there was no legitimacy to the rule of their souls over their bodies or of their city over other cities."[49]

But how, the neo-pagans shot back, could we possibly expect believers obsessed with the next world to care about the common good of this one? Against this charge, Augustine proposed the godly servant-ruler. His (or her) outstanding feature, per Augustine, is "true piety," the only source of "true virtue." Such rulers necessarily take a religious view of governance, and "there could be nothing more fortunate for human affairs than that, by the mercy of God, they who are endowed with true piety of life, if they have the skill for ruling people, should also have the power."[50]

Augustine thought Rome had been blessed with an early exemplar in the Christian emperor Theodosius I (347–395), who, as the bishop of Hippo reminded his readers, took counsel from Christian spiritual advisers. "The sons of his enemies whose fathers had been slain," he treated "with Christian love," allowing them to retain their properties and even granting "additional honors." He despaired that any wars should be fought and endeavored to bring hostilities to an end as quickly as possible. Throughout his reign, he "rejoiced more to be a member of [the] church than he did to be a king upon the earth."[51]

Theodosius's greatest act of pious governance came after one of his biggest mistakes. In the year 390, he had a large group of rioters massacred, despite having earlier vowed to pardon them at the Catholic bishops' behest. In response, the bishop Ambrose ordered him to perform penance; Theodosius complied, removing his imperial robes and tearfully begging forgiveness.

This was a political and religious earthquake whose magnitude would be hard to overstate. Theodosius's pagan predecessors demanded obeisance as god-emperors, and the good Roman citizen was also a dutiful devotee of the imperial cult. But now the emperor himself was acknowledging his sins and begging forgiveness of a quite different God and his earthly apostle. Asked Augustine: "What could be more admirable than his religious humility when . . . being laid hold of by the discipline of the church, [Theodosius] did penance in such a way that the sight of his imperial loftiness prostrated made the people who were interceding for him weep?"[52]

Theodosius's repentance was an image of the political order Augustine envisioned, and the bishop of Hippo made great use of the event in *The City of God*. Politics, though, represents only one facet of a book that stands also as a monumental achievement in theology, philosophy, history, and literature. Its arguments have been the subject of voluminous scholarship and debate across sixteen hundred years. And yet they remain fresh for every generation, owing to the universality of the problems Augustine addressed and the moral clarity and stylistic verve with which he did so.

Yet Augustine didn't live to see the fruit of his great and arduous work. Having completed *The City of God*, he watched as his earthly city was thrown into fresh chaos. In the year 429, an eighty-thousand-strong barbarian army crossed into Roman Africa, with Genseric, the Vandal king, at its head. The squabbling local leadership and imperial administration were caught off guard; there was almost no defense to speak of. Brown puts it starkly: "Roman rule in Africa simply collapsed."[53] The Vandals inflicted atrocities on the African church: the razing of cities, the raping of women and girls, the torture and killing of bishops and priests, the looting of whatever wasn't fixed to the ground.[54]

Augustine's life's work lay in literal ruins.

As a student of Scripture and Roman history, Augustine was no stranger to the ups and downs of the earthly city; he was prepared. From the depths of despair that swallowed his last years, the old man launched his message deep into the future, like a spearman hurling his projectile just before enemy forces overwhelm his position. Not long before the Vandal invasion, Augustine had begun compiling an index of all his written works. The task continued "right up to his death," on August 28, 430, while Hippo was under barbarian siege. With his archive, notes Brown, Augustine "provided the Catholic church with what, in future centuries, it would need so much: an oasis of absolute certainty in a troubled world: here was the library of a man, whose life could be regarded as a steady progression towards . . . Catholic orthodoxy."[55]

It is no exaggeration to say that Augustine set the political course for Western Christendom for a millennium to come. His theorizing gave rise to the ideal of Christian statesmanship: the ruler duty-bound to protect the weak and to serve the common good of all, who views sound governance and the welfare of souls as different aspects of the same holistic business, who seeks not after his own, transient glory but the undying glory of the city of God.[56]

Not every Christian king lived up to that ideal through the long centuries, of course. Not every ruler could be a Theodosius or, say, a Saint Louis IX, king of France (1214–1270). But the "primacy of the spiritual"[57] meant that the spiritual authority (the Church) could discipline, and even depose, the small and big would-be tyrants of Europe. By binding the political community to a higher power—the highest, in fact—Augustinian politics tamed the beast of earthly power.

GOD DOESN'T NEED anything. But the God of the Bible seeks to transfigure everything about us, including our cities. He wants to "help our political nature to find healing," in Waldstein's apt phrase.[58] That might sound like a big, scary claim to ears marinated in liberal assumptions about the purpose of politics. Then again, liberalism itself came as a shock when it claimed to totally sever politics from the shared quest for "the highest goods of human life."[59]

Today, the very words "highest good" evoke the specter of bloody religious wars and persecutions. To liberals, such ordering of human life is bound to yield intolerable "coercion"; for conservatives, or "classical" liberals, the common good is often seen as a synonym for statist oppression. The most we might hope in our common life, in this view, is to protect basic shared interests, such as security and contract enforcement, while allowing each individual citizen to pursue those goods she deems highest.

For most of us, this means wealth, career success, tech superiority, and the like. But these are private and competitive, rather than common, goods. As such, they give rise to plenty of coercion, meted out by private actors. Doesn't a large, sophisticated firm act coercively when it enforces a payday loan at 700 percent interest against a high-school-educated single mother? Is the employer who digitally monitors every second of his workers' time not coercing them? What about the eleven-year-old who encounters hardcore porn online and develops a lifelong addiction to ever more extreme and exploitative imagery—isn't he coerced, by his own defective will and the ready availability of prurient content?

Liberal societies *do* coerce, then. Even more, the notion that we can't know, much less legislate, humanity's highest end *is itself a metaphysical, even spiritual claim,* and it stands at the heart of the modern project. Its god is the unbound self. And the worship of such a god will inevitably have political consequences: vast accumulations of capital, much of it concentrated in very few hands; a ceaselessly disruptive culture offering kaleidoscopic lifestyles; a heavily armed commercial empire.

These are the conditions fueling popular discontent across the developed world in our century. And, all else being equal, this predicament would have been familiar to Augustine. What would the bishop of Hippo make of our situation? He would certainly find in the modern West "an assemblage of reasonable beings bound together by a common agreement as to the objects of their love"— namely, the love of unbound personal liberty and of wealth.

Perhaps such loves, with the help of God's good providence, can sustain our empire for a while yet. But so long as our hearts are restless for something higher, the city of God will beckon them to find rest in its geography of love.

PART II

THE THINGS OF

HUMANKIND

HOW MUST YOU SERVE YOUR PARENTS?

————

In February 2020, MarketWatch's "Moneyist" advice columnist, Quentin Fottrell, took up an anxious letter about a hairy family situation. "I am a former creative director for a global ad agency and now a freelance writer, who bills at $125 an hour," wrote "Daughter-in-Law in Connecticut." "My husband owns a graphic design firm that bills at $175 per hour." Clearly, the couple's time was valuable. And yet when her husband's parents asked for help expanding a local charity they had founded, he and Daughter-in-Law readily agreed. "It was a crushing amount of work," involving the creation of social-media campaigns, a website, PowerPoint presentations, and newsletters, as well as a decent amount of travel to develop partnerships between the organization and other nonprofits. "Understanding what a huge amount of time and energy this would take, and that we are both working full-time, my in-laws insisted on paying us." She added parenthetically: "They are well-to-do."[1]

But how much should children bill parents for help with a charitable project conceived in their senior years? Daughter-in-Law and her husband were methodical: "We invoiced them for 50% of our hours at 25% of our usual hourly rate, and we did not bill them for meetings or travel." In the end, they charged their parents $10,000, which, Daughter-in-Law was quick to add, was how much "I alone would usually charge for creating a single website."[2]

Trouble lay ahead. "When my husband's three siblings—all over age 60 and financially secure—heard that we were getting paid to do the work, all hell broke loose." The other siblings hadn't lent a hand with the nonprofit work, Daughter-in-Law huffed, but they began demanding payment from their parents for "tasks that my husband and I have always taken as loving filial duty and done for free: Driving them places, helping take the dock up at their lake house, etc." The siblings protested, "'Our time is worth something, too.'"[3] Finally, the parents put an end to the matter by cutting $10,000 checks for each of the other siblings, too.

The whole affair amounted to a latter-day, real-life reenactment of *King Lear*—except tawdry, embarrassing, and all too American. Unlike Lear's two older daughters, who go to war over their father's kingdom, the middle-aged siblings in our story fought over . . . dog-walking stipends. And there was no righteous Cordelia to be found among them: While Daughter-in-Law's account frames the rival siblings as petty and vicious, she and her husband don't come across as exactly selfless, either, what with their spreadsheet billing of parents in their eighties or nineties.

Tellingly, Fottrell didn't see anything unusual. "I have received letters from people who charge their parents for driving them to the grocery store or doctor's appointments," the "Moneyist" wrote in response. To his credit, he urged Daughter-in-Law and her husband to rise above the siblings' "penny-pinching" and to "enjoy all the time you can spare with your in-laws, and with renewed purpose."[4] One can imagine his correspondents taking that advice to heart—and using Excel to track billable hours for time spent with the parents.

Such stories are a natural consequence of a modern sensibility that sees everything, or nearly everything, as negotiable. In a commercial culture that monetizes quite literally every dimension of life, why shouldn't we put a price on the parent-child relationship? If many of our other relationships—employment, career networking, friendship, sexual flings—are transactional, then shouldn't this other relationship be subject to the same financial give-and-take? *Or do we owe something more in service to our parents?*

THE TRAGEDY OF SHUSUN BAO

To explore our question, let us travel to the Lu state of eastern China in the sixth and fifth centuries B.C. If you surveyed the natural landscape from above, you would see vast and verdant rice paddies dotted by little outposts of settlement and activity, some of the oldest cities built by humankind. At a distance, these cities would appear orderly. But look closely: Political transformation agitated the Middle Kingdom in this era, known as the Spring and Autumn period, as the reigning Zhou dynasty lost its grip to ambitious and violent regional vassals.

As the Yale University scholar Annping Chin has written, China, having already existed for two millennia, "felt old and dispirited, and was so impatient for change that she was ready to renounce all that was good about her and all that had worked for her and to let anyone have a go" at power.[5] The resulting instability spread to individual vassal states. In Lu, located in today's Shandong Province in eastern China, three leading families jockeyed for influence and increasingly hemmed in the regional ruler—an aggressive political rivalry that gave rise to corruption and moral decay.

Shusun Bao was a member of and an adviser to one of these families. A statesman of "gravity and foresight,"[6] according to Chin, he nonetheless failed miserably in his personal life. In 575 B.C., Shusun's brother tried, and failed, to use his own sway over the ruler's mother to destroy the other two leading families. This forced Shusun to flee to the neighboring state of Qi, lest he be punished for his brother's evil intrigue.

En route to Qi, Shusun had a sexual encounter that yielded a son, but by then he was long gone. After arriving in Qi, Shusun had a dream in which it seemed as if heaven itself was suffocating him under its awesome, invisible power. As he grappled with this supernatural menace, he glimpsed a man "dark in countenance with stooped shoulders, deep-set eyes, and mouth like a pig snout." Shusun cried out to this stranger: "Niu! Help me!"[7]

The hideous little man rescued him, and Shusun awoke drenched in sweat. The dream, however, stayed with him. He would go on to marry a woman in Qi and have two legitimate children with her before the ruler of Lu called him back to serve as his chief counselor. Soon after this, a woman came to Shusun's house and showed him a boy whom she claimed was his. Astonishingly, this boy resembled the pig-snouted man from his nightmare, and he "answered to the name Niu."[8]

Years passed. The child grew up—and set out to turn his aging father's life upside down. As Chin recounts, summarizing the ancient annals, the chief counselor

> indulged this child, and as [Shusun's] own health declined, Niu began to manipulate Shusun's relationship with his two legitimate sons. He fabricated the perception that these two sons had betrayed their father, and so Shusun had one killed and the other exiled. By the time he became aware of Niu's deception, it was already too late.[9]

Shusun was bedridden and too sick to manage his family, much less carry out his role as chief counselor to the ruler. So Niu took complete control of his father's affairs. Eventually, he resolved to murder the old man, and this he did by simply refusing the food and water sent for Shusun. "After three days of deprivation, the counselor of Lu died alone in his mansion."[10]

After offing his father, Niu continued to manipulate the affairs of state and the other leading families. When the legitimate son who had been wrongly exiled returned to take his father's job as chief counselor, Niu had him assassinated. In his place, Niu installed a young man named Zhaozi, another son of Shusun's from a concubine. Niu figured that a concubine's son who owed his rise to him would serve as the perfect puppet. But Zhaozi refused to play his designated role in Niu's schemes.

As soon as he took office, Zhaozi convened the family for a meeting. "Niu has brought disaster to the Shusuns," he told them. "We must kill him right away!"[11] Sensing the reversal in his fortune, Niu escaped to Qi, as his father once had done. But his kinsmen tracked him down, beheaded him, and tossed his severed head into a bramble bush. Niu's reign of terror came to a close.

When Shusun Bao died, the state of Lu was home to a thirteen-year-old boy living a hardscrabble life with his single mother. As he grew up, he heard the story of the late chief counselor and was riveted by it.[12] The Shusun Bao tragedy, and other stories of the kind, would form the basis of the civilization-defining philosophy this boy would weave as an adult. At the heart of his ideas was the question of children's obligations to parents and other elder kin—that is to say, the problem of filiality.

The boy was called Qiu Kong, though he won renown in his lifetime as Kong-fuzi, or Master Kong. In the West, we know him by the Latinized name Confucius.

"Look After the Roots"

The Shusun Bao story likely blends real history with mythic and folkloric elements, and it isn't hard to see why it continues to resonate across two and a half millennia of Chinese literary culture. For one thing, there are its psychosexual undercurrents: Shusun's sexual encounter produces a physically malformed, almost demonic offspring (whether Niu was, in fact, Shusun's biological son is one of the story's intriguing mysteries). Later, Niu appears seemingly out of nowhere to ruin Shusun.

The story also encapsulates timeless, universal problems of filiality, a keystone of Chinese culture. These include our duties to parents, as well as the relationship between respect in the domestic sphere and a sound political order. Seen through this lens, neither Shusun Bao nor Niu is the true protagonist of the tragedy. That role belongs to Zhaozi, the concubine's righteous son.

Confucius thought Zhaozi was "extraordinary," according to

Chin. By defeating Niu, Zhaozi "exercised his political purchase with only the public good in mind, which was nearly impossible to do because he owed everything—his position and his power—to private grants of favor and to men with only selfish interests."[13] Zhaozi had risen to chief counselor thanks to his conniving half-brother. A less virtuous man would have gone along with Niu, on the ground that you don't bite the hand that feeds you. But Zhaozi felt a higher loyalty to the Shusun family, the state as a whole—and his late father. By avenging Shusun Bao, Zhaozi also served the common good, ridding Lu of a malign schemer.

Early in the *Analects,* the collection of Confucian wisdom compiled by his disciples in the fifth century B.C., we find this teaching:

> It is rare for a person who is filial to his parents and respectful to his elders to be inclined to transgress against his superiors. And it has never happened that a person who is not inclined to transgress against his superiors is inclined to create chaos. A gentleman looks after the roots. With the roots firmly established, a moral way will grow. Is it not true then that being filial to one's parents and being respectful to one's elders are the roots of one's humanity?[14]

We don't know if the moral contrast between Niu and Zhaozi inspired this particular teaching, but we can read back into it the half-brothers' story. For didn't the one, Niu, begin to sow chaos by first betraying his father, Shusun? And didn't the other, Zhaozi, serve the state by honoring the memory and family of that same father? The humanity of the one and the inhumanity of the other, in the Confucian moral scheme, were both rooted in how they treated the paternal roots.

Attend to the roots, protect the filial branches, and "a moral way will grow." Confucius felt that in his time, men and women had abandoned the moral way; his calling was to help restore it. He didn't set out to teach anything new, he insisted, much less formulate any sort of theory. As he told his disciples, "I transmit but do not create. I am fond of antiquity, because I have faith in it."[15] His life's work was an expression of filial piety toward the past.

THE TEACHER BEFORE ALL TEACHERS

Confucius was born in Qufu, the capital of Lu state, in 551 B.C. "According to some reports," Chin tells us, "his early ancestors were Kongs from the state of Song, a titled family that produced several eminent counselors." Yet by the seventh century B.C., Confucius's illustrious forebears had lost political favor to the machinations of their enemies, so that they "couldn't hold their heads high."[16] Many migrated to Lu, Confucius's great-grandfather included.

In Lu, the Kongs became common gentlemen, or *shi,* which meant they had "no privileges or entitlements except for a chance to have an education."[17] Confucius's father, Shu-liang He, was a soldier. He had nine daughters from a legitimate wife and a clubfooted son from a concubine. Later in life, he convinced the head of another family to let him have his way with their daughter. The older man and the teenager copulated in the fields and brought Confucius into the world.

The boy's father died when Confucius was only three years old, leaving Confucius's mother adrift financially. From an early age, the boy had to face a hard reality: Much as with members of Augustine's class in Roman Africa some nine centuries later, the only way for men like Confucius to rise to the political and administrative halls of power was through toil. Along the way, he had to learn many "menial things," tasks he felt were unbecoming of a gentleman but unavoidable for someone of a "humble station."[18]

But rise he did, eventually becoming minister of crime in Lu. What his superiors valued most in Confucius, says Chin, was his "knowledge of the rites."[19] The concept of rites, or *li,* is difficult to convey in English. It suggests the religious or quasi-religious rituals we explored in chapter 4, as well as the notion of propriety or right conduct. The rites regulated everything from how much food a gen-

tleman should eat to when, where, and how to offer sacrifices to ancestral spirits; from the conduct of diplomacy with foreign nations to
the funeral arrangements befitting members of different classes.
Their domain, in other words, extended to the *whole* of life.

As the American sinologist Jerry Dennerline has written, *li* is "a
general concept that applies to customary behavior throughout the
Chinese world and distinguishes Chinese culture from all others."
Crucially, the rites aren't the same as local custom but denote universal standards, even though their expressions may vary dramatically;
what a modern Taiwanese family might understand by *li* is very different from what the rites meant to a family in Confucius's time. Generally speaking, however, they govern "standards for the family—its
internal relations, its external relations, birth, marriage, death." And
these familial standards have political analogues: "standards for the
workings of government and state ceremonies—internal relations,
relations between state and society, recruitment, treaties, succes-
sion."[20]

Confucius wasn't just a master of these rites, but also a great believer in their healing powers. He didn't promote them merely because "that's how we've always done things," so to speak, but because
experience had taught him that the rites were *good*—morally,
spiritually—for those who remained faithful to them. For one thing,
the rites bore the accumulated wisdom of prior generations. Adher-
ing to them could thus help preserve order and continuity amid constant change: shifts in fortune, sudden and unforeseen calamities,
cycles of life and death. Over against a topsy-turvy human condition,
Confucius felt, it was important "to learn and perform something
with well-defined structures and rules."[21]

Following the rites, moreover, promoted self-mastery and thus
could be liberating. A change in fortune, whether auspicious or tragic,
could throw anyone's life into chaos and allow emotions and baser
drives to take over. When the storms raged, the voice of the rites
whispered: *Be calm, light this candle, refrain from sex, pray this way, show
reverence to So-and-So*. The person who honored the rites possessed an

"interior," and he "understood the virtue of taking measured action and measured steps," as Chin puts it.[22]

Confucius was extremely strict about the rites and propriety, yet a moral spirit animated his apparent scrupulosity. Why, for example, did Confucius abruptly quit his cushy government job and leave the state of Lu at the height of his political powers? Contemporary annals and later hagiographers proffered differing accounts, while Chin, the modern historian, lays bare the byzantine political intrigue that may have been involved. Yet most sources agree that the Lu elites' failure to keep to the rites had *something* to do with Confucius's decision, even if he used them as a mere pretext.

At a certain ceremony, these elites didn't grant him, a senior minister, a share of the sacrificial meat, as the rites required. On another occasion, they invited eight rows of pretty girls to dance in the courtyard of their ancestral temple, a privilege that belonged only to the king, prompting Confucius to scoff: "If this can be tolerated, what cannot be tolerated?"[23] Such ritual indiscretions, troubling in themselves, were mirrored in the unjust liberties the upstart elite took in government: levying heavier taxes than the people were accustomed to, for example, and keeping much of the proceeds for themselves— that is, pursuing their own private good, rather than the common good.[24]

Even if some aspects of these accounts are the embellishments of later historians too eager to burnish Confucius's image, they nevertheless jibe with the spirit of the man as it comes through his own teachings.[25] Rites and ethics, Confucius insisted, were inseparable. In the event, in 497 B.C. he quit his ministerial job and hit the road "with no prospects and very little cash."[26]

CONFUCIUS WAS FIFTY-FOUR when he left Lu to wander the kingdom, sojourning wherever a ruler would hire him as an adviser. His disciples followed, some seeking moral enlightenment, others hoping to find their way into government by emulating Confucius. The Master accepted anyone who was truly hungry for knowledge. The glibly incurious, however, he rejected: "I can never do anything for a man who has not been asking himself, 'What should I do? What should I do?' "[27]

Unlike, say, Plato or Aristotle, Confucius never laid out his ideas systematically in writing; the Confucian "system," as it were, was the creation of disciples, who recorded his ideas in the *Analects*. Subsequent generations of scholars codified these in commentaries, and a Confucian tradition was born—though, as with any great system, there were differing schools of interpretation, organic developments in response to changing historical circumstances, and plenty of mixing with other religious and philosophical traditions.

The teachings in the *Analects* are aphoristic, episodic, bound to concrete problems that arose in Confucius's political life and that of his followers. In each instance, his ultimate aim was to nurture "the moral way." Eloquent rhetoric and intelligent ideas, he at one point told his disciples, are useless unless they "lead you to self-reform. . . . To be pleased [with someone's advice] but not to try to understand [the point of his advice]; to agree with [someone's words] but not [to let his words] bring about self-reform—there is nothing I can do with those who behave like this."[28] If a man repeated Confucius's words but disrespected his own aging mother, he was no true disciple.

Confucius didn't pretend to be a prophet. At one point, he told his followers: "Do I possess an all-knowing cognizance? I do not. If a simple fellow asks me a question, my mind at first is a complete blank, and I have to knock at both sides [of the question] until everything has been considered [and some clarity begins to emerge]."[29] Elsewhere, one of his disciples commented that "our Master" learned from *everyone;* the righteous way, after all, was embedded in the conscience of every human being, and thus the moral seeker could tap anyone for insight.[30] Could Confucians not learn about filiality, for example, by observing how "a simple fellow" honored his parents (or failed to do so)?

On other occasions, Confucius could harshly rebuke his followers. Once, after he fell seriously ill, one of his more blockheaded disciples, a man named Zilu, suggested that the band of followers pretend to be hired retainers to a great minister, to ensure that the Master would receive a minister's ostentatious funeral. This, even though Confucius was only an ex-minister and not entitled to a minister's funeral, according to the rites. When he recovered, Confucius scolded Zilu: "By pretending I had retainers when I had none, whom were we trying to deceive? Heaven?" Playacting as if Confucius had a rank he didn't possess was a ritual violation. But again, Confucius gave an added glimpse of the moral spirit behind his scrupulosity: "Besides, would I not rather die in the arms of a few good friends than in the arms of retainers?"[31] A humane gentleman would have preferred to breathe his last among spiritual and intellectual comrades, rather than political lackeys.

After fourteen years of wandering, Confucius was invited back to Lu by the state's ruler, thanks to the intervention of disciples who had entered the highest circles of power. This time, the Lu elites honored him as an elder statesman, though he didn't seek any official post or wield power directly. Then, one day, Confucius was seen pacing by a city gate, tears flowing from his eyes. He told a disciple who ran up to him, "The world has long been without a moral way. Therefore, no one is able to appreciate me. . . . I shall die soon."[32] He died a week later, aged seventy-one or seventy-two.

History would prove wrong Confucius's gloomy predictions about his own legacy. His teaching would gather prestige until it formed the bedrock of Chinese civilization, its influence unparalleled well into the nineteenth century, when many intellectuals began to hanker for Western-style ideas and reforms. Following the Communist takeover in 1949, Mao Zedong and his followers attempted to exorcise the Master's spirit, going so far as to desecrate his family cemetery in Qufu during the Cultural Revolution—to demonstrate, once and for all, that Confucius was well and truly dead. Yet today, a Confucian revival of sorts is underway in the People's Republic, and the Chinese still remember him as *xianshi,* "the teacher before all teachers."[33]

"The Root of Virtue"

How must we serve our parents, and what do we gain from serving them well?

Confucius didn't speak of his own parents in the *Analects*. Yet he discussed the experience of being a son with such authenticity that he must have had an "intimate knowledge of such things," Chin speculates. Or maybe "he possessed an uncommon ability to internalize what he had seen and heard and what other people had told him about their" parents.[34]

Certainly, his cultural milieu echoed with morality tales about children good and bad. Besides Shusun Bao, there was, for example, the equally tragic tale of Ding Jiang. A noblewoman whose own son died at a young age, Ding Jiang was made the adoptive mother of a certain ruler. This man, Ding Jiang's adoptive son, was "callous and shortsighted" in government, forcing the leading families to expel him. Before he left, he asked the priest who cared for his family's ancestral temple to "inform his forbears [*sic*] that he was fleeing the country but that he had done nothing wrong."[35]

When the priest related this to Ding Jiang, the old woman became incensed. Her adoptive son, she told the priest, "abandoned his counselors and schemed with his minions," and this was "his first crime." His second crime: "His father appointed his own counselors to be his tutors and guardians, yet he failed to show them any respect." Yet his third crime was worst of all, and it involved Ding Jiang personally: "I attended to his father's every need, waiting on his father with towels and comb, yet he treated me boorishly as if I was a [leftover] concubine. . . . Tell the ancestors that he is fleeing. But don't say to them that he has done nothing wrong."[36]

Millennia later, the heat of Ding Jiang's outrage smolders in her words as recorded in the ancient annals. Through a Confucian lens, this man's later political misdeeds, like Niu's, traced back to his failures as a son. His third crime was the basis for his first and second.

In the *Analects*, Confucius urged that "a youngster should be filial to his parents at home and respectful to his elders when he is away from home."[37] He saw the parental hearth as a school of right conduct, helping each of us grasp "the fundamentals of human relationships early in life, before one sets out into the world," as Chin comments.[38] The *Classic of Filiality,* a compendium of Confucian wisdom likely composed during the Western or Former Han dynasty (206 B.C.–A.D. 8), put this starkly: "Filiality is the root of virtue and the wellspring of instruction."[39]

How can we partake of this instruction? Confucius's followers recorded the core teachings in the early chapters of the *Analects.*

When one disciple, Meng Wubo, asked the Master about being filial, the latter told him, "Give your parents no cause for worry other than your illness." The first-century scholar Ma Rong interpreted this to mean that a good son or daughter "will not act thoughtlessly and unduly to bring grief to his parents; he allows his illness to be the only cause for their worry." Ziyou, another disciple, asked the Master about the same thing. Confucius said, "Nowadays, [filiality] is taken to mean being able to feed your parents. But dogs and horses do as much. If you are not respectful, how are you different?"[40] Caring for our parents' physical needs is necessary but not sufficient to prove filial devotion.

Still another disciple, Zixia, asked Confucius about filiality. The Master replied, "The difficult part is the facial expression. As for the youngsters taking on the burden when there is work to be done and the older ones being served first when there is food and wine, can this be called filial conduct?"[41] This third teaching echoes the second: Even if children take on their parents' burdens and serve them food and drink before helping themselves, their filial devotion is undone if the children's faces betray annoyance or fatigue. We must *want* to be filial.

To sum up: We should act in a measured, moral way, so as not to cause unnecessary distress to our parents. In some situations, that might mean granting them at least some deference when it comes to making major decisions, or choosing to remain geographically close to them. We should give high priority to our parents' material and emotional needs, and we should do so with love and joy. We mustn't dare to toss our parents aside in their old age and senescence.

AN AMERICAN TODAY might fairly wonder why the Confucian tradition imposed on sons and daughters obligations that go well beyond "being nice." Even some parents recoil at the idea of expecting such a degree of deference from their children. The question leads us to one of the luminous gems of the Confucian tradition.

One day, Zai Wo, one of Confucius's disciples, asked the Master about the extended mourning period that was supposed to follow the death of a parent. According to the ancient rites, a child who lost a parent was expected to spend the following three years in a state of dejection. He wasn't supposed to take delight in sumptuous food, or perform music, or have sex, or gather ripened grain, and so on.

Zai Wo considered these burdens needlessly onerous. "'A year,'" he said to Confucius, "'is already too long. If a gentleman neglects the [non-mourning] rites for three years, those rites will be in ruins. If he does not allow himself to perform music, it will be the undoing of music. . . . A year of mourning is quite enough.'"

Confucius shot back: "'And would you be able to eat rice and wear brocade and feel comfortable doing it?'"

"'I would.'"

"'If you feel comfortable doing it, then go ahead. But a gentleman in mourning finds no relish in tasty food, no pleasure in music and no ease in his own home. So he does not eat rice and wear brocade. But if you feel comfortable doing it, then go ahead!'"

When Zai Wo left, Confucius told the others that the disciple "'lacks humaneness. A child does not leave his parents' arms until he is three. The three-year mourning is the practice observed by all the world. Did Yu [Zai Wo] not also have three years of love and affection from his parents?'"[42]

Here lies the natural justification of not just Chinese but all traditional filiality norms. We are creatures naturally inclined to love and longing to be loved. Our parents answered this longing precisely when we were most vulnerable, when we couldn't have even survived on our own. The point of filial devotion is to honor—and return—the love we were once given.

Filiality is, or should be, a physical thing. The Han dynasty *Classic of Filiality* taught: "Our body, skin, and hair are all received from our parents; we dare not injure them. This is the first priority in filial duty." Filial devotion is inscribed in the bare fact of our bodies and in our human nature: "Parents give one life; no bond could be greater," and "therefore not to love one's parents but to love others is to act against one's moral nature."[43]

This duty to parents doesn't preclude us from serving others. Nor does it mean partiality toward one's own blood to the point of hurting our neighbor. On the contrary, filiality, at its best, allows us to grow in empathy for those with whom we don't share blood ties.

Before we could reason, our parents nourished the moral impulse inside us by their example, by caring for us in our babyhood. We didn't have to ask our mothers to breastfeed us or our fathers to rush us to the doctor when we fell ill. They just did these things, and more, out of natural love. The Confucian ideal of filiality encourages us to revive those early memories of being gratuitously loved, to help us remember our childhoods with our parents, and thus to sharpen our moral imagination amid the rancor and competitiveness of adulthood.

"Revering one's parents, one dare not be contemptuous of others," said the *Classic of Filiality*. This vision of filial empathy is especially essential for good government: "When his love and reverence are perfected in service to parents, [the ruler's] moral influence is shed on all people and his good example shines in all directions."[44] The empathy learned from, and reciprocated to, parental love ripples out into the political community.

Having learned empathy from parental love, the *Classic* taught, righteous kings dared not "neglect the ministers even of small states (much less their own . . . nobility)"; regional rulers dared not "abuse

widows and widowers (much less scholar-officials and commoners)";
and heads of families dared not "mistreat servants and concubines
(much less their own wives and children)." Living by filiality, "they
were at peace; in death, content."[45]

THE ERRANT PARENT

"We all accept that there is an enduring bond between parent and
child," the advice columnist Emily Yoffe wrote in 2013. "One of the
Ten Commandments is to 'honor your father and your mother,'
though this must have been a difficult admonition for the children of,
for example, Abraham, Rebecca, and Jacob." To Yoffe, filial instincts
make sense from an "evolutionary perspective," but we needn't act
on them if our parents egregiously violated our expectations as children.[46]

What prompted her essay was an inbox full of letters from men
and women "looking for someone, anyone, to tell them they should
not feel guilty for declining to care" for bad parents. Many confided
horrific cases of abuse at the hands of parents. "In private correspon-
dence with these letter writers, I sometimes point out that, judging
by their accounts, there doesn't seem to be any acknowledgment of
guilt on the part of the parent."[47] So Yoffe told her correspondents
what they wanted to hear.

The Confucian tradition wasn't unfamiliar with errant parents—
far from it. We have already encountered one in Shusun Bao, who
was by any measure a terrible father, conceiving and abandoning one
son, then later unjustly killing another and exiling still a third. Yet a
fourth (illegitimate) son, Zhaozi, understood that the good of the
whole family and the political community would be served by remaining filial to the memory of his errant father.

A more striking example is the parents of the mythic ancient
emperor Shun. The fourth-century B.C. sage Mencius, inarguably the
most influential Chinese philosopher after Confucius, presented
Shun as a paragon of filiality in the face of awful parents.

When he was already in his fifties and working in the rice paddies, Shun would be heard wailing to heaven and "calling upon father and mother," according to Mencius.[48] This was mind-boggling, not only because of Shun's age but because his parents simply hadn't loved him. In fact, Shun's father, stepmother, and half-brother had repeatedly plotted to kill him. They would send him to repair a barn roof, for example, then remove the ladder and set fire to the structure. Or they would dispatch him to draw water, then cover up the well. Shun survived each plot—yet he would still wail to heaven and yearn for parental love years later.

Shun's filiality toward his frankly evil parents so impressed the reigning emperor that the latter "sent his nine sons, and two daughters, together with the hundred [senior-most] officials, taking with them the full quota of cattle and sheep and provisions, to serve Shun in the fields." Eventually, the emperor turned over his throne to Shun, in part because he recognized in him a "son of supreme dutifulness," one who "yearns for his parents all his life."[49]

Does taking Confucian teaching seriously mean we have to put up with murderous parents? Absolutely not. The Shun story is quasi-mythical. It is an ideal. The important question we moderns should ask is: *Why* would tradition hold up this extreme ideal of filiality?

The answer, it seems to me, is twofold. First, Shun's filiality in the face of parental evil crystallizes the essential and impenetrable mystery of the parent-child bond: No matter how strong our differences with our parents, and even when they quite literally try to kill us, they remain our parents. We wouldn't exist without them, and this natural mystery imposes certain obligations on us—even if our mothers and fathers fail to meet *their* obligations as parents.

Second, and more important, a vital tradition *must* celebrate such an ideal, even if the vast majority of people fall short of it. Most people would run away from parents like Shun's. They certainly wouldn't wail for such parents after they died. That's fine. It's understandable. But tradition can't uphold the opposite ideal: Because it is concerned with preserving and handing down a *norm* of conduct, tradition can't allow us to base our filiality on whether or not our parents loved us as we expected them to. Individual parents might fail to demonstrate the love and empathy that is the basis for filiality, but tradition can't treat such exceptions as the norm.

To be clear, we *can* correct errant parents when they act ignobly. Indeed, the Confucian tradition urges us to do so, provided we do it gently and respectfully: When correcting parents, Confucius taught, "do not be resentful even when they wear you out and make you anxious."[50] But filiality finally mustn't be permitted to become negotiable or conditional on our parents' conduct—lest it be undone.

If we agree that our parents aren't just a random, accidental fact about our own personalities and existence, then it follows that our obligations to them are different from others we might choose to accept or reject as we please. That idea is deeply embedded in the Chinese tradition, whose wisdom insistently addresses us across vast barriers of time, language, and culture, in the sublime teachings of Master Kong.

SHOULD YOU THINK FOR YOURSELF?

———

T hink for yourself and question authority."[1] So urged the Harvard psychologist and psychedelic-drug guru Timothy Leary (1920–1996), best-known for his LSD-drenched motto "turn on, tune in, drop out."[2]

If we remember Leary at all, it is as one of the nuttier icons of the 1960s counterculture—the ur-hippie, if you will, whose influence has faded like Dad's tie-dyed T-shirt from college. But Leary was onto something when he identified "think for yourself and question authority" as the defining ethos of our age. In 1989, Leary told a live audience that, for eons, the human mind had been beholden to various disciplinary authorities: family, folkways and communal mores, institutional religion. But now you have the unthinkable freedom of "thinking for yourself." And not only thinking for yourself, but "making your own decisions, navigating your own career throughout your life, of choosing your own wife, of choosing how you dress, choosing how you live."[3]

Well, who can deny that all this is open to us, and much more besides? Three decades since Leary's talk, we are free not only to choose our own wives or husbands, but to join multiple-partner unions (with growing legal recognition)—or even to "marry" ourselves (with social approval).[4] The freedom to think the unthinkable has given way to the freedom to *do* the unthinkable. Leary thought we had the 1960s student revolts to thank for the downfall of traditional authorities and the blossoming of free thought. But in fact, these phenomena are of much older vintage, dating back more than two hundred years to the rise and entrenchment of liberalism in Europe and the United States.

"Liberalism" is notoriously hard to define. It comes in many different shades, and even liberals frequently disagree over its true meaning. But if one principle unites the varieties, it is that the individual has the supreme right and even the duty to reason through life's dilemmas on her own, her conscience unchained by authorities of whatever kind. Indeed, as one liberal intellectual historian has argued, "liberalism *is* free thought."[5]

To the liberal, the act of thinking for yourself is an inherent good, even the highest good. It is the guarantor of the flow of information, the currency of the marketplace of ideas. More than that, free thought guards the integrity of the conscience against oppressive external forces, against dogmatic principles and unproved presuppositions. To deny an absolute right to question everything is thus the most heinous intellectual crime under liberalism, the first stop on the road to tyranny.

This isn't a matter of left or right. After two centuries of liberal hegemony, absolute freedom of thought is a bipartisan pledge. Nowadays, a progressive *New York Times* columnist flatly asserts, "Personally, I can't understand anyone who doesn't question every inherited part of the culture."[6] Meanwhile, conservative publications and institutions enshrine a devotion to "free minds" in their mastheads and mission statements.

Yet, though we treat free thought as inviolable dogma, censorship is pervasive, most of it done by online mobs that can ruin lives and careers in a matter of minutes. Not surprisingly, nearly two-thirds of Americans admit they are afraid to speak their minds.[7] The old authorities have lost much of their sway or been toppled entirely, but we feel our "free minds" manipulated by commercial and political forces deploying ever-more-sophisticated mechanisms, from fake-news memes to apps and social media designed to be as addictive as possible. Conspiracy theorists make a killing in our marketplace of ideas. The loudest, most outrageous voices are rewarded. We don't know whom to believe. Yet few wonder if the habitual distrust for authority bred by liberalism has anything to do with any of this.

Something isn't working. We are very far from the ideal promised by the powdered-wig liberals of the eighteenth and nineteenth centuries. Thus, I ask: *Should we, in fact, always think for ourselves?*

A Rupture with Modernity

The statesman who personified liberalism in the nineteenth century, William Gladstone, picked a peculiar topic for his maiden speech as a newly elected member of the House of Commons. The year was 1833, and Parliament was debating a bill to abolish slavery across the British Empire. Britain had already banned the slave trade in 1807, but British plantations in the West Indies and elsewhere continued to own, exploit, and terrorize black men and women.

Rising to speak in opposition, Gladstone declared: "I would not free the slave, without assurance of his disposition to industry."[8] That is, he wouldn't emancipate slaves unless it could be shown that they could make themselves useful somehow, without the lash to motivate them. If emancipation was inevitable, then he would insist that owners be compensated for the loss of their free labor—owners like his own father, whose practices Gladstone vigorously defended.[9]

Parliament did pass the Slavery Abolition Act, and in the years that followed, Gladstone would gradually abandon the High Toryism of his political youth, though he stayed cool to abolition for the rest of his life.[10] As a liberal, Gladstone utterly dominated Victorian politics: He held a seat in Parliament for more than six decades, serving four times as chancellor of the Exchequer and as prime minister for a total of twelve years across four terms, from 1868 to 1894.

Oxford-educated, Gladstone possessed what one historian has called a "demonic energy."[11] His marathon speeches would have left Fidel Castro blushing. He read some twenty thousand books in six languages over the course of his life, translated from Italian a titanic history of the Roman state, and penned works of literary criticism on the likes of Homer and Tennyson. For leisure, he chopped down trees, prompting Lord Randolph Churchill (Winston's father) to quip, "The forest laments in order that Mr. Gladstone may perspire."[12]

Look at one of Gladstone's portraits, and his famous earnestness will radiate from the canvas: a stern chin, pursed lips, and sparkling eyes framed by muttonchops. A devout evangelical, he breathed a moralizing spirit into his causes: free trade, low taxes, hostility to aristocratic privilege and to religious establishments. He considered himself a friend of the lowly. These included the London prostitutes he visited nightly, to "rescue" them, he claimed, from the oldest profession (there was almost certainly a less-noble aspect to these encounters).[13]

Above all, he was relentless, to the endless chagrin of his ostensible boss, Queen Victoria. When voters returned him to No. 10 Downing Street on one occasion, Victoria wrote to her secretary (referring to herself in the third person in her signature style): "She will sooner *abdicate* than send for or have any *communication* with that who [would] soon ruin everything and be a *dictator*."[14] But get his way Gladstone did, pushing through numerous pieces of legislation, many of them admirable steps toward greater social justice—stronger protections for labor unions, improved sanitation and public health, and so on.

The brand of liberalism Gladstone embodied rose in tandem with British prestige, which reached its zenith in this era of rapid economic and geographic expansion. Gladstone and his ideas were plainly *winners,* at least in material terms. His achievements, moreover, made Gladstone enormously popular with the working classes, even if he repulsed the upper echelons of Victorian society. Which is why British Catholics shuddered when this man, a powerhouse in what then was the world's most powerful nation, set his sights on them.

The cause of his ire was a pair of decrees issued by the First Vatican Council (1869–1870) defining the doctrine of papal infallibility. *Pastor Aeternus,* the more controversial of the two decrees, had declared:

The Roman Pontiff, when he speaks *ex cathedra,* that is, when in discharge of the office of pastor and doctor of all Christians, by virtue of his supreme Apostolic authority, he defines a doctrine regarding faith or morals to be held by the universal Church, by the divine assistance promised to him in Blessed Peter, is possessed of that infallibility with which the divine Redeemer willed that his Church should be endowed for defining doctrine regarding faith or morals; and that therefore such definitions of the Roman Pontiff are irreformable of themselves, and not from the consent of the Church.[15]

These words, and the proceedings of the council as a whole, sent Gladstone into a fit of apoplexy. Initially, he remarked in passing that no one could now convert to Catholicism "without renouncing his moral and mental freedom, and placing his civil loyalty and duty at the mercy of another."[16] The council had made Catholics the intellectual slaves of the authority of their popes, and, therefore, they couldn't fully function as citizens of a free society.

The offhand jibe shocked British Catholic opinion, but the Right Honorable William Ewart Gladstone wasn't one to back down. In 1874, newly out of power and with time on his hands, he set to work on an essay that widened his assault. The resulting pamphlet, *The Vatican Decrees in Their Bearing on Civil Allegiance: A Political Expostulation,* remains among the most notorious anti-Catholic screeds ever published.

Gladstone took pains to show that he didn't have anything against individual Catholics: "I desire to eschew . . . religious bigotry."[17] He granted, too, that ordinary lay Catholics didn't get to choose their religious leaders or direct their church's affairs. Nevertheless, Catholic Britons owed their fellow citizens some "reply to that ecclesiastical party in their Church who have laid down, in their name, principles adverse to the purity and integrity of civil allegiance."[18]

Papal infallibility, Gladstone argued, marked a rupture with history and, worse, with modernity. The reigning pontiff, Pius IX (1792–

1878), had already issued in 1864 a *Syllabus of Errors* prohibiting Catholics from holding certain opinions, such as the notion that the pope "can, and ought to, reconcile himself, and come to terms, with progress, liberalism, and modern civilization."[19] Now Pius wanted his retrograde ideas—not least opposition to freedom of conscience in religious and political matters—to be infallibly binding on the minds of individual Catholics?

That, Gladstone charged, was tantamount to "moral murder"—an unpardonable assertion of authority aimed at "stifling conscience and conviction."[20] Left unchallenged, papal authority would short-circuit the process by which every person must freely reason through moral questions. And the collective consequences were more alarming still. When the pope teaches on faith and morals, per the Vatican declaration, his edicts are binding on his children spread across the earth, with the disobedient risking the salvation of their very souls. Could freedom be preserved if a large minority (in Britain's case) surrendered its conscience to a bishop in Rome?

As he drew to a close, Gladstone recalled with a patronizing air that "for thirty years, and in a great variety of circumstances, in office and as an independent member of Parliament . . . I have with others labored to maintain and extend the civil rights of my Roman Catholic fellow-countrymen."[21] He had done these things as a sincere believer in freedom of thought and conscience. The Roman church had repaid this liberality with treachery.

In a final passage tinged with not a little menace, he called on Catholic Britons to do in the nineteenth century what some of their forebears had done in the sixteenth and seventeenth—that is, to resist papal power and rededicate themselves to the precious liberties of their island nation. The "strong-headed and sound-hearted race" of Englishmen, he concluded, "will not be hindered, either by latent or by avowed dissents, due to the foreign influence of a caste, from the accomplishment of its mission in the world."[22]

The irony was lost on Gladstone but not on history: He had begun his career defending indigenous slavery, a crime the papacy had condemned three centuries earlier. Now he accused the popes of enslaving not bodies but minds.

His charge was not without teeth: Catholics in Britain had won legal equality only four decades earlier. Various handicaps against them remained in place. They still felt their second-class status, and they knew that residing on the other side of Gladstone's favor posed a terrible danger. *The Vatican Decrees* sold a staggering 150,000 copies.

Who could champion Catholics against this mighty adversary? Who could vindicate their honor as citizens? The task would fall to a famous convert, who, it happened, treated the conscience as the foremost thing in human affairs. This was Father John Henry Newman.

"A Higher Rule Than Any Argument"

Like Augustine, Newman told his own story in a splendid memoir that painstakingly documented the evolution of his beliefs. What mainly concerns us isn't Newman's decision, at age forty-four, to abandon the prestige of Oxford society and the Anglican priesthood to adopt a faith his Victorian peers regarded as the superstition of Irish maids. We need, rather, to probe Newman's ideas on the link between conscience and authority and what it *really* means to think for oneself.

He formulated these ideas in the fray of a nineteenth-century intra-Christian debate. Yet they remain relevant far beyond that original context, including to non-Christians, and can allow us to reconsider our own age's certainties about free thought. His scandalous conversion and his conflict with Gladstone over the question of conscience and authority were closely entangled, and so we must examine both.

Newman was born in London on February 21, 1801, the son of a banker father and a mother of Huguenot extraction. His family was what Americans might call "Bible-believing Christians." His grandmother especially inculcated in the young John Henry a lifelong love of Scripture, though at boarding school he came across Enlightenment philosophy and briefly danced at the edge of skepticism. As he recalled in his memoir, the *Apologia Pro Vita Sua*, "When I was fourteen, I read [Thomas] Paine's *Tracts against the Old Testament*, and found pleasure in thinking of the objections which were contained in them." Voltaire's arguments against the immortality of the soul made him think, "How dreadful, but how plausible!"[23]

At age fifteen, Newman was brought back to faith by writers and teachers in the evangelical, Calvinistic tradition. He enrolled at Trinity College, Oxford, where he studied math, history, the Greek and Latin classics, John Locke, and Francis Bacon. In his free time, he didn't carouse with the boys but took long walks and practiced the violin. Come exam time, he did poorly, owing to a nervous breakdown of sorts; nevertheless, he was awarded a prestigious fellowship to Oriel College.

"For the next decade," one biographer summarizes, Newman "moved within a cluster of intellectuals heavily concerned with theological questions."[24] They pushed him to abandon evangelicalism, with its do-it-your-own-way spirituality, in favor of submission to a visible, authoritative church rooted in antiquity. Antiquity—the wisdom of early Christianity (which we sampled in chapter 6)—mattered. It was, he wrote, "the true exponent of the doctrines of Christianity."[25]

He was ordained an Anglican priest in 1825. Over the fifteen or so years that followed, he wore three hats, as a minister, tutor, and intellectual-at-large at Oxford. Soon, he emerged as a leading light of what became known as the Oxford Movement, a circle of thinkers who wanted to position the Church of England as a middle way, a *via media*, between what they saw as a tradition-bereft Protestantism and Rome's "excesses."[26]

Liberal Anglicans suspected the Tractarians—as Newman's group came to be known, for the periodical *Tracts* they published—of drifting across the Tiber, whether unconsciously or willfully and conspiratorially. Newman, England's most cutting polemicist of the nineteenth century, didn't hesitate to push back and mix it up with the movement's critics.

Yet the most fateful incident of this period had nothing to do with tracts and polemics. It was, rather, the journey he took in 1832 to Sicily and the Italian mainland. The trip granted him a glimpse of religious devotion the likes of which he had never before witnessed.

"Making an expedition on foot across some wild country in Sicily, at six in the morning," Newman recalled, "I came upon a small church; I heard voices, and I looked in. It was crowded, and the congregation was singing. Of course, it was the mass, though I did not know it at the time."[27] He fell in love with the smoky awe and mystery of Catholicism, the devotion and holy abjection of God's own peasants. If only he could bring his mind to assent to Rome's teachings, he lamented in a poem he jotted down:

> *Oh, that thy creed were sound!*
> *For thou dost soothe the heart, thou Church of Rome.*
> *For thy unwearied watch and varied round*
> *Of service, in thy savior's holy home.*[28]

Newman fell direly ill on his Mediterranean journey, likely of typhoid. The doctors thought he was on the verge of death. But at one point, fevered and bathed in sweat, he awoke to inform his servant: "I shall not die. I shall not die, for I have not sinned against the light."[29] What exactly this meant would puzzle him for the rest of his life. But in the event, the kindly light did lead him back to the land of the living; he convalesced and returned to Oxford. There awaited him the decision that would dramatically alter his profile—and eventually set Newman on a collision course with the mightiest politician in his country.

IN BRITAIN, NEWMAN turned more strident in his criticisms of progressive currents in the Anglican communion. Whichever church is true at any time, he thought, must look familiar in its essentials to the earliest sages—Augustine & Co., if you will. Yet the more he tried to reconcile the Church of England to antiquity, the more the Anglican hierarchy spurned and shushed him. Finally, he concluded that the *via media* was hopeless.

Newman's romance with Rome was heating up by the day, yet still he resisted converting. Why? Because he entertained serious doubts about some doctrines, high among them the Roman devotion to the Virgin Mary. So long as these doubts persisted, "I had no right, I had no leave, to act against my conscience. This was a higher rule than any argument."[30]

For Newman, as we have said, conscience was the foremost thing. "What is a higher guide for us in speculation and in practice," he asked in his *Apologia,* "than that conscience of right and wrong, of truth and falsehood, those sentiments of what is decorous, consistent, and noble, which our Creator has made a part of our original nature?"[31]

His own conscience held him back from Rome; to go against it would have been an awful transgression. What he was certain about, down to his inner depths, was that he opposed the liberal spirit just then sweeping Europe. He detested it so much that while he was abroad, it sickened him to catch sight of the tricolor, the French revolutionary standard that had given the sanction of "Reason" to the guillotining of priests and the raping of nuns.

"My battle," he would insist, "was with liberalism; by liberalism, I mean the anti-dogmatic principle," the "lawless" notion that every first principle, every dogma, every authority, and every hierarchy was up for questioning.[32] Thus, Newman held in his mind two seemingly contradictory beliefs—first, that the conscience was sacred and inviolable; and second, that unlimited freedom of thought was not a good but rather a wellspring of error and chaos. This (apparent) tension would prove crucial in his duel with Gladstone decades later.

For now, he had to work out his own salvation. While still pursuing the *via media,* Newman had a sudden, and perhaps providential, moment of clarity. It came thanks to Augustine himself. A Protestant friend had pointed Newman to a passage in Augustine's letters, in which the bishop of Hippo had written, *"Securus judicat orbis terrarum"*—roughly, "The whole world [i.e., the universal Church] judges rightly." His friend, Newman recalled, "repeated these words again and again, and, when he was gone, they kept ringing in my ears. . . . For a mere sentence, the words of St. Augustine, struck me with a power which I never had felt from any words before."[33]

The spiritual import was clear: The individual soul was called to submit to the authority of an apostolic body tracing to Christ's first followers, and that body's judgments couldn't be wrong. Antiquity's voices sang in unison on this. Yet it would take several more years for Newman's conscience to admit that if Augustine & Co. were to time-travel to the nineteenth century, they would find the closest resemblance to their own church in the Roman communion.

It was Rome that had preserved apostolic celibacy among its priests, Rome that insisted on the sacraments and dogmas of the primitive Church, Rome that could justly boast of universality. And the things that appeared as Romish "excesses," including the Marian doctrines, hadn't been conjured out of the blue over the long centuries but were natural, logical developments of the faith of the Church Fathers and early Christian communities.

He wouldn't strong-arm his own conscience but allow it to take its course, aided by copious reading, reflection, and prayer—until, in 1845, John Henry Newman was received into full communion with Rome and ordained a Catholic priest not long after.

GIVEN THIS (WELL-PUBLICIZED) personal history, it made sense for Newman's friends to urge him to pick up the gauntlet against Gladstone. Yet by 1874, when *The Vatican Decrees* convulsed Britain, Newman was an old man, not as energetic as he once had been and reluctant to enter what struck him as "a scene of war."[34] Still, he couldn't live with himself not to engage, and so he did, publishing his counterblast as a letter addressed to the (Catholic) Duke of Norfolk.

In it, Newman set out to prove that Gladstone's accusations against the Catholic hierarchy were "neither trustworthy nor charitable"—and, more fundamentally, that there was no conflict between following one's conscience (rightly understood) and submitting to authority (ditto).[35]

To repel Gladstone's onslaught, and thus help guard Catholic Britons' right to participate in the public square *as Catholics*, Newman had to mount two defensive maneuvers. First, he had to show that, far from a radical power grab, the conciliar claim of papal infallibility was in unbroken continuity with Christian history. Second, and more pertinent to our discussion, Newman needed to show that absolute freedom of thought of the kind advocated by Gladstone and other leading liberals was an illusion—and a pernicious one at that. We will focus on this latter maneuver.

Conscience, Ancient and Modern

Every so often, I hear from my wife that our Max has gotten into a playdate tiff over some toy. Whether it's the other boy or girl who has grabbed the toy out of Max's hands or vice versa, the scene will have ended in sobbing, time-outs, and clashing shouts of "It's mine!" or "No, it's mine!"

That last—the assertion that "it's mine!"—is far more interesting than most adults realize. Even when they act like brutes, kids somehow feel compelled to give a *reason* for it, to appeal to principles of justice. This tells us something profound about human beings.

If the playdate took place at our house, for example, and it was Max who grabbed the toy, then implicit in his assertion is that the other child had taken something that really belonged to him. If, on the other hand, the playdate took place on some "neutral" ground—say, at a playground—then implicit in Max's assertion might be that "I had this toy *first*." Each child firmly believes that there is a solemn, unwritten Law of Toddler Land that the other has transgressed. Even as they disagree passionately over who should keep the toy, they are in passionate agreement that there *is* such a law.

For Newman, as for his fellow Briton C. S. Lewis a century later, the fact that children and, for that matter, adults act this way gave proof of an objective, universal standard of ethical conduct that was somehow branded into human nature from the beginning.[36] "The divine law," Newman wrote to the Duke of Norfolk in 1875, "is the rule of ethical truth, the standard of right and wrong, a sovereign, irreversible, absolute authority in the presence of men and Angels."[37]

The conscience, he argued, is just this law "as apprehended in the minds of individual men."[38] It is the mental agent of the law that gauges our conduct according to the law's standard and tries to get us to comply with its precepts.

Of course, there are all sorts of different human personalities, as well as a vast range of familial and cultural conditions that nurture them. In the Christian telling, moreover, original sin hobbles the human conscience. The universal law "may suffer refraction in passing into the intellectual medium of each." Yet "it is not therefore so affected as to lose its character of being the Divine Law."[39]

Newman would grant the widest liberty to this inner awareness of an objective, universal law embedded in our nature. But that *wasn't* what his adversaries had in mind when they spoke of free thought. For them, liberty of conscience meant merely the liberty to form one's own judgments as a free citizen of Britain, regardless of whether those judgments aligned with the dictates of the universal law.

In the liberal age, he went on, "a large portion of the public" has come to believe that freedom of conscience is

the very right and freedom of conscience to dispense with conscience, to ignore a Lawgiver and a Judge, to be independent of unseen obligations. It becomes a license to take up any or no religion, to take up this or that and let it go again, to go to church, to go to chapel, to boast of being above all religions and to be an impartial critic of each of them. Conscience is a stern monitor, but in this century, it has been superseded by a counterfeit, which the eighteen centuries prior to it never heard of and could not have mistaken for it, if they had.[40]

This counterfeit wasn't freedom of conscience—it was "the right of self-will."[41]

The right of private judgment, first asserted during the Reformation with respect to how people read and interpreted Scripture, had been dilated three centuries later to encompass all of our moral dealings. Conscience had thus been privatized and *subjectivized,* as it were, without regard for the potentially hideous consequences. For, Newman wondered, "what if a man's conscience embraces the duty of . . . infanticide? or free love?"[42]

Relax, the liberals of the era pooh-poohed their critics: "The good sense of the nation would stifle and extinguish such atrocities."[43] But slippery-slope arguments are no fallacy if a society does, in fact, end up sliding down to a moral abyss. Today, in Britain and across the liberal world, the right to extinguish unwanted children in the womb and the right to all sorts of "free love" are enshrined in law, and they were enshrined precisely as Newman had predicted: on the ground that one citizen's conscience may approve of such conduct, while another's might disapprove, and no one can say for sure which of the two consciences is in the right.

If *that* is what is meant by conscience, Newman concluded, then "it seems a light epithet for the Pope to use, when he calls such a doctrine of conscience *deliramentum*"—delusion, nonsense. "Of all conceivable absurdities it is the wildest and most stupid."[44]

THE GREAT ALLIANCE

So much for the conscience. But what about authority? Let's return to Max briefly—he appreciates your indulgence.

In very young children, the conscience is not yet developed, which is why they need grownup guidance. If my Max, for example, force-fully grabs a toy from his friend, he is following the law of "it's mine!" His mother, by putting him in time-out, is helping hone his under-standing that there are other laws (such as "share and play nicely") that he needs to follow. That is, Mom's authority helps to tune and amplify the interior voice of Max's nascent conscience. About this, and countless other quotidian examples of the kind, John Henry Newman would say that *authority forms the conscience*—contra the lib-eral ideology that constantly pits the two against each other.

Put another way, conscience and authority are friends and allies, not enemies. Indeed, the conscience is itself an authority, per New-man, and thus in some ways, the two are really the same thing.[45]

But note that in Newman's scheme a personal authority is an au-thority only insofar as it upholds the conscience and the dictates of the universal law. If a mother punishes a child wantonly, then she isn't exercising any authority at all but merely wielding a vicious power. Authority can do much more than coerce, for it can persuade. But insofar as both raw power and authority do coerce, the latter does so with much greater legitimacy.

Instead of a right to say or do absolutely anything that popped into their heads, the premoderns had this firm, dynamic alliance between conscience and authority for a bulwark against unjust power, includ-ing power over the mind. And here lies the big distinction between Newman's idea of mental freedom and the one advanced in liberal doctrine.

Today, we adore stories of individuals who heroically defied unjust powers: whistleblowers, conscientious objectors, and others who re-fused to follow evil orders. Many are truly heroic and deserve our admiration; think of Oskar Schindler or the tobacco-industry whistle-blower Jeffrey Wigand. Such figures risked their lives or careers for moral principles—ones they viewed as objective, absolute, and more authoritative than the raw powers above them. But a worldview in which the conscience is thoroughly subjective ends up removing the scaffolding of authority on which these sacrifices rest.

If "conscience rights" encompass letting the old and infirm commit suicide-by-doctor, say, or the view that any religion is as good as any other or none, then what authority, really, does the conscience have? We like to tell ourselves that thinking for yourself and questioning authority will make Oskar Schindlers out of all of us. But if we discard all the old, inconvenient authorities that restrained the beastly side of our natures, isn't it more likely that we will end up becoming beastly people?

Which brings us back to the inconvenient authority of the papacy. In his pamphlet, Gladstone had accused the nineteenth-century popes of having allegedly " 'condemned' the 'maintainers of the Liberty of the Press, of conscience, and of worship.' "[46] But as Newman pointed out, the popes didn't oppose such liberties *in toto*. Nor, for that matter, did even Britain's fast-liberalizing regime endorse it *in toto*. Censorship still had some force, especially in the colonies.

When the popes criticized "liberty of conscience" (always in scare quotes), "they were speaking against it in the various false senses, philosophical or popular, which in this day are put upon the word,"[47] for example, those whose "liberty of conscience" led them to take up Satanism or child sacrifice. But the papacy couldn't have attacked the freedom of the *true* conscience without undermining its own authority. Christians obeyed papal authority, after all, out of fear of divine retribution and a horror of guilt that prowled *their own consciences*. Thus, Newman wrote, "did the Pope speak against Conscience in the true sense of the word, he would commit a suicidal act. He would be cutting the ground from under his feet."[48]

What the popes have always done is to insist on limits and boundaries. Pius IX's successor, Leo XIII (1810–1903), for example, felt called to address the abject condition of workers in his time. Exploitative wages in the nineteenth century condemned the urban working classes to almost universal penury, yet the owners of industry shamelessly defended this state of affairs: It was a "free market," and workers could "choose" to accept or reject employment contracts. "No!" insisted Leo XIII in his 1891 encyclical *Rerum Novarum*. There had to be *limits* to profiteering, and the mere fact of "free agreements" didn't obviate employers' duty to provide a living wage.[49]

The *true* conscience is aware that exploitation is wrong, that poverty wages violate the universal law. Leo XIII merely used his authority to amplify the conscience's voice and widen its ambit to cover a new human problem: workers' rights under industrial capitalism. Yet while some nineteenth-century liberals like Gladstone were sensitive to social injustice, such exercises of authority horrified them—only because they tended to forget how truly new and radical their own view of conscience and authority was. "The grant of liberty," Newman argued, "admits of degrees."[50] But liberalism wants to "force upon the world a universal"—an anarchic vision of the "conscience," unbound by any of the authorities that traditionally guided it.[51]

That liberal vision of absolute free thought and "conscience," Newman argued, would never be realized anyway. It was a mirage. Some orthodoxy or other will inevitably lord over our societies, and likewise, some authority or other will inevitably demand our obeisance. It is our good fortune if the orthodoxy in question is one that reverences the true conscience, and if the authority is a true authority, rather than some huckster trying to make a buck or a demagogue who would lead us to perdition.

Conscience First, the Pope Afterward

So, should we always think for ourselves? Newman would answer that we should always exercise our consciences—again, properly understood as the interior awareness of an objective moral law—upon the big and small moral dilemmas life throws everyone's way. But in doing so, he would add, we must form our judgments according to sound authorities, as most people did until relatively recently in the moral history of our species.

What might that look like?

Writing in praise of the Anglican churchman and poet John Keble, Newman recalled that his friend was "a man who guided himself and formed his judgments, not by processes of reason, by inquiry or by argument, but, to use the word in a broad sense, by authority." Keble turned to his own conscience, of course, but there were other sources to consult: "The Bible is an authority; such is the Church; such is Antiquity; such are the words of the wise; such are hereditary lessons; such are ethical truths; such are historical memories; such are legal saws and state maxims; such are proverbs; such are sentiments, presages, and prepossessions."[52]

To protect the free conscience, we must ring it with true and tested guardians of the kind Newman listed. We must treat those guardians as absolute—lest our defensive barrier give way to the battering ram of external powers (tyrants, advertisers, demagogues, etc.), or lest the counterfeit conscience subvert the true one. This is why Newman railed against liberalism as "false liberty of thought": While "liberty of thought is in itself good," he wrote, human reasoning can go astray unless certain things are left standing as authorities.[53] Question authority enough, and soon, magazines pitched to *teenagers* will publish primers like "Anal Sex: Safety, How-Tos, Tips and More," and TED speakers will urge us to view pedophiles in a sympathetic light.[54] Question authority enough, and large numbers of men will abandon their wives and children and tell themselves their "conscience" approves.

Even following Newman's model, however, we will at times find ourselves torn between conflicting authorities, between a sincere conscience and the command of a superior exercising legitimate authority: say, a pastor. Can we defy the superior in these scenarios? Newman's answer was yes—provided that we first "vanquish that mean, ungenerous, selfish, vulgar spirit" of our nature, "which, at the very first rumour of a command, places itself in opposition to the Superior who gives it."[55]

In other words, we mustn't *start* with a spirit of skepticism or presume that there is a conflict where there may be none. (Many Catholics today sadly adopt just such an opposition-from-the-get-go attitude whenever Pope Francis opens his mouth to teach.) And we mustn't wish to "exercise a right of thinking, saying, doing" whatever we please, "the question of truth and falsehood, right and wrong, the duty if possible of obedience . . . being simply discarded."[56]

Having done all that, we can securely follow our consciences. Indeed, we *must* follow our consciences. Or as Newman put it in perhaps his most famous saying: "If I am obliged to bring religion into after-dinner toasts, (which indeed does not seem quite the thing) I shall drink—to the Pope, if you please—still, to Conscience first, and to the Pope afterwards."[57]

NEWMAN WAS MADE a cardinal four years after his great duel. At the end of his life, as the heat of his various debates with fellow Christians dissipated, he beheld all around him a country and a continent losing faith in God. He died on August 11, 1890. In October 2019, Pope Francis declared John Henry Cardinal Newman a saint.

Gladstone was elected to No. 10 three times following the *Vatican Decrees* controversy. In addition to a rather unjust, if popular, invasion of Egypt in 1882, the quest for regional autonomy (home rule) for Ireland consumed his governments. It was the best cause Gladstone ever took up, and he repeatedly failed to achieve it. In 1894, after his final failure, he resigned and said he was entrusting it all "with God. His blessed will be done."[58] He died four years later.

The immediate threat of Gladstone's invective passed over Britain's Catholics. By the end of the nineteenth century, full Catholic emancipation was secure. Today, Catholics participate at all levels of British society (save for the throne). Yet Gladstone would have his revenge, as his ideas took ever deeper root in the West. A century later, the student activists of the 1960s would capture their quads under the banner of "think for yourself." Yet far from making a radical break, their uprising merely reaffirmed and accelerated the logic of liberal society.

The cultural rupture between conscience and authority heralded by the likes of Gladstone is now complete. People are still mercifully born with consciences, of course, and that won't ever change. But the imperative to always think for yourself leaves many consciences mal-formed, if not altogether unformed.

It is impossible to be one's own pope. For some, the moral life becomes an endless, solipsistic quest to figure out "what my *true* self stands for." Many feel they have to reinvent the moral wheel daily, which is the height of arrogance, not to mention utterly exhausting. Still others externalize all of the conscience's furies, directing them against the faults of others or those of social and political systems. Worse, too many simply learn to tune out the conscience's voice, now lowered to a murmur for lack of authoritative supports.

The think-for-yourself culture celebrates all of these groups for their "free minds." Yet we know that most people sway, feather-like, to the prevailing winds of news and social media, fashion and fad-dism, public and "expert" opinion, P.R. and propaganda. Large corpo-rations, especially, want nothing more than for our minds to be *independent*—that is, unmoored from absolute, unbendable moral au-thorities that might challenge corporate agendas. And how much the better for the powers-that-be if pliant consumers and docile workers fancy themselves rebels and radicals.

WHAT IS FREEDOM *FOR*?

———

In March 2020, while the novel coronavirus ravaged the world and claimed its first victims in the United States, brothers Matt and Noah Colvin had a flash of entrepreneurial inspiration. As *The New York Times* reported, Noah drove across their home state of Tennessee and into Kentucky, "filling a U-Haul truck with thousands of bottles of hand sanitizer and thousands of packs of antibacterial wipes" that he bought from out-of-the-way stores—items that had sold out at most other places and that their fellow citizens badly needed amid a viral outbreak.[1]

Matt, meanwhile, began to list the items for resale on Amazon and eBay. It was a brilliant success at first, with bottles of hand sanitizer commanding prices of $8 to $70 each, "multiples higher than what [they] had bought them for." That is, until the online retail giants pulled the listings under public pressure, leaving the brothers Colvin with "17,700 bottles of the stuff [and] little idea where to sell them."[2]

The *Times* noted that the Colvins were "one of probably thousands of sellers who have amassed stockpiles of hand sanitizer and crucial respirator masks that many hospitals are now rationing." What made their crisis-profiteering both amusing and infuriating were their self-justifications: "Just because it cost me $2 in the store doesn't mean it's not going to cost me $16 to get it to your door," Matt explained. "I honestly think it's a public service. I'm being paid for my public service," he later added.[3]

The story sparked a massive online outcry—but why? The brothers were only guilty of taking our concepts of freedom and the supremacy of the market to their logical ends. Under "normal" conditions, our whole society follows the same logic: The supreme goal is to be free, and the less restricted and disciplined, the freer we are. The political right prizes autonomy in the economic sphere. The left is equally zealous for autonomy in the sexual and cultural sphere. The two partisan camps oppose each other furiously, and the end result is the expansion of autonomy in *both* spheres, the boardroom and the bedroom.

To be sure, we admire those who exercise their individual rights for altruistic ends, and we might shake our heads at those who use them selfishly. But we dare not question our "neutral" concept of maximal individual liberty. Indeed, the dream of freedom without ends or limits holds such sway over the Western mind that anyone who questions it is instantly accused of being either a reactionary or a radical.

The openness of the liberal West thus coexists, paradoxically, with a dogmatic faith that maximizing individual rights is nearly always and everywhere good—the One Thing Needful to help us lead fulfilled lives. A pair of Tennessee hucksters who perhaps took an idea a little too far during a pandemic don't come out looking like angels. We might even judge their plan an egregious abuse of freedom. But even so, like some invisible magnetic field, a thick layer of intellectual conformism protects our fundamental faith in unlimited, or nearly unlimited, individual freedom as an unalloyed good.

Yet for some of us—especially those who have experienced both lawless tyrannical states and the dizzying legal freedoms of the West—the dismal state of our common life raises a nagging question: *What is freedom* for?

BITTER TRUTHS

Commencement addresses rarely make headlines, because most speakers do little more than string together clichés and bromides. But when Alexander Solzhenitsyn addressed Harvard University's graduating class of 1978, his words traveled far beyond the collegiate precincts of Cambridge, Massachusetts. For months afterward, the "Harvard speech" was all Western opinion-makers could talk about, and not in a good way.

Solzhenitsyn was probably the most famous writer in the world at the time, celebrated for his novels, histories, and exposés of the gulag, the network of forced-labor camps in which the Soviets imprisoned some 18 million people, including him. His personal courage in the face of Communist tyranny had won him the admiration of the good and the just the world over—and the unremitting hostility of the KGB and the USSR's Western apologists.

Ever since his arrival in the West four years earlier, he had been inundated with interview requests, speaking invitations, honorary degrees, and the like. He tried his best not to be beguiled. He was a deeply private man, and he didn't want his writing projects to fall by the wayside, his craft to rust. Why were they bothering him anyway? As he recalled in his memoir of exile, "I had already said everything that was important in Moscow."[4]

Harvard was a different story, though. The school, he knew, was among the world's preeminent academic institutions. Harvard administrators had been trying for years to coax him into speaking (and accepting an honorary degree). Finally, the Nobel-winning author of *One Day in the Life of Ivan Denisovich* and *The Gulag Archipelago* relented, setting the scene for the marquee intellectual event of the year, if not the decade.

His hosts assumed he would follow a certain script. Having documented the horrors behind the Iron Curtain before making his home in the Land of the Free, he was expected to sing his variation on the immigrant's ode to America. Solzhenitsyn recalled: "What was mainly expected of me . . . was the gratitude of the exile to the great Atlantic Fortress of Liberty."[5] But he wasn't one to follow ideological scripts, else he would have thrived as a court writer under Communism. Nor was he inclined to flatter anyone.

On the day, an audience of some twenty thousand—students, par-

ents, professors, and others, plus a large contingent of journalists—
packed Harvard Yard to hear him. Dressed in a drab military-style
jacket, with his penetrating gaze and Rasputinesque beard, the great
man must have cut an intimidating figure among the Ivy elites. A
heavy rain fell as Solzhenitsyn stood up to speak. No one scurried
away to avoid the downpour, though many hadn't brought umbrel-
las. After a long and preemptive standing ovation from the audience,
he delivered his address in Russian, with a simultaneous English
translation broadcast over his piercing voice.

Harvard's motto, he began, is *Veritas* ("Truth"), and he had come
there to share "bitter" truths.[6] The rain, it turned out, had been a sign
of a brooding message to come.

The title of his speech was "A World Split Apart," evoking the division, in that age, between two nuclear superpowers, the one he had
fled and the one he had fled to. Yet he devoted the bulk of his speech
to the latter—to diagnosing what had gone wrong *in the West*.

He saw in the West an ever-expanding culture of what he called
legalism, one that allowed, even encouraged, everyone to pursue his
own selfish ends up to the limit of the law. Having lived under a lawless regime, he knew how invaluable the rule of law was. Even so, "a
society with no other scale but the legal is one also less than worthy
of man," for such a society "fails to take advantage of the full range
of human possibilities."[7]

He saw a West captive to a tyrannical notion of rights. "The defense of individual rights," he warned, "has reached such extremes as
to make society as a whole defenseless against certain individuals."[8]
Terrorism ran rampant, because there were lawyers and judges less
committed to society as a whole than they were to maximizing the
rights of defendants who, if they had their way, would destroy society
and all rights. Oppressive regimes like the one that had thrown him
into the gulag took advantage, too, hiring lawyers, lobbyists, and other
profiteering henchmen to advance their interests in the West—legally.

He saw an abusive Western media whose "overriding concern"
wasn't in serving the truth or readers, but their own agendas. Though

the media defended the maximal possible freedom for themselves, they were accountable to no one when they "misled public opinion by inaccurate information" or even "contributed to mistakes on a state level." At the same time, major outlets maintained a narrow corridor of acceptable opinion, its boundaries set by intellectual fads and corporate interests. "Unrestrained freedom exists for the press, but not for the readership, because newspapers mostly transmit in a forceful and empathetic way those opinions which do not openly contradict their own and the general trend." What a "surprise for someone coming from the totalitarian East"![9]

Solzhenitsyn saw a West where the clamor of intellectual fashion shut out true intellects, where shallow public opinion swallowed true excellence. "Your scholars," he charged,

> are free in a legal sense, but they are hemmed in by the idols of the prevailing fad. There is no open violence, as in the East; however, a selection dictated by fashion and the need to accommodate mass standards frequently prevents the most independent-minded persons from contributing to public life and gives rise to dangerous herd instincts.[10]

If all *this* was what Westerners meant by bringing freedom to the Soviet Union, Solzhenitsyn said, then the nations trapped behind the Iron Curtain would be wise to decline the offer. And this was the most shocking part of the Harvard address: "Should I be asked . . . whether I would propose the West, such as it is today, as a model to my country today, I would frankly have to answer negatively. No, I could not recommend your society as an ideal for the transformation of ours."[11]

"A TERRIBLY HOMESICK RUSSIAN"

While a few hisses rose up from Harvard Yard as the author spoke, his words for the most part elicited bursts of applause from the audience. But afterward, the media and the commentariat he had lacerated

went to work. Soon, it would become clear that the whirlwind Solzhenitsyn launched at Harvard had permanently unsettled his own
reception in the West, turning him from celebrated dissident into re-
viled reactionary and kooky mystic.

The reviews, as they say, were bad. The upshot was that while Solzhenitsyn was undoubtedly a master writer and a braveheart of a
man, his social and political ideas were not only wrong but positively
sinister—the product of a peculiarly Russian type of obscurantism
and a lack of appreciation for what the free world was all about. In so
many polite turns of phrase, the prestige press framed him as a theo-
crat and an authoritarian.

While Solzhenitsyn had undoubtedly "earned the right to call the
West to a moral reckoning," granted a *New York Times* editorial, his
worldview "seems to us far more dangerous than the easygoing spirit
which he finds so exasperating." Indeed, it was precisely to forestall
"zealots like Mr. Solzhenitsyn" that America's "Founders took such
pains to disperse power and safeguard individual freedom." Maybe
the newcomer should stop preaching to the free society and learn,
instead, to appreciate its "precious and abiding strengths."[12]

The Harvard speech displayed "a gross misunderstanding of Western society," charged *The Washington Post*. Worse, Solzhenitsyn was
taking advantage of "the tolerance and diversity that are the splendor
of the West to attack tolerance and diversity."[13]

"A cranky spiritualism is the classic affliction of great Russian men
of letters," snarked an editorial in the now-defunct *Washington Star*.
The conservative *National Review* was more sympathetic, noting that
"Solzhenitsyn is a towering presence on the landscape of twentieth-
century literature and politics, and this address is likely to be read,
pondered, and discussed a century hence." Still, *NR*'s editorial posed
several pointed questions to Solzhenitsyn, the gist of which was that,
whatever the merits of his complaints, it was hard to imagine a better
alternative "in space or in time" to the liberal model—as if any critique of our arrangements is invalid unless it comes with detailed al-
ternatives.[14]

The one adulatory take came from the right-of-center columnist George Will, who wrote: "Solzhenitsyn's philosophy has a far more distinguished pedigree than does the liberalism that is orthodoxy in societies that owe their success, so far, to the fact that they have lived off the moral capital of older and sounder traditions." Will railed against the "flaccid" American consensus, which was "a study in intellectual parochialism" and no match for the Russian's "restatement of the most honorable and ancient theme of Western political philosophy."[15]

The *Star*'s Mary McGrory, however, spoke for many more columnists when she simply dismissed Solzhenitsyn's ideas with a personal swipe. "We would be better off," she said, "if we stopped grappling with the politics and even the morality of what Solzhenitsyn said at Harvard and look at it in a different way—as the personal statement of a conservative, religious and terribly homesick Russian."[16]

What could a soul nurtured in Russia's despotic soil teach a people for whom freedom is a constitutional birthright? Very little, as far as Solzhenitsyn's critics were concerned. As he confided in his memoir, to the Western liberal mind "I presumed to judge the experience of the world from the point of view of my own *limited* Soviet and prison-camp experience."[17] Could a gulag serve as a school of freedom?

A GOOD DAY

Alexander Isayevich Solzhenitsyn was born in the North Caucasus in 1918. Educated as a mathematician, he served as an artillery officer in the Red Army during World War II. All along, he remained faithful to the Soviet state and ideology—that is, until February 1945, when his (fairly mild) jibes at Joseph Stalin in private letters made it into the hands of the secret police. The authorities sentenced him to eight years' hard labor.

During his involuntary sojourns through the gulag network, Solzhenitsyn spent three years, from 1950 to 1953, working as a bricklayer and foreman at a political prisoners' camp in Kazakhstan, the experience that would form the basis of his novel *One Day in the Life of Ivan Denisovich*. First published in 1962 (after Stalin was dead) in the literary magazine *Novy Mir*, the thinly fictionalized account shook the Soviet Union. And once its descriptions of Communist torture, mass arbitrary detention, and other crimes against humanity made their way to the West, it became impossible to defend the regime for all but its most abject apologists.

Compared to the methodical historiography of *The Gulag Archipelago*, the novel *One Day* is the more philosophical witness to one of humanity's worst-ever atrocities, and for that reason remains, as I see it, the more timeless of the two masterpieces. The Soviet gulag is now gone, thank God (though China's and North Korea's Communist regimes maintain similar networks in our time). What remains vital in *One Day* are Solzhenitsyn's lessons on how we can remain absolutely free even under the most repressive circumstances—and the difference between true and false freedom. Seen through this lens, the novel is only incidentally about the gulag.

As the title suggests, the book recounts a single day, from reveille to lights out, among a tightly knit group of camp prisoners—Gang 104. Our protagonist, Ivan Denisovich Shukhov, has been hurled into the gulag by mistake: Captured by the Germans as a POW during the war, he is subsequently accused by his own side of having spied for the enemy. He has done no such thing, but there is no appealing Soviet "justice." His sentence: ten years' hard labor.

Solzhenitsyn weaves many philosophical threads into this deceptively simple tale, and we can't unspool all of them. But one main thread is the author's observations about how different human types navigate the prison-camp experience. The life of the *zeks* (convicts) is dominated by constant hunger, backbreaking labor, freezing tundra temperatures, bodily ailments, cruel disciplinary officers—the physical and psychological degradations inherent in a system *designed* to make them feel less than fully human.

Degradation: Shukhov awakes later than usual, to a body aching all over. His tardiness earns him punishment in the form of having to wash the floors of the warders' quarters, work the lazy orderly refuses to do. He doesn't exactly do a stellar job of it—he can barely feel his hands after drawing water outside in minus-thirty weather—and so the warders add insult to his misery: "Did you never see your old woman clean a floor, you filthy pig?"[18]

Degradation: "Meals" consist of hard bread—the cooks invariably supply fewer than the regulation 550 grams per prisoner—and thin, watery soups of oatmeal or rotten-fish gruel, complete with fish eyeballs swimming in the stuff and loads of tiny, indigestible bones. "And the worst of it was that if there was anything left in a bowl, you couldn't help licking it."[19]

Degradation: The guards force the *zeks* to stand for interminable roll calls, before they go to work and afterward. There are constant full-body searches, requiring the condemned to remove their clothes; did I mention the temperature was thirty below? When a naïve newcomer complains that this goes against his rights under the Soviet penal code, it is cause for a good laugh—and ten days in the "hole" (freezing solitary confinement) for the complainer.

Degradation: Often, it is unnecessary for the disciplinary officers to brutalize their charges, because the *zeks* do it to each other. When, at the end of the workday, a Moldavian from a different gang can't be found—he has fallen asleep somewhere—none of the others can go back inside until he is located. The Moldavian's foreman sends him staggering with a one-two punch (this, to save him from what the guards might do), only to have a Hungarian from the same gang practically kick the life out of the laggard. Then another roll call commences.

Degradation: Worst of all, perhaps, the gulag system steals almost every waking minute of these men's days. "Apart from sleep," says our narrator (who sometimes assumes Shukhov's interior voice), "an old lag can call his life his own only for ten minutes at breakfast time, five at lunchtime, and five more at suppertime."[20]

How does one preserve one's humanity in such circumstances, where the margins of freedom and human dignity are so narrow as to be almost nonexistent? That, for Solzhenitsyn, is the great moral challenge of the gulag. A *zek* can either refuse to succumb to the baser side of his nature, despite all the external pressures and temptations—or he can just let loose that base nature, to do as it might to himself and to the other prisoners. The one course of action leads to *inner freedom,* the other to a slavery worse than any gulag, because it enchains the mind and heart.

The author illustrates this using character contrasts, the starkest one drawn between Shukhov and another member of Gang 104 named Fetyukov. The latter never misses a chance to add self-degradation to the degradations inflicted by the gulag. Tobacco is rare, and when one of the wealthier *zeks,* Tsezar, lights up, Fetyukov clings to the smoker like a lost dog, "standing right in front of him and staring hot-eyed at his mouth."[21] At the mess hall, Fetyukov hovers like a fly around men with extra bowls of gruel, hoping to swipe one or even to lick their finished bowls. At the worksite, Fetyukov is the least reliable and therefore most hated member of Gang 104. No one likes to work for free, of course, much less for a gulag state that imprisons men for decades on the flimsiest charges. But if they don't show solidarity, if each doesn't do his bit, they all suffer. Fetyukov is incorrigibly lazy, however, "deliberately tilting the handbarrow . . . and splashing mortar out to make it lighter."[22] This earns him a beating, of course. Fetyukov ends the day in a pitiful state: After dinner, he has his mouth boxed for trying to lick other men's empty bowls— again. "He walked past the whole team without looking at anybody, not trying to hide his tears, climbed onto his bunk, and buried his head in his mattress."[23]

Trying to take every little advantage, to scrounge every morsel of food and take every last drag off every cigarette butt, Fetyukov has no dignity, no interior peace. This, even though his wiliness probably makes him "freer" than many other *zeks.*

Shukhov is just as wily, but his simple, conscientious insight into what is right and wrong, decorous and indecorous, saves him many indignities and finally leaves his interior castle of freedom intact and undefiled. Forced to get on his knees and wash the warders' freezing floors, he deflects his superiors' humiliating insults with jolly humor. He swipes extra bowls at the mess hall but is happy to give the spoils to the newcomer who can't fend for himself. He doesn't engage in bribery, though bribery is the order of the day in the camp.

And Shukhov works—harder and better than anyone else in Gang 104. Bricklaying in frigid weather is crushingly difficult, because the mortar can freeze before it can glue the bricks together. Shukhov operates rapidly and efficiently, with almost Zen-like precision, never making a mistake. He spots the irregularities in each brick the second he picks it up and instantly decides "which way round" it should be laid down and "which spot in the wall [is] just waiting for it." Thanks to his perfectionism, each new brick ends up "flush with the outside of the wall and dead-level widthwise and lengthwise."[24]

The reader can almost feel Shukhov's satisfaction in a job meticulously well done. Whom does Shukhov serve by throwing his flesh and soul into bricklaying in a gulag? The Union of Soviet Socialist Republics? Stalin? Well, yes, I suppose, in an abstract sense. But mostly he is serving his comrades in Gang 104. Within the narrow margin—a slit, really—of autonomy the gulag affords him, he chooses to do what he *ought* to do. He acts out of the unspoken love between fellow prisoners, not servility to an evil regime.

Where does he mine the spiritual resources to carry on in this way?

Admirers of Russian literature might recognize in Ivan Denisovich Shukhov a certain Russian *type:* Other iterations include Sonya, the soulful prostitute in Fyodor Dostoevsky's *Crime and Punishment,* and Platon Karataev, the humane and cheerful peasant who flits in and out of the final chapters of Leo Tolstoy's *War and Peace.* Sonya and Karataev both stand for the rootedness and resilience of Russia's poor, reminding cerebral, restless intellectuals that amid adversity, it suffices to savor one's daily bread, give glory to God, and love one's neighbor as oneself.

Shukhov likewise finds freedom—in a gulag!—by way of a peasant's goodness and natural religiosity. For him, faith in a higher power comes as easily as watching the night sky during a storm. For, "how can anybody not believe in God when it thunders?" he asks.[25] If there is a higher power and an enduring moral law, then no one can take away his inner freedom. He is obliged not to degrade himself, even if he might cut little corners to survive and help comrades.

By the end of the day, Shukhov has his reward, going to bed "pleased with his life," even having "enjoyed working on the wall."[26] What could a survivor of the gulag teach the West about freedom? What, indeed.

FREEDOM UNTO SERFDOM

As a prisoner, Solzhenitsyn had lived through and witnessed firsthand much of what he recounted in *One Day*. Far from misunderstanding freedom, he had gained that profound appreciation for it that can only come with near-total deprivation. And contrary to his critics' claims, he emphatically didn't favor tyranny or oppose democracy, having suffered the Soviet Union's "centralisation of all forms of life," particularly the life of the mind, which he thought amounted to "spiritual murder."[27]

But could it be that the liberal West, having reduced freedom to a bare legalism and the absence of natural and traditional barriers, was also unfree, only in a different way?

This was Solzhenitsyn's early intuition, and the more time he spent in the West, observing its ways and attempting to navigate them, the more the thought gathered strength in his mind. The loss of many barriers against the individual will, he concluded, had paradoxically robbed Western life of its true freedom. An excess of rights had paved the road to a new serfdom, creating a society in which the Fetyukov type thrived.

He saw this, first, in the misdeeds of the Western media. Reporters mobbed him from the second he arrived at the Bavarian home of the German novelist Heinrich Böll, his first destination in exile. Aware of how vulnerable his friends and loved ones were back home, Sol-zhenitsyn declined all interviews—that is, except with one reporter who had assisted him greatly in Russia. This sent another journalist into such a fit of jealousy that he published a story claiming that the reporter who had been rewarded had brought Solzhenitsyn a secret letter from his wife.

That was an outright falsehood. It could have endangered Sol-zhenitsyn's wife, who was then trying desperately to protect the author's hidden archives from the KGB in Moscow before escaping herself. And it jeopardized the ability of the honest reporter to work in the Soviet capital. Yet neither the envious reporter who had written the false story nor his outlet took any responsibility or showed any remorse. Solzhenitsyn recalled in his memoir, "Every encounter I had with the media in my first days in the West filled me with bewilder-ment."[28]

Then there was the mean legalism that permeated the West's commercial practices and its social climate. Solzhenitsyn's books were global blockbusters, but he had written them with a moral and spiritual purpose: namely, to awaken the world to the evils of the So-viet Union and to help liberate his compatriots. He had put together *One Day in the Life of Ivan Denisovich* and *The Gulag Archipelago* in the bricklaying spirit of his character Shukhov, an outpouring of solidar-ity, a writerly act of true freedom ordered to what he ought to have done, given his God-given talents.

Yet in one country, bookshops refused to honor his request to sell *Archipelago* at a lower markup than they would books of similar length (so more people could read it). In another country, one publisher kept bringing out pirated, mangled, badly translated editions of his works. Why? To profit off his literary labor, the research and writing he had done in defiance of the KGB, often in secret, under conditions of censorship and repression that no Western publisher or editor could begin to fathom.

In America, one of the largest corporate publishers tried to nickel-and-dime him at every turn, drawing up staggeringly one-sided publishing contracts, in which every risk and even the smallest costs were laid on the author's shoulders. *We honor your sacrifice, Mr. Solzhenitsyn, but as the contract signed on your behalf says here, the author must bear all incidental postal charges for mailing review copies and for the production of an index. . . .* Most of the sophisticated hucksters who took control of his books' foreign rights, including one especially predatory Wall Street figure, were "quite indifferent to the literary and political aspects of the matter." All they cared about was that "something of material value is lying untapped, and that a hefty profit can be made from it."[29]

To assert his rights, he would have to go to court against publishers that treated his blood equity as a commodity, and "God, how I balk at this with my entire soul."[30]

Western-style litigation, he concluded, was "a profanation of the soul, an ulceration. As the world has entered a legal era, gradually replacing man's conscience with law, the spiritual level of the world has sunk. The legal world! Nothing but chicanery!" The various publishers even went to war among themselves over his material, and when he tried to reconcile them, they would insist on fighting to the last in the courts: "The Western court system is drowned in a litigious quagmire, choked by the letter of the law, the thread of its spirit lost, so often affording crooks and swindlers an advantage."[31] In the West, the spirit of Fetyukov so often triumphed, legally, over the spirit of Shukhov.

Most shocking of all was how this obsessive profiteering motive even worked to the advantage of the Communist regimes. He saw this crisply soon after his arrival in the West, when a Swiss trading company dismissed one of its interpreters—over complaints from a Soviet client. The client had attacked Solzhenitsyn's writing, and the interpreter had asked: "But have you read Solzhenitsyn?" Which was enough to get her fired. And this, in "the oldest democracy in Europe, independent and free!"[32]

At one point, Solzhenitsyn was even taken advantage of by the contractors he hired to build his house in rural Vermont, where he settled after leaving Europe.[33] They dragged out the work, did a shoddy job in places, and stung him with an unaccountably fat invoice. There is something bitterly humorous in this: the writer who had outsmarted the KGB on a thousand occasions, who had survived hard labor in the frigid cold, bested by the deviousness of small-town American contractors and the "ordeal of the Western financial system."[34]

Finally, there was the sheer disorder that sullied the West's moral and physical landscape. On a tour of Italy, Solzhenitsyn saw the country's monumental glories "covered with graffiti, painted with hammers and sickles, slogans and threats: 'Police Are Killers!' 'Death to Fascist Christian Democrats!'" Columns that had survived barbarian invasions and Lord knows what else now blared: "Long Live Proletarian Violence!"[35]

The slogans must have especially irked a man who had tasted "proletarian violence," but worse was the question these displays must have raised in the author's mind: Was *this* what he and his compatriots had fought for in defying Communist repression?

IT WAS THIS simmering pot of emotions and observations that boiled over when Solzhenitsyn addressed the Harvard grads. In the gulag, he had surveyed the moral heights people could reach by doing what they ought to have done, despite the pressures exerted by a lawless prison state. In the West, meanwhile, he saw free men and women and society as a whole failing to make any distinction between freedom to do what ought to be done and the freedom to do what ought not.

And here lay the philosophical heart of his critique of the West. As he put it at Harvard, "today's Western society has revealed the inequality between the freedom for good deeds and the freedom for evil deeds."[36] The two, freedom for good and freedom for evil, aren't the same thing. Indeed, the latter doesn't even qualify as freedom, since it breeds self-degradation. Solzhenitsyn saw this in concentrated form in the lives of prisoners like Fetyukov, but the idea stretches all the way back to the Bible: "Everyone who commits sin is a slave to sin" (Jn 8:34).

How had the West come to mistake false freedom for the genuine article? Solzhenitsyn traced the error back to Renaissance humanism and its "benevolent" hope that "man—the master of this world—does not bear any evil within himself." That hope had found political expression in the European Age of Enlightenment and "became the basis for . . . what could be called rationalistic humanism or humanistic autonomy."[37]

Put another way, human beings took themselves as their own moral scale and—surprise!—concluded that they were pretty good. This soon led to the erasure of the ancient distinction between freedom for good and license for evil: If humans were good on their own, naturally so, then an unbound humanity, free to exercise autonomy in every realm and every direction, could only be a good thing.

Western-style liberalism and Communism shared this faith in the basic goodness of the autonomous human being. Both hallowed the autonomous human "as the center of all."[38] Despite their differences over how to free humanity from all natural and traditional constraints, whether to do so collectively or individually, the two ideologies were twin children of the same parent philosophy.[39] In this sense, the Cold War world was, in fact, united. Its two halves were riffing on the same melody in two different keys.

It was easy to see how Communism's vision of unbound human rule had in practice led to the absolute loss of true freedom—to the gulag, to the killing field, to the torture chamber. The West's deformations were more diffuse and subtle but no less real. In the West, Solzhenitsyn reflected in his memoir, "the notion of *freedom* has been diverted to unbridled passion, in other words, in the direction of the forces of evil (so that nobody's 'freedom' would be limited!)."[40]

The only limit is law, and law exists to maximize individual autonomy up to the point of harming others (and sometimes beyond it). Law gives the advantage to a thousand advantage-seeking Fetyukovs: "The reigning ideology, that prosperity and the accumulation of material riches are to be valued above all else, is leading to a weakening of character in the West." Poor Fetyukov, at least, had the excuse of gulag conditions. What excuse have those who use their freedom to chip away at "the whole and the high," ultimately to enslave themselves?[41]

IN THE DECADES since Alexander Solzhenitsyn issued his jeremiad (in the true prophetic sense) at Harvard, the conditions he diagnosed have only worsened. We have demolished many barriers in the name of freedom, and the demolition job has paradoxically left us less free.

Our market fundamentalism, for example, has penetrated deep into the popular psyche, hence the Colvin brothers' profiteering amid the pandemic and their grotesque Milton Friedman–esque self-justifications. More systematically, it has abetted the rise of a tech oligarchy that seeks to reshape not just how and how much people work, but how and how much they think—all while draping itself in the banner of multicultural and sexual-liberationist virtue. Market fundamentalism has likewise blinded us to the suffering of Americans with no more than a high-school education in the new economy.

Even for the materially successful, there are few, if any, patterns to follow as they seek the good life. Let's try another look into the future: Imagine that my post-college Maximilian has been dating a young woman for several years. Is he expected to marry her? (Well, maybe.) Have children? (Possibly.) What if that hampers his career mobility? (Then no.) What if he gets tired of his would-be wife? (Well, they could always divorce later.) What if he just tires of her while they are still dating, and "dumps" her wantonly and cruelly? (That's okay.) What if she does that to him? (That's okay, too.)

All the profound questions of life are unsettled; young and old alike lack a stable basis for answering them. In economic life, entrepreneurial autonomy has generated vast wealth for the innovative. But the downsides are increasingly evident. Even the well-educated stagger under the weight of hypercompetition. Great acts of true freedom—that is, freedom for the good—require knowing that one stands on solid ground, a confidence that we too often lack.

Are we too free? Solzhenitsyn would say that insofar as our disordered concept of freedom hamstrings moral excellence and promotes its opposite, insofar as it encourages us to be base and Fetyukov-like—then *we aren't free enough*. And we certainly aren't free merely because we are unconstrained and unrestricted.

The current state of affairs is here to stay, barring a philosophical sea change on the scale of the Enlightenment, and that seems unlikely. Meanwhile, we might ask ourselves: Does blurting out whatever I wish to Internet strangers truly fulfill me, or am I taking a perverse pleasure in conflict? Is that sixteenth hour in the day spent toiling for a corporate boss an act of freedom and mastery, or is it merely depriving my spouse and children of my presence? Am I truly free to watch digital phantasms having sex, or am I perpetuating the exploitation of real people and digging myself deeper into a degraded hole? Am I free to refuse to carry my cross or commit to any sacrificial responsibility—or in so refusing, do I in fact diminish my moral stature, habituating my nature to the narrow, selfish horizon of a Fetyukov?

Each of us has to work within the sphere of life entrusted to us, to carefully discern true freedom from its seductive counterfeits. Then we might give a new, and true, meaning to our common aspiration to a Land of the Free.

ALEXANDER SOLZHENITSYN RETURNED to his native land on May 27, 1994, following the collapse of the Soviet Union. As *The New York Times* reported, he chose to land, first, "in the Siberian northeast, in Magadan, the former heart of the gulag."[42] And the first thing he did was to touch the bloodstained soil in tribute to the 60 million victims of the Soviet system. He died in 2008 in Moscow, having outlived the gulag state by seventeen years.

IS SEX A PRIVATE MATTER?

———

The 2010s were a time of sexual schizophrenia. It was the decade that saw Western societies embrace, with a fresh and uncompromising ardor, the previous century's project of sexual liberation. This, even as the downsides of our liberated sexual ethic became glaringly apparent.

In the last decade, corporations, major media outlets, universities, and other elite institutions promoted a vision of near-absolute sexual autonomy. The euphemism "sex work" supplanted the more judgmental term "prostitution" in polite discourse. Polyamorous partnerships received ever more, and ever-more sympathetic, coverage in the prestige press. Fetishes once confined to the fringe, such as sadomasochism, burst into the mainstream. (*Fifty Shades of Grey* topped global bestseller lists, and even a think-tanker at the right-wing American Enterprise Institute came out as a kink practitioner.) Online smut exploded. At the start of the decade, according to a University of New Hampshire study, nine out of ten boys were getting exposed to porn before turning eighteen.[1] "Sex-positive" feminism rode high.

At the same time, the decade opened our eyes to sexual exploitation and hidden criminality. The year 2018 brought the Catholic Church's "summer of shame," as victims brought forth a cascade of credible historical allegations against abusive clergy, demons in Roman collars, including an American cardinal, Theodore McCarrick. This was also the decade of #MeToo, which saw courageous victims expose some of the most powerful men in Hollywood, fashion, politics, and the media as serial abusers and harassers. It was the decade of Jeffrey Epstein, the billionaire hedge-funder who, it turned out, had served also as a procurer of underage victims for the rich and powerful. It was the decade that saw younger Americans recoil at the sexual boorishness of the Boomer generation of their fathers. It was a decade of surging paranoia, of hushed wonderings in high quarters about who might be the next to fall because of his past misdeeds.

Both sets of phenomena—a radical sexual autonomism and a new awareness of sexuality's dangers—were real and definitive, and they pressed in opposite directions. How did Western culture reconcile them? Well, it didn't really. The post-#MeToo sexual consensus holds that accused harassers and abusers are to be swiftly punished, even if that means abridging their procedural rights—and even if some innocent or falsely accused men end up paying, as well. And for all that, many of #MeToo's victim-advocates lament that the movement has largely failed to bring about lasting change at the level of ordinary life.[2]

But the liberationist credo has lost none of its sway. We still hold these truths to be self-evident: that sex is basically good and healthy; that sex of nearly every kind is intrinsically harmless, provided we carefully seek our partners' consent and adhere to the latest hygienic guidelines to avoid disease; above all, that what people do in the privacy of their bedrooms has nothing to do with how we arrange our social affairs and certainly is nobody's business to regulate. But as we reckon with the high costs of easy sex, we might as well pose the more fundamental question: *Is sex nothing more than good, private fun?*

"Hot, Hot City"

In July 1985, the National Organization for Women—the group founded in 1966 by the feminist author Betty Friedan and some two dozen other activists—held its annual convention in New Orleans. As far as the organizers were concerned, the choice of New Orleans for the location was only incidental; NOW was holding its conference there in the same spirit as the Chevron Corporation might have picked Milwaukee for one of its gatherings.

But for one of the attendees, the grimy realities of the surrounding area mattered profoundly, and feminism stood or fell on whether it took notice of them and drew the right conclusions. *The New York Times* described her as one of America's "most radical feminists," an object of fear and revulsion not just among old-school chauvinists but even among many liberals and fellow activists.[3] This was Andrea Dworkin. She was thirty-eight years old.

The Big Easy was, she recalled, a "hot, hot city in every sense." Just beyond the conference site, with its genteel panel discussions and Robert's Rules–governed politicking, lay Bourbon Street, where Dworkin observed "trafficking in women in virtually every venue." In daytime, the neighborhood thronged with "middle-aged men in suits roving as if in gangs, dripping sweat, going from one sex show to the next, searching for prostitutes and strippers."[4]

For the clients, typically whiter and more affluent than the working women they patronized, Bourbon Street was an adult playground. It was a zone of sexual fantasy and release, where, for not a lot of money, women donning translucent heels and not much else posed submissively for the men, grinding on them and pretending to like it. For a little more money, the women would take the men by the hand, guide them to shady little bedrooms, and pretend to like that, too.

The women, in other words, became objects, blending their own existence with the fantasies swirling in the men's imaginations and swelling their genitals. And for Dworkin, that was the problem: Prostitution (and pornography) took the baseline objectification and devaluation of all women and amplified it across life's realms. As she wrote in her 2002 memoir, *Heartbreak,* "The worst immorality is to use another person's body in the passing of time."[5]

Something had to be done. The impetus came from a black woman employed at the hotel where the NOW convention was being held. Knowing the guests were there for a feminist conference, she asked

Dworkin and a few others "if we would march down Bourbon Street with the workers in the hotel . . . to protest the pornography and prostitution so densely located there."[6]

Dworkin knew that "New Orleans is like most other cities in the United States in that the areas in which pornography and prostitution flourish are the areas in which the poor people, largely people of color, live." Standing with the local activists against the "despoiling of their living environment" was thus an "overwhelming mandate."[7] Persuading the more liberal and less radical elements at NOW to support the march proved more challenging, and in the end, Dworkin and only about a hundred others took part.

As the *Times* reported, Dworkin led the march "wearing her trademark blue denim overalls, bullhorn in hand." The women (and a few men) shouted, "Hey, hey, ho, ho, pornography has got to go!" and carried signs that read, "Say no to por-NO!"[8] Then, someone in the NOW leadership called the police to complain of an unauthorized march. The cops came and broke up the protest; one male feminist was arrested and spent a night in jail.[9]

THE EPISODE, AND many others of the kind, solidified Dworkin's status as a cultural bête noire and even as an "inverted sex symbol," as the writer Ariel Levy has noted. There were other feminists who opposed prostitution and pornography with equal vehemence, "but nobody else could elicit the same disgust and fascination from the public as Andrea Dworkin did—they didn't have her overalls or her anger; they weren't as *big*."[10]

Pimps and pornographers naturally detested her. *Hustler* magazine portrayed her in cartoons as a grotesque lesbian, to which Dworkin responded by launching a $150 million libel suit (a federal trial court dismissed the complaint, and the liberal Ninth Circuit upheld the decision on First Amendment grounds).[11] Polite liberal opinion kept her at a distance, too, with many publishing houses spurning her work lest her forthrightly restrictionist position jeopardize their own free-speech rights. Even ostensible comrades in the feminist movement shunned her, with Eleanor Smeal, the NOW president, going so far as to suggest there were "fascist overtones" to Dworkin's anti-porn crusade, especially since it brought Dworkin into alliance with the enemy: social conservatives.[12]

As the new millennium dawned, it was clear that Dworkin's brand of anti-porn, anti-prostitution feminism had utterly flopped. Levy quips, "With the possible exception of the Shakers, it is difficult to think of an American movement that has failed more spectacularly than anti-pornography feminism." What had still been the viewpoint of a small but resolute minority at the 1985 NOW convention—that porn and prostitution could even be empowering, provided women took charge—became the mainstream position. Its proponents called themselves "sex-positive" feminists explicitly in reaction against Dworkin's tendency.[13]

Dworkin was unfortunate to live long enough to see herself reduced to a cultural stereotype: Much as Solzhenitsyn had been branded a Mystical Russian Reactionary (see chapter 9), the liberal mainstream decided that Dworkin belonged to the role of Fat, Sex-Hating Radical. As Levy recounts, people who had read not a single word of Dworkin's prose associated her name with two things: "overalls and the idea that all sex is rape."[14]

Dworkin's position was undoubtedly radical. The use of "another person's body" was what took place in those back rooms of New Orleans. But it was also ubiquitous in advertising, which commercialized human bodies, female ones especially, to sell *things*. The sexual conquest of women was a mainstay of the culture, highbrow and low, which held up the act as a rite of passage, as "natural" and invigorating, banal and fun. Bourbon Street traded on using another person's body for pleasure—but so did Broadway and Madison Avenue. And so did Main Street: For, Dworkin believed, what happened in the shady back rooms of New Orleans's French Quarter was little different from the goings-on behind the closed doors and shuttered curtains of the wholesome American boudoir.

Yet the radicalism of a viewpoint isn't proof alone that it is incorrect. Nor, indeed, that the viewpoint in question is necessarily new. For while Dworkin was on the hard left of the modern American political spectrum, her ideas—that what men and women do in the privacy of the bedroom is in fact inherently public and inherently troubling—were as old and as radical as the vision of sex found in historic Christianity. And recent events have amply vindicated her critique.

CIRCLES OF HELL

Anyone habituated to a certain East Coast experience will have met—or been—the girl Dworkin started out as: the Jewish girl from Jersey; a middle-class family life, though overshadowed by the Shoah for her émigré elders; a vaguely liberal worldview instilled by her mother; small rebellions against teachers who didn't get her, against the mildly Christian ambiance at school; summers on the Jersey Shore; tangerine lipstick.

How does that girl, that Andrea, become *Andrea Dworkin*?

The answer lies in the combination of a keen intellect and more than a few harsh encounters with reality—starting with her molestation by a stranger in a movie theater when she was nine. There was abuse, too, within that otherwise ordinary Jewish milieu. An uncle, she would learn, molested his children when they were infants, disquieting knowledge that years later would prompt one of those classic Dworkin lines: that a man who abuses babies "belongs in [Heinrich] Himmler's circle of hell."[15]

In high school, a devilishly charming male teacher preyed on her and two other female friends. He would give the girls "passes to get out of classes we didn't like, and we'd get to spend time with him learning real stuff: sex stuff or sexy stuff." Oblivious to the power he wielded over teenage girls, the "pedophilic teacher," as Dworkin called him, drove her to the brink of suicide at one point, when "I didn't think he loved me." She changed her mind at the last minute, and he later reassured her that he did, in fact, love her.[16]

There was more to Andrea's childhood and teenage years than sexual trauma, of course. She had an ear for music, though she was self-aware enough to know from a fairly young age that her reservoir of talent wasn't full enough for a career as a classical pianist—whereas she could write brilliantly.

One of the great tragedies of the Dworkin-as-sex-hater stereotype is that it smothers the force of her writing, its poignancy and playfulness, her facility with metaphor, her jazzy meanderings in prose that exploded in thundering, Beethovenian climaxes. Here, for example, is how Dworkin described falling in love with the voice of the blues legend Bessie Smith:

> Her detachment equaled her commitment: she was going to sing the song through your corporeality. Unlike smoke, which circled the body, her song went right through you, and either you took what you could get of it for the moment the note was moving inside you or she wasn't for you and you were a barrier she penetrated.[17]

Much the same could have been said about Dworkin's own writerly voice.

In 1964, she enrolled at Bennington College as a member of the last all-women freshman class before the Vermont liberal-arts school went co-ed. There, she had her first inklings that sexual intercourse—and not just abusive intercourse, mind you, but sex as such, given the raw nature of the act—somehow steals women's dignity, turns them into objects of male domination, and thus renders true equality impossible.

While she was still pursuing music, her adviser at Bennington was the composer Louis Callabro. Adviser and advisee struck what seems to have been a true friendship and disclosed their souls to each other. But, Dworkin concluded, "the equality between Lou and myself, our mutual recognition, was no part of the school's agenda," which included mostly male teachers having copious sex with their favorite female students. Callabro told her as much: that no man she slept with would ever treat her as an equal.[18]

Young adulthood had more formative traumas in store. In her freshman year, she joined the burgeoning protest movement against the Vietnam War. Arrested at one rally in New York, she was taken to the Women's House of Detention in Greenwich Village and there subjected to a humiliating internal examination. Her fellow anti-war activists, mostly male, were unsympathetic. But Dworkin wouldn't let the incident drop, taking her case against the jail authorities to the *Times* and eventually to a grand jury.

The jurors declined to act on her complaint, but her refusal to stay silent led to the institution's being closed down a few years later. Not long before her death in 2005, she reflected on this turn of events: "You tell the truth and people can shit all over it, the way that grand jury did, but somehow once it's said it can't be unsaid; it stays living, somewhere, in someone's heart."[19]

EVEN A WRITER of great courage and lucidity can sometimes fail, or refuse, to follow the twists and turns of her own life to their ironic, unexpected conclusion.

That seems to me to have been the case with Andrea Dworkin. For she was, in many ways, a creature of 1960s and '70s radicalism, of the Baby Boomer ferment against traditional sources of moral authority and restraint. And yet the worst abuses she suffered and documented were meted out not by the stodgy, remnant avatars of tradition—but by the radical men, by men who claimed to have discovered a new morality or else to have transcended the moral altogether.

The "pedophilic teacher" of her high-school years was one such man. Another was the poet Allen Ginsberg. Dworkin met him while she was in college, and the beat icon took an interest in her and even invited her to visit him in the Big Apple. They spent a long night at his apartment talking poetry and art and jazz and everything else, and he bewitched her. But he was also, quite openly, a predator of young boys.

This wasn't a matter of literary gossip; Ginsberg told her as much and related his belief that all sex was good, even and perhaps especially sex between men and boys. As Dworkin later recalled, Ginsberg "did not belong to the North American Man-Boy Love Association out of some mad, abstract conviction that its voice had to be heard." No, "he meant it."[20] Years later, Ginsberg and Dworkin were reunited when they were both asked to serve as godparents to a mutual friend's baby. By then, she was a literary star in her own right, and Ginsberg, imagining she would be simpatico, complained to her, "The right wants to put me in jail." She shot back: "Yes, they're very sentimental; I'd kill you." Ginsberg joked to others, "She wants to put me in jail." She didn't let up: "No, Allen, you still don't get it. The right wants to put you in jail. I want you dead."[21]

Then there were the sexually liberated, radical men she contended with during a postgraduate stint in the Netherlands. In Amsterdam, Dworkin came to know an American hippie whose daughters, ages thirteen and eleven, were sent to him by their mother (because their stepfather was making moves on them). Instead of caring for them, Dworkin recalled in her memoir, "the hippie man had given each kid [about $55], set them loose, and told them to take care of themselves. He just could not be with them without fucking them." The "hippie man" worked as a sound engineer for various rock bands, and it came to light that before throwing his daughters out, he was allowing the rockers to have their way with the older of the two.[22]

Dworkin ended up having to care for the two girls for a time, even though she herself was living in dismal poverty, in an Amsterdam apartment with quite literally no furniture or amenities. She had been driven to such a state by another liberated radical: a Dutchman she had married, the most calamitous decision she ever made.

Dworkin's husband was a self-proclaimed anarchist who "envisioned social change as circles on a canvas; the idea was to destabilize the circles by adding ones that didn't fit—the canvas would inevitably lose its integrity, and some circles would fall off, a paradigm of social chaos that would topple social hierarchies." What did such liberatory "chaos" look like in practice? The Dutchman beat her savagely, often to the point of unconsciousness, and used lit cigarettes to burn her chest, "leaving open sores on my breasts" that bled for months afterward.[23]

Here was another candidate for Himmler's circle of hell. She eventually escaped and returned Stateside, where she set out to write some of the most ferocious books in the American feminist tradition. Andrea the girl you knew had become *that* Andrea Dworkin.

ANYTHING BUT BANAL

Dworkin's unhealed scars supplied the raw material of her philosophy and lent it a burning anger and urgency. Yet to reduce her philosophy to her scars—to suggest that it was just her wounds speaking through her words—would be the tawdriest sort of maneuver. She was a thinker and a literary critic, not merely a symptom or a victim, and her ideas had an ancient pedigree, even if she herself denied and disparaged that pedigree.

What she opposed utterly was the notion that intercourse is harmless, private fun. In other words, she set herself against a modern American consensus on sex that transcended conventional divisions of left and right in her time—and still reigns supreme today, even if some cracks have appeared in the edifice since #MeToo.

"In Amerika [*sic*]," she wrote (she spelled it with a "k" after Franz Kafka), "there is the nearly universal conviction . . . that sex (fucking) is good and that liking it is right: morally right; a sign of human health; nearly a standard for citizenship."[24] That was the premise she interrogated, and demolished, in her 1987 polemic, *Intercourse*, the hugely controversial book that sealed her reputation as a hater of men and of sex.

It wasn't just Woodstock types or the radical children of 1968 who promoted the modern view of sex as an inherently harmless source of joy that shouldn't be repressed. Dworkin wrote:

Even those who believe in original sin and have a theology of hellfire and damnation express the Amerikan [*sic*] creed, an optimism that glows in the dark: Sex is good, healthy, wholesome, pleasant, fun; we like it, we enjoy it, we are cheerful about it; it is as simple as we are, the citizens of this strange country with no memory and no mind.[25]

Dworkin gave the example of Marabel Morgan, the author of *The Total Woman*, a massively popular, now blessedly forgotten, 1970s manual pitched to evangelical women about how to please their husbands, complete with tips on how to greet men returning home from work (hint: dressed in lingerie). She quoted Morgan's advice that " 'sex is for the marriage relationship only, but within those bounds, anything goes. Sex is as clean and pure as eating cottage cheese.' "[26]

We might cringe today, but Dworkin argued that Morgan's view of sex, draped though it was in cornpone '70s evangelicalism, aligned rather well with that of *Playboy* founder Hugh Hefner or sundry sex-positive feminists. Disagreements, if any, were at the margins. As Dworkin observed:

On both right and left, a citizen best be prepared to affirm her loyalty to the act itself. Ambivalence or dissent impugns her credibility; a good attitude is requisite before she is allowed to speak—in magazines, on television, in political groups. The tone and general posture of the Dallas Cowboys Cheerleaders set the standard for a good attitude; not to have one is un-Amerikan [*sic*] and sick, too. The social pressure to conform is fierce, ubiquitous, and self-righteous.[27]

Those tempted to dismiss Dworkin's complaint as an artifact of the 1970s or '80s ignore the thrust of a culture that still bombards us with hypersexualized images and ideas.

Take advertising. It is true that nowadays, the overtly sexist ad is rare. Advertisers detect the slightest tremors in public opinion, after all, including elite culture's current preference for reversing or subverting stereotypic roles, at least in representation. Typical is the Equinox gyms' ad from 2018 that showed a statuesque black woman with a white, Wall Street–type guy in a suit over one shoulder and another under her arm, like a huntress carrying her limp prey.

But note well: The men are fully dressed, while the woman is in a bikini and platform stilettos. Then, too, the value of these representational shifts is discounted by the fact that Pornhub attracts more than 100 million viewers *each day,* and that videos of women and teenage girls being slapped and brutalized are among the most popular categories.

Yes, we are much more sensitive to consent and representation, at least when our web browsers aren't set to incognito mode. But if anything, we are *more fervent* in the belief that the worst sin is "repression," as Dworkin wrote, because it "leads to authoritarian social policies." We are as committed as ever to the idea that sex itself is "freedom," that it is a "private act engaged in by individuals and has no implicit social significance," that intercourse is just about "pleasure" and has "no deeper meaning."[28]

None of the cultural developments since Dworkin published *Intercourse,* then, gets us around her central argument.

SEX INVOLVES A terrifying existential nakedness and vulnerability, Dworkin thought, especially for the woman—for the one being penetrated. We call it "making love," but too often, the lust to dominate women is the real substance of this "love." Man and woman are supposed to find communion in sex, but the very nature of the act can, and frequently does, turn the latter into an object for the use of the former. Even the marital bed can be a site of violation when compulsion is part of it.

To illustrate this darker vision of human sexuality, Dworkin turned to literature. She analyzed, among many other works, Leo Tolstoy's notorious 1889 novella, *The Kreutzer Sonata.* In it, a man recounts for fellow train passengers his murder of his wife—a crime of which he has been acquitted on account of the woman's suspected adultery. Dworkin wasn't so much interested in the antihero's jealousy as she was in his views on how lust blinds men to the humanity of women, thus foreclosing true equality.

Before Tolstoy's protagonist got married, Dworkin noted, he "valued the absence of any moral dimension to sex as freedom. The absence signified the inferiority of the woman, because relations with a human on the same level as oneself always have a moral dimension."[29] Love and matrimony didn't abate this tendency, for, as the murderous husband confesses, lust made it impossible for him to see his wife's individual personhood—that is, until that all-too-brief moment when he drove a dagger into her flesh and the life went out of her.

Dworkin granted the possibility that, occasionally, sex could give us a taste (an illusion?) of true communion.[30] But when communion isn't there, sex is "hatred" and "revenge," "fucking is hell: a destruction in violence and suffering of self-knowledge and self-esteem."[31] For a woman, every encounter entails the risk of having her personal integrity and personhood dissolve under the battering force of male lust, of male thrusting.

So no, sex is *not* meaningless, banal fun. Rather,

it is intense, often desperate. The internal landscape is violent upheaval, a wild and ultimately cruel disregard of human individuality, a brazen, high-strung wanting that is absolute and imperishable, not attached to personality, no respecter of boundaries; ending not in sexual climax but in a human tragedy of failed relationships, vengeful bitterness in an aftermath of sexual heat, personality corroded by too much endurance of undesired, habitual intercourse, conflict, a wearing away of vitality in the numbness finally of habit or compulsion or the loneliness of separation.[32]

Andrea Dworkin, Traditionalist

The passage of time might tempt us to dismiss Dworkin's claims even more firmly than her contemporaries did: These are the "extremist" declarations of a wounded and angry American feminist from the '70s and '80s, right?

Sure. But Dworkin may well have been issuing them from deep within the Judeo-Christian tradition. The early Christian sages, especially our friend Saint Augustine (chapter 6), worried about the same problem, a fact that didn't escape Dworkin's notice—hence her complaint in *Intercourse* about how, in our thoughtlessly pro-sex culture, "critical thought or deep feelings" on sex "puts one into the *Puritan* camp."[33] ("Puritan" here is American shorthand for Christian.)

The problem is lust. For Augustine as for Dworkin, lust generally, and the lust for domination especially, renders *moral* sex unattainable, or nearly so. Catholic saint and radical feminist alike were also troubled by how this lust undoes even our best aspirations—for example, the aspiration to a society that honors the equal dignity of men and women.

Dworkin approvingly quoted *The City of God* on this very point. "Lust does not merely invade the whole body and outward members," the bishop of Hippo had observed. "It takes such complete and passionate possession of the whole of man, both physically and emotionally, that what results is the keenest of all pleasures on the level of sensation; and at the crisis of excitement, it practically paralyzes all power of deliberate thought."[34]

The point is this: Once the "sex-passion" takes over, it beats into submission our noblest convictions about human equality and dignity, about restraint and self-mastery. All else gives way to the heat of the moment. As a result, we fail to notice how the profound intimacy of what is taking place coexists with a deep sort of alienation. For the man thrusting relentlessly toward climax, the actually existing woman before him disintegrates into her constituent bodily parts, her breasts or backside or vagina standing in for the whole of her—or else she melts into some imaginary woman (a past lover? some erotic fantasy?) other than who she is, *this* person, flesh and soul. "What can it matter" to the man, asked Dworkin, "that in entering her, he is entering this one, real, unique individual"?[35]

The moral conscientiousness that ordinarily operates in the mind breaks down; restoring it requires viewing the situation objectively, from outside the passionate bodily experience of intercourse—a mental feat that, even if achievable, is bound to result in limpness, deflation, a severe turnoff. Thus, sexual intercourse almost requires a bracketing off or putting on pause of the conscience and moral imagination.

And yet sexual intercourse is how human beings reproduce. It is the bodily cornerstone of society's foundational unit: man, woman, child. For Dworkin, it was thus the height of folly to think of sex as a private matter. How could we? How could we treat as purely private pleasure a human experience in which personhood—female personhood, to be precise—is existentially at stake? In which one group uses another's bodies for its own enjoyment? How could we possibly build a decent society if its foundation, usually hidden, is lustful domination?

This was the issue for Dworkin—and for Augustine. Indeed, she could be considered an Augustinian moralist of a kind. As the University of Notre Dame's John Cavadini, perhaps America's preeminent orthodox Augustinian scholar, has noted, Dworkin's "radical" suspicion of sex as such "gets closer to the approach Augustine takes than the rest of us do, content as we are to isolate 'sexual pleasure' as though it were an unimpeachably fixed quantity innocent of political dynamics, far from being contoured or warped by ideologies of power."[36]

Like Dworkin, the Christian intellectual tradition saw "private" sexual intercourse as intractably bound up with public power and domination. In *The City of God,* for example, Augustine mocked the ideology pagan Rome had built around sex between newlyweds. In Roman mythology, the bride and groom's bedroom on their wedding night was far from private. On the contrary, a host of deities crowded into it to guide the couple.

And why, Augustine asked, did the whole polytheistic host need to show up in a space that was supposed to be private? Was it "that the thought of the presence of the gods should make the couple more concerned to preserve decency? Not at all." Rather, wrote Augustine (in words that could have been penned by Dworkin), they were there to enforce compliance "in ravishing the virginity of a girl who feels the weakness of her sex and is terrified by the strangeness of her situation." Venus was there, "so named, because 'not without violence' (*vi non sine*) can a woman be robbed of her virginity." The minor god Subigus manhandled the bride and made sure she was "subdued to her husband." Prema pressed her "tight to keep her from moving."[37] And so on. As Augustine archly noted, all this divine exertion left very little for the happy Roman groom to do.

The passage, says Cavadini, is proof that lust in the Christian tradition "is exposed not as something merely 'personal' and 'private,' but something which is in effect a cultural project."[38] For Augustine, the earthly city's *libido dominandi*, its lust for domination, has its first image in the *libido dominandi* of the bedroom. Or as Dworkin put it, sex "is not a private act at all—it is a social act in conformity with a social requirement." Lustful domination is "a building block of society as a whole."[39]

The worst immorality is to use another person's body in the passing of time. And yet, it seems such immorality is unavoidable if the fallen city of man (and woman) is to perpetuate itself down the generations.

SEX WITHOUT LUST?

So how do we redraw this age-old pattern? Can we? I wish I could offer simple, Marabel Morgan–style advice. But I can't.

I affirm with Augustine and the whole Judeo-Christian tradition that "it was part of God's original intention that human beings live together in embodied experience, reproducing by means of sexual intercourse," as Cavadini has written.[40] The injunction to "be fruitful and multiply" came before the Fall (Gen 1:28) and was reiterated afterward (cf. Gen 9:1). Biology and instinct seem to issue the same injunction. Yet this fruitfulness entails an act with high costs, which a rational, moral creature feels obliged to tally. Sex can be painful and destructive, and its dangers are *intrinsic* to it, owing to the act's apparent inseparability from dominating lust.

That was Dworkin's insight—and, again, also Augustine's. Both questioned pro-sex ideologies that pulled a reassuring blanket over a complicated, morally fraught reality (as all ideologies do). For Dworkin, the dominance of male lust and, therefore, sexual indignity for women were indivisible from the mechanics of the act. Intercourse was thus the organic base of larger male-supremacist structures, which, in turn, shielded and reinforced the violations inherent to the act.

Augustine never went so far as to condemn the biological mechanics of intercourse. Rather, he traced what had gone wrong with sex to the Fall and the resulting defects in our will: our inability to resist the temptation of dominating lust, our wills divided against themselves, even when we approach our sexual partners with the purest intentions. As his sardonic critique of the Roman bedroom scene shows, he, too, deplored the public ideologies constructed to legitimate lust and saw the force of lust rippling out to society, far beyond the bedroom.

Historic Christianity and Dworkinian feminism both condemn lust as a *public* problem (though the latter goes much further in striking at the bodily act itself). Insofar as they agree, the question becomes whether we can reimagine sex without lust. Is it possible to remove lust from our enjoyment of an act that is central to our bodily experience?

The bishop of Hippo sure tried. Augustine held that before the Fall, the sex act was "committed '*tranquillo arbitrio*,' that is, with a will undisturbed by passion."[41] As Cavadini tells us, that is *not* the same thing as sex devoid of feeling. "But it is without passion, and it is altogether without fear or sadness, since there was nothing to occasion such emotions."[42]

In this way, Augustine speculated, "the seed of children" could have been "sown without the sickness of lust. . . . Without feeling the goading of seductive and burning agitation, the husband would have come to rest on his wife's bosom in tranquility of mind and without any corruption of her body's integrity."[43] (In *Intercourse,* Dworkin, relying on a lousy translation, read this very passage to mean that the man was the aggressive one "on top" even before the Fall, and the misinterpretation informed her rejection of the Judeo-Christian tradition's attempts to "solve" or mitigate the problem of lust.)[44]

Dworkin tried to imagine a different kind of sex, too. One was "female-first" intercourse, advocated by the American suffragette Victoria Woodhull (1838–1927), in which the woman is "entirely self-determining, the controlling and dominating partner, the one whose desire determined the event, the one who both initiates and is the final authority on what sex is and will be," as Dworkin summarized.[45] Dworkin also floated the sexologist Shere Hite's vision of sex without male thrusting: a "mutual lying together in pleasure, penis-in-vagina, vagina-covering-penis, with female orgasm providing much of the stimulation necessary for male orgasm."[46]

I don't know. Devoted as I am to Augustine—I chose him as my patron saint upon being received into the Catholic Church—I just can't see how we might reenact Edenic, pre-Fall sex. Augustine himself seems to have been aware of how daunting a challenge this was. With some embarrassment, he admitted that even trying to picture sex without lust was enough to conjure . . . lust.[47] Dworkin, meanwhile, granted that the Woodhull and Hite models are inconceivable "in real life with real men."[48] Maybe, she wondered, sexual intercourse is just "immune to reform."[49]

Another solution, promoted in Dworkin's time and with renewed vigor today by sex-positive feminists, is to impose drastic consent requirements, for example, demanding that men seek affirmative consent at every step of the sexual encounter. But Dworkin was skeptical of that, too. Without a more humane sexual ethic, she said, consent standards are "pallid, weak, stupid, second-class."[50] She had a point: If degradation of human dignity is inherent to certain acts, no amount of affirmative consent would overcome such degradation.

So what's left? Should we abolish sexual intercourse altogether? That isn't remotely plausible, of course, and it would go against our nature. Plus, as Dworkin foresaw, new "reproductive technologies" that attempt to sever sex from childbearing have wrought still more monstrous exploitations.[51] Men and women (or other family arrangements) no longer necessarily receive the gift of life from natural intercourse. But the *libido dominandi* still grips our society. Without even conception to bind them, men feel "free" to give vent to their lust in new ways that would have shocked the Roman bridegroom and his host of perverse gods.

REGULATING LUST

Andrea Dworkin burned her way through the rosy clouds that fogged the moral realities of sex in modern society. At the same time, a fierce hostility to tradition was baked into her philosophy. She treated all traditional teaching on sex as a manmade creation lending bogus legitimacy to male supremacy. To be sure, she was happy to strike narrow tactical alliances with traditional believers on discrete causes, such as pornography, but she went no further.

This prevented her from seeing the full extent to which tradition was her ally—how, for example, a Saint Augustine had perceived the same trouble with male sexual domination fifteen centuries earlier and even described it in terms resembling her own. Dworkin's anti-tradition cast of mind meant that her intellectual armory lacked the swords tradition had sharpened through long ages to at least *try* to subdue the beast of dominating lust.

For starters, there was the natural law. First articulated in classical thought and developed much further by the Church, natural-law theory says that human sexuality should be ordered to the true, natural *ends* of the human person: namely, the forming of families and the nurturing of children. Put another way, just because a man can do all sorts of things with his penis doesn't mean he *should* do them. Nor, for that matter, should women do whatever they please with their sexual powers—something Dworkin barely grappled with, female desire remaining her one big blind spot. As rational creatures with free will and consciences, man and woman can discern what their sexual powers are meant for, and public rules should assist and encourage them in that discernment. Natural law aside, traditional societies of all kinds put up various walls between the sexes—modesty norms and separate spaces, for example—to tightly regulate when and where the "sex-passion" could be unleashed.

Yeah, right, Dworkin in effect scoffed in *Intercourse*. With a too-quick sweep she dismissed natural law and the other regulations as means for promoting "the power of men over women" and keeping "women sexually subjugated (accessible) to men."[52] Oh? Even laws against adultery? Against incest? Even the Christian prohibition against husbands lusting after their own wives? A thinker acutely suspicious of pseudoscientific attempts to justify sex-liberationism, Dworkin claimed with scant evidence that tradition's only motive for regulating male lust was cynical: namely, that if all men did as they pleased sexually, they would upset the male-supremacist order. In other words, traditional regulation restrained male dominating lust—but only to maintain the exploitation of women.

Or something like that. Her theory is muddled. It is a sign, I suspect, that as with the threat of "liberated" men, she refused to take things to their logical conclusion: Traditional sexual regulations did far more to domesticate male lust than any modern alternative on offer. Even if marred by hypocrisy in its application, traditional teaching was at least alert to the dangers of sexuality and erected some protective barriers. Conversely, we might ask: Has the downfall of those barriers ushered in a new era of sexual dignity and equality? Or did it create conditions favorable to the Harvey Weinsteins and Jeffrey

Epsteins of the world, to Pornhub and the mass pornographization Dworkin rightly decried?

If Dworkin's diagnosis was mostly correct—and the daily #MeToo headlines suggest it was—then the best we can do might be to begin rebuilding some of the barriers foolishly torn down by our parents and grandparents. "Conservative," religious Americans should set aside their reflexive hostility to all things feminist and resist the tendency to treat a sexist, boorish, and essentially libertine ethic of relatively recent vintage as somehow ordained by Scripture, antiquity, or "nature." By the same token, feminists and men and women of the "left" would be wise to take a second look at tradition, rightly and broadly understood, as a source of sexual restraint and regulation, ordered especially to the protection of women and children.

Sadly, Dworkin's spurning of tradition left no exit from the cul-de-sac of her diagnosis. If human beings were endowed with a conscience—the voice of some objective standard of conduct (see chapter 8)—then lust, bad as it was, came with "shame" and thus "left a door open to repentance," as Cavadini says.[53] There was no such opening in Dworkin's moral universe. Her prognosis was supremely bleak: "Men are shits and take pride in it."[54]

With no loving God or transcendent horizon, there was no hope of redeeming intercourse on heaven or earth.

I PREFER REDEMPTION, and I can't view embodied sexuality as such as evil. Having said that, if the choice were between Dworkin's brand of moral seriousness about sex, on one hand, and our giddy pro-sex ideology, on the other—well, the morally serious person should choose the company of the woman who spoke unpleasant truths. And it wasn't as if Andrea Dworkin ever *promised* to be pleasing.

You tell the truth and people can shit all over it. . . . But somehow once it's said it can't be unsaid; it stays living, somewhere, in someone's heart.

WHAT DO YOU OWE YOUR BODY?

———

As I write, much of the world has been coping with varying degrees of coronavirus lockdowns and social-distancing restrictions for close to half a year. The essentials are by now familiar to all of us: Stand at least six feet apart from other people. Put on a mask. Don't shake hands. Closures and cancellations. Those who can, work from home. Be sure to wear pants while on that Zoom call, in case your lower body accidentally comes in view of the camera.

And remember, we're all in this together.

That last—"we're all in this together"—was an inspiring slogan when the lockdowns first began. But soon, it lost much of its charm and promise of solidarity. For one thing, it became clear that, economically speaking, we weren't, in fact, all in this together. Those who were most zealous for protracted lockdowns tended to have jobs that mainly entailed manipulating information on screens—and financial cushions to fall back on in case of layoffs and furloughs. By contrast, jobless rolls swelled with downscale workers (in retail, hospitality, service, and similar industries). "Essential workers," meanwhile, had no choice but to expose themselves to the danger of the virus.

Beyond the class and economic disparities, however, there was another, more general sense in which it felt as if we weren't in it together: We couldn't physically *be* together. More than one single friend of mine in New York City reached out to me with an anguished complaint: They hadn't had so much as a hug for months. They desperately missed the sensation of pressing someone else's body to their own. Of course, these friends could "see" their distant loved ones on FaceTime or Zoom or Skype, and they availed themselves of these options as much as possible. But all admitted that virtual hugs and virtual happy hours and virtual parties "weren't the same." These substitutes certainly weren't enough for too many mentally ill people and those with substance-abuse problems. Overdose deaths and suicides increased.[1]

Human beings are social animals, and the lockdown experience was a reminder that our sociality depends on bodies, on embodied experience. We don't just want to hear a human voice; our ears yearn for the *natural* voice, unmediated by digital equipment. We don't just want to see other human beings; we want to see them up-close, in the flesh. We don't just want to love and be loved; we want to express our love with hugs and kisses and backslaps and high fives.

Yet even before the pandemic, our hypertechnological societies were drawing us rapidly away from embodied experience of all kinds. An ever-greater share of human activities took place in a virtual realm: working, shopping, studying, socializing, and on and on. Many of us—me included—have one or more online avatars, which we cultivate more carefully than we do our embodied personas. And in the aftermath of COVID-19, these trends look poised to accelerate, as firms expand remote work, Zoom drinks become routine, cities depopulate, and "attending university" takes on a primarily Internet-based connotation.

Perhaps not accidentally, these trends coincide with a modern ethic of the body, according to which our bodies and our embodied relationships are open to being remade, rewritten, or reconfigured according to our desires. Our true selves, in this view, are immaterial entities housed—or trapped—inside our bodies. One clear expression of it is the modern account of gender, which is premised on a rupture between who we are interiorly and the sexed bodies we receive from nature. A more radical version can be found in "transhumanist" ideologies, which see the human body as an impediment to full human development. The body, in this telling, is a flawed vessel: prone to decrepitude and disease, in constant need of sleep and organic fuel to keep operating, *stuck* in time and space. The sooner we can transcend it, the better.

If lockdown trends hold, the mental side of our existence—our memories, intelligence, personalities, and emotions—could eclipse our bodies as the primary or even sole locus of our being. In the future, selfhood could even be treated as mere information—souls or personas that can be stored, copied, transmitted, and modified. At that point, who is to say where my Max's true self lies?

But is all this desirable? Is it reasonable to say goodbye to more and more of the embodied experiences our ancestors took for granted? *Or do we owe the body something more?*

The Assignment

Can a single homework assignment form, and then re-form, a person's cast of mind? It did for the philosopher Hans Jonas. In the 1920s, Jonas was a graduate student at the University of Marburg, the world's oldest Protestant university, nestled in the lush, fairy-tale hills of west-central Germany. But Marburg's idyll was a mirage: This was the same intellectually vibrant but socially and economically volatile Weimar Germany we spoke of in chapter 3; the Third Reich lurked just around the historical bend.

For Jonas, what was supposed to have been a weeklong project during his time at Marburg turned out to be a years-long calling. The assignment would send him deep into antiquity's religious and philosophical crypts, a labyrinth of forgotten ideas. To find his way, he took with him the insights of modern philosophy as a sort of map. But when he returned from his quest, he realized that the ancient world had handed him a map of the modern ruins around him.

The fateful assignment came in a New Testament seminar. Almost anywhere else but at Marburg in the '20s, Jonas's presence in that class would have been unusual. For one thing, he was an aspiring philosopher, not a theologian. Then as now, many of philosophy's leading lights saw their pursuit as completely unrelated to the things of God. As Jonas recalled decades later, the "necessity of becoming an atheist in order to become a philosopher" was taken for granted and considered a source of intellectual "freedom."[2]

Yet at Marburg, Jonas had the benefit of a pair of unusually brilliant teachers, men who were in the business of reevaluating the whole course of Western thought. And that meant paying very close attention to ancient sources, especially religious ones, even if their interpretations of the texts were hardly orthodox. One teacher was the philosopher Martin Heidegger (1889–1976), the other the Lutheran New Testament scholar Rudolf Bultmann (1884–1976).

Both men were associated with the movement—or, rather, the sensibility—that later came to be known as existentialism. Its defining feature was a feeling of radical contingency: in the world and between human beings, with neither God nor metaphysics able to preserve a stable life horizon. In the existentialists' telling, we humans are thrown into this world without asking for it, and we find that all our striving, our hopes, our grasping for meaning, finally our whole existence come up against the unyielding wall of finitude called death.

For the existentialists, the self was an unstable category. What did it mean to be a person, to possess a self? Whatever the answer, it couldn't be found in anything prior to the existence of the individual—no preconceived notion or essence could lend meaning to human existence. This predicament had profound psychological and moral consequences. The individual had no assurance about her place in the world, which mocked her with its indifference and offered no answers to her questions about being. At the same time, this meant she could discover and become who she truly was on her own terms; indeed, this *becoming* was her true calling.[3]

The existentialist sensibility was thick in the heady atmosphere at Marburg when Jonas studied there in his twenties. Heidegger dominated the whole scene, and he was the object of almost cult-like adoration among his students. Jonas himself had followed the forceful and enigmatic thinker from the University of Freiburg, in southwest Germany, where he had done preparatory studies under Heidegger.

Heidegger's project—to rethink all of philosophy, which he believed had gone wrong almost from the beginning when it came to the question of being—required going back behind all the settled interpretations of the great texts. On any given day, he might have had students closely read and analyze Aristotle's *On the Soul* (in the original Greek) or Aquinas's commentaries on Aristotle (in the Latin).[4] It wasn't at all unusual, as a result, for one of Heidegger's philosophy students to take theology courses with Bultmann, who was famous for his close reading of classical Christian texts in their original languages.

Indeed, there was in play at Marburg a fascinating Heidegger–Bultmann symbiosis. As Jonas wrote, it was fashionable "among certain of Heidegger's disciples to go also to Bultmann and study New Testament theology and, if admitted to enter, Bultmann's seminar on the New Testament, and vice versa."[5] At Marburg, unlike at most other universities of that time, the border between philosophy and theology, reason and revelation, was refreshingly porous.

Still, as a Jew, albeit not one deeply educated in the Jewish tradition, Jonas had another reason to feel out of place in a Christian seminar. He wasn't the only one in his cohort. Joining Jonas around Bultmann's table was the political philosopher (and Heidegger's sometime lover) Hannah Arendt, who would go on to international fame with her book *The Origins of Totalitarianism* and her reportage on the trial of a Nazi war criminal, *Eichmann in Jerusalem*. "The seminar," Jonas remembered in his memoir, "was packed, of course, with Protestant theologians and certified goyim, while we two, who to begin with were philosophers not theologians, but above all Jews, really didn't belong there."[6]

Born in 1903 into a tiny, highly assimilated Jewish community in far west Germany, Jonas had had his share of run-ins with German anti-Semitism. He refused to submit to it as a fact of life or to believe that Jew-hatred would eventually subside in the course of historical "progress." As the only Jewish boy in his public school, "I was a holy terror," mustering "Maccabean rage" when classmates insulted his religion.[7] In the aftermath of World War I, when Jews became the scapegoat of choice for the country's defeat and humiliation at Versailles, Jonas was certain that his people would never belong in Germany—that the Jews had to establish a state in their ancient homeland. He arrived at Marburg a committed Zionist.

In the event, Bultmann welcomed his two Jewish seminar members with the utmost high-German courtesy. And as Jonas was soon to discover, there was much that could absorb a philosophical mind in his study of Christian scriptures.

One day in 1924, Bultmann asked Jonas to research the Greek phrase *gnosis theou*—literally, "knowledge of God"—in the Gospel of Saint John.[8] What did this term, "gnosis," mean in the historical context of the New Testament? What kind of knowledge was it? How did gnosis relate to philosophical knowledge? Jonas would dedicate the next three decades of his life to this one set of questions, emerging in the process as the first modern philosopher to interpret the ancient religious phenomenon known as Gnosticism.

THE *OTHER* SISTINE CHAPEL

Gnosticism emerged as a distinct religious movement in the first few centuries following the advent of Christ. It infiltrated, and vied for influence with, Judaism, Christianity, and classical paganism. Had it, rather than orthodox Christianity, prevailed out of Late Antiquity's wars of religious ideas, our civilization would have taken a very different aspect. As Jonas speculated, we might have ended up with an alternative Sistine Chapel, its "images different from the biblical ones on which the imagination of the beholder was reared, but strangely familiar to him and disturbingly moving."[9]

Michelangelo's Sistine Chapel portrays God reaching out with a life-giving touch to Adam, an Adam who beholds his creator with a symmetrically loving gaze. Next to that panel is the creation or raising of Eve out of a sleeping Adam's flesh, flesh of his flesh. The other Genesis events—the separation of light from darkness, the creation of the heavens, the Flood, etc.—flow into and out of this bond between a loving God and these two creatures molded after his own divine image. Yes, creation is fallen, and sin strains the bond between creator and creature. But the bond remains intact; creation is *good,* and creatures can know and understand their creator through it.

The gnostic Sistine Chapel would have looked familiar in some respects (as Jonas noted) but unsettlingly different and downright bizarre in others. For starters, God wouldn't have appeared in the picture at all, because gnostic religions held the deity to be "absolutely transmundane," as Jonas found, "its nature alien to that of the universe."[10] This deity wouldn't have appeared in a gnostic account of creation—because he had nothing to do with it.

Second, the gnostic creator of the world—who *wasn't* God—wouldn't have looked anything like the loving, fatherly figure painted by Michelangelo. Rather, he would have been depicted as a mean and/or clueless demon, who created the world and humanity out of malice and/or folly. And the created world itself would have the aspects of a prison, with many layers of dungeons, each guarded by a demon.

Finally, man and woman would have appeared as creatures oppressed. Just as the world that envelops them would have been portrayed as a prison, a dungeon with many dungeons inside it, so their bodies would have appeared as fleshly traps, lacking all the nobility of Michelangelo's bodily forms. The narrative arc of this alternative Sistine Chapel wouldn't have involved communion between creator and creatures, but rather the latter's escape—from embodied existence as such. Taken together, these images would have represented some of the weirdest, most radical answers ever given to the timeless problems of being human.

The Context: The Marriage Feast of Alexander

The Alexandrian conquest created the hothouse conditions for the flowering of these strange faiths. In the late fourth century B.C., the Macedonian king Alexander III and his men swept the Mediterranean region, the Middle East, and North Africa, even making inroads into Central Asia and the Indian subcontinent. Afterward, they self-consciously fused Western and Eastern cultures, in some cases quite literally: At a wedding ceremony in Susa, Iran, presided over by Alexander himself, ten thousand of his troops married women from the newly defeated Persian Empire.

Initially, there followed a "period of manifest Greek dominance and oriental submersion," Jonas explained. But soon, the East mounted a "kind of spiritual counterattack into the West and reshaped universal culture." As we saw earlier in this book, the East, especially in its Judeo-Christian strain, had an answer to the questions about unchanging principles and uncaused causes that haunted Greco-Roman philosophy: namely, God. And the East would learn to account for its faith in this God with the rigor and vocabulary of Greek philosophy. The result, explained Jonas, was the "synthesis carried into the Middle Ages": the Alexandrian marriage of *fides et ratio*, faith and reason.[11]

Still, a conquest is a conquest, no matter how reciprocal or cosmopolitan the winners. Conquered peoples chafe under new overlords. In the Middle East and North Africa, Greek cultural ascendancy, coming on the heels of military defeat, produced in addition a "subsurface stream" of religion, a "secret tradition" or "invisible East."[12]

This stream carried all sorts of new religious currents. Many had Judeo-Christian admixtures but with elements of astrology, magic, pagan polytheism, and so on thrown in and mashed together. They were *secret* faiths, both in that they sometimes resembled underground cults, with an inner circle of members who knew more than those in outer circles, let alone the average unenlightened man or woman—and in the very nature of the knowingness they claimed to possess: namely, hidden knowledge.

In the 1920s and '30s, when Jonas undertook his work, historical and archaeological information about these movements was scarce. Much of what was known about Gnosticism came via polemics against it penned by the Church Fathers: We already encountered Augustine's break with the Manichaeans, a quintessentially gnostic sect; but even earlier, such Greek Fathers as Irenaeus and Hippolytus and Latin ones such as Tertullian had picked up the gauntlet against what they considered a Christian heresy.[13]

In 1945, however, after Jonas had already completed his dissertation and the first volume of his monumental study on Gnosticism, *Gnosis and the Spirit of Late Antiquity,* a man and his brothers in southern Egypt, out digging for a type of soil they used as fertilizer, uncovered a large, sealed jar containing, among other texts, fifty-two ancient gnostic treatises. The discovery of the so-called Nag Hammadi Library massively expanded modern knowledge of Gnosticism. Even before the Nag Hammadi find, Jonas had been accused of getting ahead of the archaeology and historiography with his analysis, which attempted to identify a singular religious impulse behind all gnostic movements.[14] Afterward, the attacks intensified. Critics charged Jonas with distilling a unitary faith out of a multiplicity of religious phenomena too diverse to be boiled down together. More recently, some scholars have gone so far as to suggest that the very term "Gnosticism" is "premature" and best "dismissed and replaced."[15]

Did Jonas make small mistakes? Yes. Did he at times have a tendency to identify nearly every religious phenomenon of Late Antiquity as "gnostic," to project what he wanted to see onto the historical material? Sure.[16] Even so, Jonas went boldly into uncharted territory and made a penetrating analysis of what he found; I suspect much of the criticism is the nitpicking of the pioneer by latecomers.

There is a reason his study remains the foundational classic. Even those who aren't entirely uncritical admit that once they "see" the unity Jonas found in such disparate religions, they can't un-see it.[17]

The gnostic religions themselves, as we have said, were a hodgepodge of Jewish, Christian, pagan, magic, astrological, and other obscure sources. Jonas, however, pinpointed the human longing animating the various systems, notwithstanding their differences in belief and their practical similarities with mainstream Judaism, Christianity, and paganism. To define that longing was to define Gnosticism.

What was it? It was a desire to go beyond the world and thus to overcome the "absolute rift between man and that in which he finds himself lodged," as Jonas explained. He called this longing "acosmism": the sense that self and world are radically at odds, that humans aren't at home in creation but must go beyond it altogether. All the other main features of gnostic religions served this one, acosmic impulse: to "revolt against the world and its god in the name of an absolute spiritual freedom."[18]

THE FOREMOST FEATURE was the transmundane God. If believers viewed creation as oppressive and bad, something to be transcended, then of course they couldn't ascribe creation to the true deity. Rather, they held the true God to be alien to the world. Jonas explained: "The concept of the alien Life"—alien to created or earthly life—"is one of the great impressive word-symbols which we encounter in gnostic speech, and it is new in the history of human speech."[19]

Take, for example, an opening formula of the prayers of Mandaeism, a gnostic sect that revered John the Baptist (but not Jesus) and whose members still persist in small numbers in today's Iran and Iraq. It begins: "In the name of the great first *alien Life* from the worlds of light, the sublime that stands *above all works*."[20] The phrase "above all works" immediately sets apart this alien principle of Life from the creator-God of Genesis, whose works are familiar and legible. The Genesis God rests from his works; the alien deity doesn't work at all.

Or take the names for the true deity used in Marcionism, an explicitly Christian form of Gnosticism founded by Marcion, a mariner from the Black Sea region of today's Turkey. Adherents of his religion called the true deity the "alien God," "the Alien," "the Other," "the Unknown," "the Nameless," "the Hidden," and the "Unknown Father." This deity had nothing to do with the "inferior and oppressive creator" of the world.[21]

Marcion (A.D. 85–160) had a supremely literal mind: After reading the Hebrew and Christian scriptures, he concluded that the God of the Jews couldn't possibly be the same God who sent Jesus Christ. The Hebrew God stood for law and justice, whereas the New Testament God proclaimed love and grace. To Marcion, law and justice were incommensurable with love and grace. Therefore, we were dealing with two different deities, one inferior and mean, perhaps a vicious angel; the other superior, loving—and unknown.

We couldn't know this true God, and, crucially for Marcion's scheme, we weren't even his children. In orthodox Christianity, God sends his only Son to redeem a creation that ultimately belongs to him. But Marcion taught that since the true creator of this world was an evil angel or lower God, we couldn't have been the children or heirs of the God of Jesus Christ. Rather, the alien God sent Jesus out of sheer unmerited goodness, not even really knowing us as human beings, to "buy" us from the inferior deity, who otherwise had full legal title to humanity.

Marcion compiled the first-ever canon of the Bible. It consisted only of some Pauline epistles—which, read literally and in isolation, seemed to support Marcion's view of the law as bad—and a truncated version of Saint Luke. That's it. The Old Testament he omitted entirely. Church Fathers like Tertullian mocked Marcionism and similar sects for editing the Bible *just so,* to bolster their own eccentric interpretation.[22] Marcion's Bible prompted the early Church to develop its own canon, which very much included the Old Testament.

Yet Marcionist communities survived, especially in the East, well into the fifth century.[23] They were sustained by their bizarre, fanatic reading of Jesus's words in Luke that "no good tree bears bad fruit" (6:43).[24] The worldly "fruits" they saw around them were orderly and rotten—rotten *because* orderly and constraining—and thus they couldn't have issued from a good tree, a loving creator. No, creation was contemptible: "a grand production," they snarked, "and worthy of its God, this world," with its "miserable elements," the whole thing a "puny cell of the creator."[25]

WHICH BRINGS US to the second main feature: the prison cosmology. For the gnostic faiths, Jonas found, the universe was "like a vast prison whose innermost dungeon is the earth, the scene of man's life." Beyond the prison of ordinary life stood other cosmic structures—stars, firmaments, and other invisible bodies—that further enclosed the human spirit. And this was by malicious design of the demons, evil angels, or "archons" (governors) who condemned men and women to the "universal Fate" of imprisonment.[26]

The Naassene Psalm, a text associated with an early Christian cult, characterized the world as a "labyrinth of evils" to which the soul is confined, not knowing "how she shall get through."[27] The prison cosmos, however, wasn't crushingly and obviously oppressive in all gnostic accounts. In other texts, the very comforts of the world formed the fetters that chain humankind.

Jonas considered the third-century *Hymn of the Pearl* a supremely lyrical expression of Iranian-variety Gnosticism. The protagonist of the story is a prince born in some higher and nobler dimension, whose royal parents send him on a mission to Egypt—that is, our lower world, a house of bondage. He is supposed to retrieve a pearl guarded by a serpent, the slithering, moist, poisonous embodiment of the malign forces that rule the human domain. (The pearl itself, it seems, acts almost like a MacGuffin plot device, its significance never quite disclosed; what matters is the quest, not its prize.)

Our hero dons "filthy garments" to prevent the Egyptians, servants of the serpent, from recognizing him as a being from the upper world. The trick works, for the Egyptians indeed mistake him as one of their own. But soon, he reports, they "ingratiated themselves with me and mixed me drink with their cunning and gave me to taste of their meat." Their food and drink cause the prince to fall "into a deep slumber."[28]

The pleasures of the lower world, in other words, intoxicate the prince, so he altogether forgets that he is the son of a king from a higher realm on a mission. It takes the intervention of his kin from the beyond to save him. They send him a letter—and here we find some of the *Hymn's* most magically poetic imagery—that "rose up in the form of an eagle," to awaken the prince and remind him of his true identity and mission.[29] *Wake up!*

Now our hero can free himself. Seizing the pearl and escaping the lower world, he removes the worldly clothes and puts on, instead, his otherworldly "robe of glory" that fits him like a second skin—indeed, the robe that was always a part of him or a projection of him, his true self, which he had shed when he set out for our world.[30] The "filthy garments" of the Egyptians, in other words, were nothing other than bodily and sensory experience as such. And that experience—taste, digestion, strong drink, etc.—was humanity's deepest prison in this profoundly gnostic vision. Embodied, the person was vulnerable to deception, whereas the "robe of glory" was the truest part of him all along, and it didn't belong to the bodily world.

This leads us to the third and, for our purposes, most important feature of the gnostic faiths: suspicion, even hatred, of bodies and the bodily. In the ancient gnostic imagination, the human body mirrored the prison structure of the universe as a whole. The body, and in some cases even the soul, trapped the divine, alien spark, just as layers of cosmic dungeons confined the human person to the earth.[31]

Thus, in a Mandaean text, the alien Life laments its predicament: "Who has made me live in the [earth], who has thrown me into the *body-stump*?" Elsewhere, the Mandaeans described a sleeping Adam receiving a gnostic wake-up call: "Arise, arise, Adam, put off thy *stinking body,* thy garment of clay, the fetters, the bond. . . ." Adam himself rages at one of the lower deities who oversee the lower world: "Why have you carried me away from my place into captivity and cast me into the *stinking body*?" A lower deity even expresses regret over what he has done: "Who has stultified me, so that I was a fool and *cast the soul into the body*?"[32]

Then there were the Manichaeans, who outstripped all other gnostic movements in their revulsion at the body generally and sex and sexual reproduction especially. The followers of Mani, you will remember from chapter 6, saw the world as being sharply divided between light and darkness, with the sparks of the divine kingdom of light trapped everywhere in the kingdom of darkness, our physical world.

Having stolen away bits of the light in an original struggle, according to the Manichaean cosmic myth, the king of darkness had to figure out some way of holding on to his spoil, which was ever at risk of slipping back to its divine source. What form, the darkness wondered, could serve as "the safest prison for the alien force"—that is, the divine spark? The answer: Adam and Eve, embodied man and woman, into whom the darkness "pours all the light left at his disposal."[33]

The contrast with mainstream Christianity couldn't be sharper. As the Christian faith developed into orthodox doctrine, the Church Fathers went out of their way to underscore the bodily nature of the Christ event: The second Adam, the incarnate Son of God, was fully God *and* fully man, endowed with a real, functional human body. His mother really bore him to term in her womb, and when her own earthly mission was complete, she retained her bodily integrity and was assumed into heaven in embodied form. Through Jesus and Mary, God granted the children of Adam and Eve a share of heaven *in bodily form*.

But for the Manichaeans and many other gnostics, the body had no claim to heaven. Rather, each baby conceived in Eve's womb formed a new, fleshly prison cell for the heavenly spark.

THE FLIGHT FROM RESPONSIBILITY

We owe the word "cosmos" to the Greeks. For us, it is just a synonym for "world" or perhaps "ordered system." For the Greeks, though, "cosmos" was a term of *praise*. It wasn't a neutral term, as ours is, for order implied hierarchy, nobility, perfection, soundness.

The cosmos appeared beautiful and harmonious. Things seemed to happen for a reason. Every thing had a proper function, an *end* to which its existence was ordered: the sun and the moon to shed light, the fruit tree to yield good fruit, beasts of burden to serve human-kind, flowing waters to quench tree, beast, and human alike. More-over, the rational human mind could contemplate the orderliness of the cosmos and take pleasure in it. Our minds, then, had a share in cosmic order. When the Greeks venerated the cosmos, they really venerated "the whole of which man is a part," as Jonas put it.[34] There was communion between whole and part.

As part of a rational, harmonious whole, human beings possessed within themselves, in their nature, a capacity for perfection (bod-ily, spiritual, political, etc.). These perfections or virtues—*arete*—constituted the right functioning of the human person, just as there were *arete* proper to those other natural things (heavenly bodies, trees, horses). For the *rational* creature, the highest perfection was wisdom: to discover the role he was destined to play, to know the truth.[35]

One part of the "East" enthusiastically took up this cosmic vision and, as it were, completed it, offering an explanation as to *why* order existed in the first place, and *why* the individual couldn't achieve per-fection or know the fullness of truth without divine assistance. That was the story in chapter 2, of the synthesis of faith and reason that reached its pinnacle in the mind of Thomas Aquinas. But the gnostics rebelled against the whole Greek way of *being* in the world, against cosmos, against order.

For the secret faiths of the East, "cosmos" was a dirty word. There *was* order, yes, and it was malign, designed by mad or evil demiurges, presided over by oppressive demons and archons. The order implied by the term "cosmos" was "tyrannical and evil, devoid of meaning and goodness, alien to the purposes of man and to his inner essence, no object for his communication and affirmation."[36] The cosmos, as we noted, was a prison, the human body its inmost dungeon.

So what did it mean, ethically and practically speaking, to treat the cosmos with such contempt and long to take flight from it altogether? It meant to treat moral responsibility with equal contempt, to seek to take flight from the responsibility that came with being part of the cosmic whole.

Gnosis was knowledge that saved: Once the gnostic believer awakened to the true nature of reality, he was freed from bonds of responsibility—and guilt. He "knew" that the rules proclaimed by the prophets and seemingly wired into human nature were pointless, indeed, evil: Nature itself was evil or mad, after all, and the prophets served the evil or mad creator of nature. Hence why gnostic moral doctrines typically paid so little attention to natural virtues or perfections (*arete*).

Arete took for granted an account of the human person, a composite of soul *and* body, as being sensible, purposive, end-directed. That was the account Greco-Roman philosophy promoted, which the Church incorporated into her moral teachings. But "it is obvious," Jonas found, "that Gnosticism had no room for this conception of human virtue. 'Looking toward God' has for it an entirely different meaning," namely, "jumping across all intervening realities": mundane social bonds, loyalty to the people and communities that depend on us, the human body—all were "nothing but fetters or obstacles, or distractions or temptations, or at best irrelevant."[37]

Starting from these premises, some gnostic cults enjoined a rigorous asceticism. Recall, for example, the Manichaean rigors Augustine encountered (in chapter 6). Agricultural labor, sexual intercourse, eating meat, and the like only prolonged the imprisonment of the light in darkness and were for that reason prohibited. Other cults promoted a total and shameless libertinism: The moral law was nothing "but the means of regularizing and thus stabilizing" our worldly affairs, after all, when the real point was to transcend the world.[38] So believers could do as they pleased: Their deeds in this cosmic realm had nothing to do with their salvation.

Though they diverged on what to do, practically speaking, the secret faiths were in agreement on a more basic point: Since there was no perfection in human nature, good and evil had no meaning as *natural* categories. Rather, as the Church Father Irenaeus summarized the thought of one gnostic teacher, "things are evil or good simply in virtue of human opinion."[39]

Summa cum Laude

"Your dissertation is excellent."[40]

So whispered Heidegger to Jonas one night, as the philosopher squeezed past his student to get to his seat at a concert hall in Marburg. It was the winter of 1928, and Jonas had been waiting for months to hear back about the dissertation he had submitted to Heidegger. "It didn't trouble [Heidegger] in the slightest that a student had been waiting in fear and trembling to hear how something he'd spent years working on would be received."[41]

The topic had grown out of Jonas's assignment in Bultmann's Bible seminar four years earlier. Bultmann had been so impressed with the initial research that he urged Jonas to expand it into a dissertation. Jonas didn't exactly dream of becoming an expert on the Hellenistic world's secret faiths, but Bultmann was insistent: "Let me talk this over with Heidegger!"[42] Soon it was settled: Jonas would render a philosophical interpretation of Gnosticism. Heidegger would serve as his primary adviser, with Bultmann on hand to make sure he got the ancient sources right.

Heidegger, it seems, wasn't all that interested in the nitty-gritty of Gnosticism per se. "Keep up the good work; it seems you are on the right track" was about as much periodic feedback as Jonas ever received.[43] What obviously pleased Heidegger was the fact that one of his disciples was about to unveil a novel interpretation of Gnosticism, and that Jonas would examine this ancient and obscure phenomenon through his (Heidegger's) existentialist frame.

That is what Jonas did. He descended into the dusty and forgotten crypts of the gnostic, drawn by the growing suspicion that he would find an ancient, primitive expression of his master's modern philosophy of cosmic alienation. And this intuition proved correct. The deeper he went, the more he was struck by what could only be described as a case of philosophical déjà vu. He had already heard acosmic talk before—from Heidegger. He had already met the idea that human beings are thrown into a cruel world against our will and that this "thrown-ness" constitutes our chief predicament—it was Heidegger's idea.

The dissertation he wrote (and later expanded into *Gnosis and the Spirit of Late Antiquity*) treated Gnosticism as an early precursor of modern existentialism. In his dissertation, Jonas wasn't critical of the acosmic impulse he discovered in the gnostic crypts. Rather, it cheered him. These visionaries and spiritual entrepreneurs of Late Antiquity had anticipated the same radical rejection of cosmic order—and the same longing to discover and become the true, "authentic" self—that animated the modern philosophy then in vogue at Marburg. Naturally, Heidegger was pleased with Jonas's dissertation, so much so that he awarded it the *summa cum laude*.

Two decades later, however, Jonas would render a darker moral judgment of acosmism, in both its ancient and modern-existentialist varieties. The great crimes of Nazi Germany prompted this change of mind. On April 1, 1933, the day of the Brownshirts' anti-Jewish boycott, Jonas resolved to leave Germany and immigrate to Mandatory Palestine, where the Zionist movement was laying the foundations of an independent Jewish state. (He later moved to America, where he taught for many years at the New School for Social Research in New York.)

Before he emigrated, he took a Christian girlfriend on a hiking trip in Bavaria. At an inn where they stopped to eat, Jonas and his date heard the brawny, drunken Germans sing: "When Jewish blood from the knife blade spurts / Then all will be well again." Jonas's irrepressible "Maccabean rage" surged again, and he turned to the thugs and dared them: "Come on, pull out your knives. Here I am. Here's a

Jew." One of them, the regional commander, sputtered about escorting Jonas and his girlfriend out of the district; the pair, though shaken, walked out of the inn "in triumph."[44]

When he left his native land, Jonas promised that he would never again set foot on German soil—except as part of a conquering army. And he kept this vow, returning to Germany in 1945 as a member of the British Army's First Palestine Anti-Aircraft Battery, drawn from Zionist émigrés like himself. The sight of Germany in ruins filled him with no pity. How could he pity the land and the people who had deported his mother, first to a Jewish ghetto in Poland and then to Auschwitz, where she had been murdered?

To this personal betrayal, Germany had added a philosophical one: Martin Heidegger, his erstwhile mentor, had joined the Nazi Party in 1933 and remained a member till war's end.

In the 1950s, Jonas, now settled in America, connected the dots between the gnostics' rejection of cosmic order and moral responsibility, on one hand, and Heidegger's modern political irresponsibility on the other. The acosmic, anti-world, anti-body, anti-order attitude common to both, he now believed, was tantamount to nihilism. The gnostic labyrinth led finally to the same moral dead end that had disgraced Heidegger.

In a 1952 essay, Jonas would take his intellectual revenge against his former adviser. "The essence of existentialism," he wrote, "is a certain dualism, an estrangement between man and the world, with the loss of the idea of a kindred cosmos." And the same "radically dualistic mood" was to be found in the "gnostic attitude," fusing its various types into one religion. That shared attitude was the problem, for if the human person isn't part of an orderly cosmic whole, but thrown into an indifferent or malign cosmos against her wishes, then she has no orderly nature, and "that which has no nature has no norm."[45]

Wasn't that the basic attitude of Heideggerian existentialism: that we are hurled at birth into a world that is alien and indifferent to us? Didn't the existentialists, Heidegger very much included, stress that we can and must define our own nature via the "authentic" decisions we make in the moment?

Submitting to a law-governed and law-constrained cosmic order meant submitting to limits, norms, and responsibilities. That was the attitude of, say, an Aristotle or an Aquinas. But if such an order is ruled out, if self and reality are irreconcilably at odds, well, then those "oppressive" limits can go to hell. Behind Heidegger's constant emphasis on *willing* and *becoming* lay a disdain for cosmic being in the present tense, with all its rules and many limitations. In this, Heidegger was all too representative of the restless spirit of German modernity, which, for all its philosophical virtuoso, had culminated in the moral disaster of Nazism.

To be clear, Jonas never suggested that Heidegger became a Nazi *simply because* he was an existentialist. Jonas's mind was far too subtle for that. What he argued was that Heideggerian existentialism shared with ancient Gnosticism an element of total moral irresponsibility, indeed, of nihilism. This raised a disconcerting possibility: that the desire to leave behind human limitations and responsibility would always find some religious or philosophical outlet.

GNOSTIC LIBERALISM

So what do we owe our bodies? Are they just fleshly vessels, which can be manipulated or even discarded in service to the mental or spiritual selves they contain? Do our bodies have *any* claim on who we are? Having explored Gnosticism at its ancient wellspring, and the gnostic attitude's resurgence in one strand of twentieth-century philosophy, perhaps we can now reformulate our starting question: What are the moral consequences when we insist we *don't* owe our bodies any duties of loyalty?

Gnosticism is stubborn. As the contemporary moral philosopher Robert P. George has written, "The idea that human beings are nonbodily persons inhabiting non-personal bodies never quite goes away."[46] Today, the old gnostic voice resounds loudly in modern gender ideology, with its account of gendered being as an interior state that is unrelated to bodily sex (reframed as "sex assigned at birth").

But not just there. Having defined Gnosticism's deepest yearning, we can see how, for example, the transhumanist techno-utopia championed by the likes of the inventor and Google "futurist" Ray Kurzweil is, well, fundamentally gnostic. The gnostic yearning is hard to miss, for example, in Kurzweil's dream of digitally resurrecting his own father, a music teacher, composer, and conductor who died in 1970, when the inventor was twenty-two. Since then, Kurzweil has gathered a storage space full of his father's personal ephemera: various documents, photographs, even old bills. As *The Wall Street Journal* reported, he hopes to combine this material with living memories of his father, his own and others', "to assemble an avatar more like his father than his father ever was—exactly the father Mr. Kurzweil remembers."[47]

Kurzweil views his father's self—and his own—as mind-software that happens to be tethered to flesh-hardware. Soon, he believes, it will be possible to untether the two and thus to allow the mind to have its own independent, and infinite, existence, freed from the body's tendency to decay. This is pure neo-Gnosticism. But I don't mean to pick on Kurzweil. The fact is, his vision is merely a more crystalline expression of the acosmic impulses behind our hyperindividualistic, technologically empowered lifestyles.

The general tendency of modern life is to defeat or circumvent the inconvenient *material* realities standing between us and our desires. Digital currencies, for example, add a new and radical layer of abstraction to commerce and money exchange; for the Bitcoin-flush, doing business need no longer be tied to nation-states—and, therefore, to political communities that might make moral demands (like economic equity). Thanks to new logistics technologies like drones, meanwhile, activities like dining and shopping are unbound from the limits of neighborhood—and, therefore, of neighborliness. The digital classroom, flourishing even before "social distancing" entered our lexicon, is sounding the death knell for education as an embodied experience. Online communities, organized around mutually agreed-upon rules and an ever-narrowing range of shared interests, are increasingly supplanting old-fashioned, historical, and material communities shaped by inconvenient customs and inherited boundaries. And on and on.

In tandem with these economic and technological developments, social liberalism ceaselessly alienates the individual from the natural—from nature as an *ordered, end-directed* reality. This is especially true when it comes to the family, now almost entirely open to reconfiguration in ways that were unthinkable as recently as a decade ago. The next frontier appears to be "chosen families"—biologically unrelated people who form pseudo-families, assuming the roles of mother, father, or sibling for each other, with or without sexual involvement.[48] Many such people have legitimate reasons to stay away from their natural families, to be sure. But the deeply gnostic impulse remains: to overcome, to replace, to forget *embodied* relationships and their moral demands.

Of course, these latter-day tendencies don't share the old Gnosticism's faith in a transmundane God. Nor does "gnostic liberalism," as George calls it, thrill to mythical stories about archons and mad demiurges and whatnot. But today's varieties *do* share with the old Gnosticism something of that acosmic attitude or longing, the inkling that the true self is other than the bodily, with the consequence that the body itself is, "if not a prison to escape, certainly a mere instrument to be manipulated to serve the goals of the 'person,'" the trapped spark within.[49]

That is as purely gnostic a notion as any held by the Manichaeans. And it entails the same moral dangers Jonas detected in the old Gnosticism and again in modern existentialism. George contends,

> If we take the Gnostic view, then human beings—living members of the human species—are not necessarily persons, and some human beings are non-persons. Those in the embryonic,

fetal, and early-infant stages are *not yet* persons. Those who have lost the immediate exercise of certain mental powers—victims of advanced dementias, the long-term comatose and minimally conscious—are *no longer* persons. And those with severe congenital cognitive disabilities aren't now, never were, and never will be persons.[50]

All these vulnerable groups of human beings, after all, lack the *spark* of interior subjective self-ness that the gnostic, ancient and modern, identifies as the "true" person, over against the merely bodily and material.

At the individual level, our gnostic liberalism authorizes the same rejection of norms pinpointed by Jonas: If I don't like my body, well, I can trade it in for another one. If my desires violate the limits imposed by my human nature and the ends to which that nature is ordered, well, I can violate natural limits and go beyond the natural ends as I please. If I weary of my immediate family and community, well, I can escape to other, virtual communities of shared interest, at the expense of kith and kin.

The human body is an image of moral responsibility. To accept the body—with all its beauty and brokenness, its miraculous capacities and its shortcomings, its natural functioning and purposes—is to accept the self as we receive it: bounded, limited, enmeshed in intervening natural realities that include our ancestors, from whom we receive the particular shapes of our bodies, and our progeny, who receive the shapes of their bodies from ours. The urge to reject the bodily—to seek to transcend it, whether through transhumanist projects, or obsessive surgical modification, or what have you—is thus always an invitation to irresponsibility, and a very old temptation, indeed.

WHEN HE RETURNED to Germany as an occupying soldier, Jonas was reminded of much that morally disgusted him: the unblinking bigotry of Nazism, Heidegger's betrayal. But there were broken shards of humaneness buried under the rubble. Upon entering Marburg, Jonas immediately went to check on Bultmann, his other great mentor. Bultmann's wife opened the door. At first, she didn't recognize him. Then, after a beat, she cried out: "Herr Jonas, it's you, Herr Jonas!" She recounted all they had suffered, hunger and poverty and national shame, how she and her husband had prayed for Germany's defeat.[51]

Bultmann had literally shrunk into his old clothes from wartime malnutrition. The sight of his Jewish former student overjoyed the Christian scholar. Then Bultmann noticed a book under Jonas's arm: "May I hope that's the second volume of your Gnosticism book?"[52] It wasn't, but the question shook Jonas. It was as if the great dialogue of philosophy and religion had never been interrupted, as if they were picking up the old seminar just where they had left it a day earlier.

Bultmann's question—"the evidence of this man's loving loyalty, which had outlasted the liquidation of an entire world"—restored Jonas's faith in humanity.[53] It was impossible to sound the depths of depravity into which the Nazis had plunged Europe. But friendship was still real. Ordinary bonds of loyalty were no demiurgical deception. Creation was no prison.

In time, Jonas even came to make peace with Heidegger. In 1969, the pair had a brief meeting in Zurich. Mostly, they reminisced about the old times at Marburg, "while the matters that were of decisive significance to me weren't mentioned," Jonas recalled. "If I'd hoped that anything would be said about the events after 1933, about the fate of the Jews in Germany, about my mother's death, I was bitterly disappointed. . . . Any clarification on his part, let alone a word of regret, was not to be."[54]

The teacher remained unrepentant. Nevertheless, his student felt he had "reconciled with Heidegger."[55] In giving Heidegger an opening and seeking reconciliation, Hans Jonas had gone beyond the demands of natural responsibility, deep into the realm of grace.

The assignment was complete.

WHAT'S *GOOD* ABOUT DEATH?

———

Throughout this book, on our journey from medieval Europe to Soviet Russia, ancient China to tribal Africa, the Jim Crow South to Weimar Germany, we went searching for wisdom—the traditional wisdom of limits. At each step, we witnessed the working out of a strange paradox: how across life's realms, the push for ever-greater human mastery has degraded humanity's real stature, put us at odds with nature and our fellow human beings, and frustrated our longings for community—and for truth.

With C. S. Lewis, we explored the limits of scientific knowledge. Thomas Aquinas showed us how the arrogance of reason unbound from religion diminishes both. At Abraham Joshua Heschel's Sabbath table, we tasted the liberating promise of Sabbath restrictions. We followed Victor and Edith Turner into the African bush, to discern how structured ritual undergirds community. We saw how submission to divine authority safeguards human dignity, at the level of the individual (Howard Thurman) and the political community (Saint Augustine).

The Confucian tradition urged us to serve our parents to become more humane. The Newman–Gladstone debate showed how "thinking for yourself," in the modern, liberal sense, undermines the true conscience. Alexander Solzhenitsyn related his hard-won lessons on how liberty without ends or limits traps us in its own kind of gulag. Andrea Dworkin's audacious life and thought exposed how our ideology of sexual freedom masks a deeper unfreedom. Hans Jonas warned of the dangers of disdaining the limits imposed by embodied existence.

The last leg of this journey will return us to our starting point. Recall that we began with the story of Saint Maximilian Kolbe and the perfect freedom he found in voluntarily laying down his life for a stranger in a Nazi death camp. My ultimate aim in this book was to make sensible the path of a Kolbe and thus to encourage a rethink of our own, modern path. The life of the mind amounts to vanity, or something worse, if it doesn't actually improve how we live. And not just how we live, but also how we die.

In a book about the wisdom of submitting to limits, there remains one final limit we have yet to explore: namely, death, which is every earthly life's ultimate barrier. It shouldn't be surprising that the same modern outlook that would demolish various barriers erected by nature and tradition during a lifetime would also seek to defeat death—or to defer, for as long as possible, our reckoning with it.

I don't mean this as a merely theoretical exercise. I mean it literally. As you read these words, there are scientific projects underway the aim of which is to biotechnologically extend the average human life span, to defer death by means of our own ingenuity. Nearly two decades ago, geneticists had already identified the single gene that could be used to extend the life of earthworms and flies, a gene we mammals share with those lower species.[1]

"Scientists eagerly seek ways to extend the maximum and average human life expectancy," noted one bioethicist in 2005, in an article praising these developments. "French scientists have produced mice through genetic engineering that can live 26 percent longer than normal," while "others have shown that mice, rats, and primates live significantly longer while on a low-calorie diet. Still others believe that by genetically engineering the telomeres of our chromosomes, reducing the level of free radicals, or replacing human growth hormone, the changes associated with aging can be slowed down or reversed."[2]

More recently, a clinical study conducted by researchers at UCLA opened the possibility of reversing the human body's internal genetic clock. The scientists found that "a cocktail of three common drugs—

growth hormone and two diabetes medications"—slashed an average
of two and a half years from participants' biological age and rejuve-
nated their immune systems, though the sample size was admittedly
small.[3]

The immediate aim of such projects is to defer natural decrepitude and death; the ultimate, if unstated, goal is human immortality.

Much of the criticism directed against these efforts, and the de-
fenses raised up by proponents, center on the social and economic
consequences: Can our retirement systems withstand an enormous
elderly bulge? How will it affect labor markets? And so on. Other bio-
ethicists grapple over whether such measures represent a natural ex-
tension of medicine's therapeutic aims, going back to the advent of
the profession, or something else, more like enhancement.[4]

Much less commonly asked is our final question: *What, if anything,
is good about death?*

DEATH AS A WAY OF LIFE

Let us venture once more to ancient Rome—this time, to Rome in
the mid-first century, during the bloody and debauched reign of the
emperor Nero, when the life of even high-ranking Romans was dirt
cheap, and dying gruesomely was, well, a way of life.

Death descended upon Nero's Rome on a massive scale in the year
64, in the form of a great fire. It flared up in the Circus Maximus, the
chariot-racing stadium near the Palatine and Caelian hills, and soon
dashed through the whole city, abetted by a gusty wind. The historian
Tacitus, writing in the second century, described the fatal pandemonium that ensued: "the wailings of terror-stricken women, the feeble-
ness of age, the helpless inexperience of childhood, the crowds who
sought to save themselves or others, dragging out the infirm or waiting for them, and by their hurry in the one case, by their delay in the
other, aggravating the confusion."[5]

Amid the pandemonium, they couldn't even stop to gather their
wits or glimpse the unfolding horror:

Often, while they looked behind, they were intercepted by flames on their side or in their face. Or if they reached a refuge close at hand, when this too was seized by the fire, they found that even places which they had imagined to be remote were involved in the same calamity. At last, doubting what they should avoid or whither betake themselves, they crowded the streets or flung themselves down in the fields, while some who had lost their all, even their very daily bread, and others out of love for their kinfolk, whom they had been unable to rescue, perished, though escape was open to them.[6]

Where was the emperor while the flames consumed the Roman people? Not quite fiddling, as the figure of speech has it. But close. Nero was at his coastal birthplace of Antium, half a day's walk from the Eternal City, when the fire broke out. Upon returning, he took some immediate measures to alleviate the suffering: opening public buildings and some of his own estates to the refugees, importing supplies from other regions, and selling food to the people at a steep discount. But this belated magnanimity did little to assuage public anger, Tacitus noted, since word had spread that "at the very time when the city was in flames, the emperor appeared on a private stage and sang of the destruction of Troy, comparing present misfortunes with the calamities of antiquity."[7]

A modern political consultant would say that Nero had a problem of colossally bad optics. And it was about to get worse. Some believed the fire was the work of arsonists acting at the emperor's behest, perhaps so he could finally redesign the urban landscape to suit his whimsy. Tacitus, and modern historians after him, haven't been able to decisively prove or disprove the theory, but in the event, public rage was at a fever pitch.

"To get rid of the report" of imperial arson, Tacitus wrote, "Nero fastened the guilt and inflicted the most exquisite tortures on a class hated for their abominations, called Christians by the populace."[8] The emperor pulled the charge from thin air; Christians were an unpopular group, and that was enough to render them suspect. Having "confessed" to the crime under duress, the scapegoats were executed by appalling methods: some forced to wear animal skins and mauled to death by hounds; others burned to death; still others crucified in the manner of their lord and savior.[9] Then Nero had the corpses lit up to brighten his garden at nighttime. So grotesque was the sight that it even kindled sympathy for the Christian martyrs among the pagan public, which concluded that the tortures and executions had taken place not "for the public good, but to glut one man's cruelty."[10]

The P.R. problem having been dealt with, the emperor set about rebuilding the city. A new "fire brigade and an improved water supply" were among the reconstruction projects, per the British historian Francis Caldwell Holland. But mainly Nero focused on a lavish new residence for himself, a "Golden House" taking up a vast amount of space—and vast sums of money, just when the recent conflagration had decimated the public treasury. To fund his palatial extravagance, Nero exacted heavy and unjust taxes, both on Romans and on the provinces.[11]

The Great Fire and its aftermath offered only a snapshot of Nero's wanton cruelty and profligacy. There was so much more where that came from. This man, having already won infamy as a matricide and a fratricide, was now quite literally killing Rome, killing Italy, killing the empire. He had to go, by daggers thrust into him by good Romans—and not a minute too soon.

Or so concluded a group of eminent statesmen the following year. The conspirators resolved to assassinate Nero and replace him with the senator Gaius Calpurnius Piso: literate, dashingly handsome, courteous to rich and poor alike, exceedingly popular. Alas, their prudence, fortitude, and cunning didn't quite match their sense of duty, and Nero and his allies unraveled the inept plot before it could be carried out. Piso committed suicide by slicing his veins, and many of his co-conspirators confessed at the mere sight of torture devices. Others saved themselves by denouncing their comrades.

Most tragic of all, for Romans who cared about good government and the philosophical life, the exposure of the conspiracy gave Nero the excuse he had been looking for to destroy his erstwhile tutor and chief adviser. This man was a friend of Piso's and the uncle of the poet Lucan, also involved in the conspiracy. He may have been aware of the operation and surely would have cheered if it were successful, but the historians' consensus is that he almost certainly wasn't actively involved. Nevertheless, Nero sentenced him to death.

This man had spent his whole life thinking and writing about death—and preparing to meet his own end. He taught his friends and the whole Roman world to live each day as if it could be the last, and in this way, to make peace with mortality. Now fate had brought him what it rarely grants philosophers: a chance to practice what they preach.

He was known as Seneca the Younger, or more simply, Seneca.

THE STOIC

Lucius Annaeus Seneca was born circa 4 B.C. in Cordoba, Spain, the middle son of the rhetor, or teacher of public speaking, Marcus Annaeus Seneca. Seneca the Elder was a conservative pagan, devoted to the Roman past, "orderly, austere, and methodical." His wife, Seneca's mother, was a vivacious and intelligent woman, and it later pained her son that his father had barred her from higher learning.[12]

The family was by all accounts tight-knit and happy. When Seneca was a boy, his father moved his wife and three sons to Rome, to ply his rhetor's trade, training would-be lawyers and politicians. By then, Seneca the Elder lamented, the Roman art of rhetoric had lost none of its prestige and material benefits but most of its nobility. Under the old republic, rhetoric was a truth procedure, embellished only with eloquence. Now all that was left was the embellishment, underwritten by bad actors who hired public speakers to destroy their enemies on the basis of flimsy accusations.

But Seneca the Elder eschewed these base methods and the baser ends to which they were applied. When his two elder sons set their sights on political and administrative careers, he approved heartily but not without fatherly admonitions. In a rhetoric-instruction book addressed to his sons, he warned them that such careers have their "dangers," that they should pursue them "within the strictest limits of honor."[13]

Seneca's older brother came to be known as Gallio (after Seneca the Elder's friend Junius Gallio, who adopted him) and rose to the Roman consulship in Achaea, on the Peloponnesian peninsula. The New Testament would immortalize Gallio as the Roman official who declined to prosecute Saint Paul in the Book of Acts (18:15).

Seneca the Younger devoted himself to philosophy in his teenage years, and it remained his principal pursuit, notwithstanding his worldly ambitions and achievements. Beginning in his thirties, he seized politics by the horns and became fabulously wealthy in the bargain. Had he done so because he recognized his own talents and yearned to make a mark on the city at the center of the world? Or because he figured the commanding heights would offer a thinker the best vantage point for observing human nature? Yes.

As a philosopher, Seneca cut his teeth in the Stoic school, founded some three centuries earlier by Zeno, a Phoenician who enthusiastically took up the Greek promise of cosmopolitan rationality. In the classics scholar James Romm's summary, "The Stoics taught their followers to seek an inner kingdom, the kingdom of the mind, where adherence to virtue and contemplation of nature could bring happiness even to an abused slave, an impoverished exile, or a prisoner on the rack."[14] Mastering the passions—*all of them*—was the Stoic's lifelong calling.

In the popular imagination, the Stoics stand for the renunciation of earthly goods (wealth, honors, bodily pleasure). But that isn't quite right. Rather, they saw these other goods as "desirable only in that they allowed one to keep one's thoughts and ethical choices in harmony with *Logos,* the divine Reason that, in the Stoic view, ruled the cosmos and gave rise to all true happiness."[15] This is why Seneca didn't consider it a violation of his Stoic principles to advance in politics, winning a senatorial seat under Caligula and rising to imperial adviser to Nero.

Still, Seneca did practice some of the austerities of the Stoic: He kept clear of decadent foods such as oysters ("they are not food, but condiments"), didn't use ointments and fragrances ("the best odor of the body is the absence of odor"), didn't go to the hot baths or drink wine. As he related to a friend in one of his *Moral Epistles,* among the chief extant works by which we know his philosophy, these habits were the "fragments of that high enterprise" that he held on to, even after he outgrew his early asceticism.[16] Other indulgences he kept to strict moderation, a feat he considered "perhaps even more difficult in practice than total abstention, for certainly it is often easier to abandon a habit altogether than to keep it within modest bounds."[17]

Seneca's "health throughout his life was delicate."[18] He wasn't a weak man—that much is apparent from a bust of him handed down to us from antiquity, showing a voluptuous, untroubled face capped by a great big dome. But he suffered from a pulmonary illness he called *suspirium,* literally "sigh" or "deep breath," which seems to have sent him into fits of breathlessness so severe, he felt like he was on the verge of death. "This is not illness," he wrote to a friend, "that's something else entirely." His *suspirium* felt more like "the loss of life and soul."[19] Recounting the thoughts that went through his mind during one of his fits, Seneca wrote: " 'What's this?' I say to myself. 'Does death make trial of me so frequently? Let it: I've done likewise to death, for a long time.' "[20]

This constant proximity to death had a paradoxically invigorating effect on his philosophy. To constantly feel as if his very life were departing him, that his airways were choked and his body would soon run out of air, was a kind of simulation or training for the real thing. It compelled him to get to know death well, almost as he would an old friend or companion, and this lent his writings on the subject a calm sobriety and objectivity very nearly unrivaled in all literature, ancient and modern.

"No Journey Is without an Endpoint"

To study Seneca's meditations on death is to delve into the real-world events that often inspired them and thus to stand at the intersection of philosophy and history. Four lessons on death especially stand out.

The first: Those who prepare for death can overcome the indignity of being forcibly expelled from the land of the living. Whereas those who cling to life in a base, desperate manner compound their indignity—and end up getting expelled anyway.

Early in his career, while serving as a senator under Caligula, Seneca witnessed a searing illustration of this principle. The senator Julius Canus was widely respected for his personal dignity and strength of character. One day, in a public debate with Caligula, he utterly bested him. When the senator turned to take his leave, the emperor held him back. "Just so you don't take comfort from an absurd hope," Caligula said, "I've ordered you to be led away for execution." To which Julius Canus calmly replied: "Thank you, best of rulers."[21] The other senators couldn't have missed the sarcastic undertone. All were perfectly aware of Caligula's "freakish cruelty," as Caldwell Holland has put it.[22] The emperor emphatically wasn't the best of rulers.

But to Seneca, there was more to Julius Canus's sarcasm than a desire to have the last word. It suggested also that the condemned was "embracing the sentence joyfully, like a grant of freedom." When the time comes to die, Seneca observed, it is going to happen anyway—so what is to be gained from struggling? Rather, this way of thinking "is a virtue: I'm being thrown out, but let me take my leave nonetheless. The wise man is never thrown out, for to be thrown out is to be expelled from a place that you leave unwillingly."[23]

Sure enough, ten days later, when a centurion showed up to take Julius Canus to be executed, the latter calmly stopped playing checkers, counted the pieces, saw that he was ahead by one point, and told his competitor, "See that you don't cheat and say you won after my death."[24] Just before the sentence was carried out, he promised his friends to study his own soul's flight from the body and to return and tell them about it if he learned anything interesting. Then he died.[25]

By embracing the inevitable, Julius Canus denied Caligula's tyrannical dominion over his mortality. By contrast, those who desperately cling to life often do so at the exorbitant cost of their dignity, a debased attitude captured by the poet and culture minister Maecenas (c. 70–8 B.C.): "Just preserve my life, even if / I sit on a sharpened stake."[26] Sitting on a "sharpened stake" refers to a method of torture used in Seneca's time, in which the victim was impaled through the genitals.[27]

To be clear, there are times when holding out against indignity and pain is a mark of fortitude. But to tolerate *any* indignity or sin merely to hold on to life was to Seneca's mind beyond pathetic:

> Go ahead, then—deny that it's a great gift of Nature that we must die. But many are ready to swap worse things for it: to betray a friend in order to live longer, or to hand over their children, with their own hands, for lechery, just to see the next dawn—a dawn that's privy to their many sins.[28]

THE SECOND LESSON: Seneca taught that fear of death is not only pointless, it prevents us from keeping the right perspective on our lives.

Seneca certainly didn't recommend the mindset of the foolhardy jackass, or an unreasonable confidence in one's ability to defy mortality at every turn. Quite the opposite, in fact: We shouldn't fear death, he contended, precisely because death stalks us at every turn. Hurricane, plague, violent crime, political and economic collapse, hunger, sudden poverty—"we are wrong to think any part of the world is excused or immune from these perils; all regions are under the same law."[29] To live fearlessly, then, we need to make peace with the fact that death is ever-present. When all things are held to be potentially fatal, no one source of terror can swell to such magnitude as to paralyze us.

Again, Seneca's political experience had reinforced this lesson. In addition to his chronic lung ailment, he also had a few close brushes with murderous strongmen, the kind his father had warned about when he and Gallio first set out on their political careers. One episode involved the emperor Caligula, who, as we saw earlier, couldn't tolerate being embarrassed in public debate or speechifying—and was prepared to murder those who did so.

One day, Seneca delivered a rousing speech before his fellow senators and Caligula. The emperor, who was a very good orator but considered himself a master, had a fit of insane jealousy. Caligula had always hated Seneca's Latin style. He famously derided it as "sand without lime": that is, full of striking declamations but lacking flow and transitions.[30] Now he was tempted to silence that voice and that style—forever. And Seneca "would have paid the extreme penalty had not one of the imperial mistresses persuaded her lover that Seneca was in a rapid consumption and must shortly die in any case."[31] Seneca's pulmonary disease proved his savior from immediate execution.

The paradoxical nature of his salvation (thanks to an illness!) imparted a clear teaching: If one potential cause of death had rescued Seneca from the jaws of the other, what point was there in fearing any single mortal threat?

A second close encounter with the executioner came at the hands of Caligula's successor, Claudius. The new emperor—"fearful to excess, apathetic to such a degree that no insult could rouse in him resentment nor suffering move him to pity, greedy and sensuous"—recalled from exile a pair of nieces who had been banished by his late nephew. The move, and particularly the return of the "beautiful and ambitious" imperial niece Julia, sent Claudius's wife, Messalina, into a jealous rage.[32] She persuaded her husband to exile Julia again and, soon after, to have her executed.

Seneca had made the mistake of siding with the newly returned Julia against Messalina and thus "shared her disgrace" when she lost.[33] The emperor—or really, Messalina and her allies—accused Seneca of having carried on an illicit affair with the married Julia. He was condemned to death, a sentence Claudius commuted to exile on the island of Corsica. In an instant, Seneca lost his seat in the Senate, the already enviable estates he had gathered to his name, and all his popularity as a rising political star.

Little is known about Seneca's daily life in exile, but we can safely speculate that it was one of relative deprivation compared to his charmed, wheeling-and-dealing life in Rome. Yet he apparently spent this time in unflappable contemplation. We know that, because it was during this period that he wrote his famous *Consolation* to his mother, reporting to her that he was happy and urging her not to mourn his situation. He could suffer from misfortune, he told her, only if he fell for the deception that fortune was ever truly his, his forever, to begin with. But if he considered fortune and misfortune alike ephemeral, their human titles provisional and delimited strictly by death, then he could muster the strength neither to revel in any good fortune nor to wallow in any misfortune.[34]

Claudius, meanwhile, for all his fearfulness, succumbed to an unseen threat. With Messalina having been executed in the course of palace intrigue, circa A.D. 48, he married Caligula's sister Agrippina. The new empress was a woman of stunning looks and almost incomprehensible ruthlessness, who in due course attempted to assassinate her imperial husband with his favorite delicacy, mushrooms. As Tacitus narrated this episode, when the poison seemed to have failed, she "availed herself of the complicity of Xenophon, the physician," who "under pretence of helping the emperor's efforts to vomit . . . introduced into his throat a feather smeared with some rapid poison."[35]

Once the deed was done, Agrippina spared no time in locking up Claudius's natural children until the principate was secured for her own son from a previous marriage, Nero.

THE THIRD LESSON: Not everyone dies the same way, but death itself is a form of equality. It establishes a democracy of sorts among people of all generations, all who have ever lived, live now, and will live in the future. "You were born under this law" of death, Seneca wrote in an epistle. "It happened to your father, your mother, your ancestors, everyone before you, everyone after you. An unbreakable sequence, which no effort can alter, binds and tows all things. How great a throng of those yet to die will follow your footsteps! How great a crowd will accompany you!"[36]

To try desperately to defer death bespeaks a kind of arrogance, an undemocratic spirit, a refusal to join the great human throngs. Why would any one person be justified in stepping out of the great procession and walking in the opposite direction? This recognition prompts us to link arms with those who march next to us. And this Seneca did in his own life and political career, particularly during the rule of Nero.

Before she offed her husband, Agrippina had convinced Claudius to recall Seneca from Corsica after eight years of exile. She did this, partly so "she might not be conspicuous only by her evil deeds" and partly so she and the young Nero might benefit from the celebrated philosopher's "counsels in their designs on the throne," according to Tacitus.[37]

When a seventeen-year-old Nero was crowned emperor in the year 54, Seneca composed his maiden Senate speech and emerged as one of his two advisers, alongside Burrus, the praetorian prefect. Nero was utterly lazy and dissolute, and, at least initially, he didn't care a whit about the administration of his empire. That was good news, because it left day-to-day governance in the hands of Seneca and Burrus, whose "single object" was "the public good."[38]

The pair pursued an ambitious program of reforms. Among other steps, they restored some of the Senate's ancient legislative functions; repealed or reduced heavy taxes; cut down on the use of confidential informants; regulated lawyers' fees; stiffened penalties against forgery; and introduced a right to appeal judicial decisions to the Senate.[39] Combined with Nero's blessed indifference, these efforts yielded five years of general happiness and prosperity, a period many historians later counted as among the best-governed in Rome's entire imperial history.[40]

Unfortunately, Nero eventually took a more active role in "government." (I use scare quotes because the young emperor's notion of rule included leading a group of friends, all of them dressed as commoners, on raiding parties to rob the homes of ordinary citizens; an escort of praetorians would be kept at a distance in case the victims decided to fight back.) Soon, the boy-emperor became the Nero of historical infamy, whose name to this day is a byword for misrule.

In time, Seneca and Burrus were sidelined in favor of thuggish advisers whose counsels more closely aligned with the emperor's degenerate character. Yet Nero wouldn't permit Seneca to retire to the life of philosophy and friendship he pined for. From Tacitus and modern historians, the impression we gather of Seneca in these dark final years is of a man who did everything within his power to restrain the worst of Nero's instincts. When he finally could do no more, he locked himself up in his room, eating only fruits and other simple foods safe from the poisoner's art.

Having met with calm resolve two close calls with the executioner and a long stint in exile, not to mention his daily bouts of breathlessness, Seneca could act vigorously in defense of the common good and of his fellow marchers in the grand procession of mortality. Knowledge of death had compelled him to serve the Roman people—and left him unafraid to stand up to the powerful, emperors included.

THE FOURTH AND final lesson is this: Death gives sense to life. It is a destination without which life's path meanders to the point of intolerableness. An excess of life, Seneca thought, is a kind of curse, giving rise to the confusion we associate with tales that have no clear beginning, middle, and end. "No journey is without an endpoint," he argued. And "just as with storytelling, so with life: it's important how well it is done, not how long."[41]

This lesson, the simplest, is the one that I find most compelling. It is also the one most out of tune with the spirit of our age, with its quest for medications that might reverse our biological clock, not to mention the profusion of physical exercises, barely edible concoctions, plastic surgery, skin creams, and other supposed aids to living longer or masking the physical symptoms of aging.

Seneca couldn't have anticipated such modern developments. And yet nearly two millennia ago, he debunked their underlying philosophical assumptions with the common wisdom and plain voice of classical thought. Those who long for natural immortality, he argued, should beware of what they wish for. Because at some point, earthly life just gets tiresome—and boring:

> There is nothing you would find new, nothing with which you're not sated to the point of disgust. You know the taste of wine and of mead. It doesn't matter whether a hundred amphoras' worth passes through your bladder or a thousand; you're just wineskin. You know very well the taste of the oyster and the mullet; your self-indulgence has set nothing aside, untried, for coming years. Yet *these* are the things you are torn away from only against your will.[42]

The longer and more tenaciously we try to hang on to the lifeline once it has reached its endpoint, the more trouble we make for ourselves and others. People who try to hold on by any means, Seneca suggested, are like those who, "swept away by a gush of water, clutch even at thorny plants and other rough things." Instead of doing that, "make your life joyful by putting aside all your anxiety about keeping it."[43]

Which brings us to the costs of our latter-day efforts to extend the human life span by ever-longer increments. Doing so would strain our pension systems, grossly distort labor markets, delay intergenerational transfers of wealth, hinder redistributive justice, and on and on. Those are some of the "thorny plants" and "rough things" with which the contemporary seekers after immortality must wrestle. But such downsides don't quite get at the more fundamental problem that Seneca put his finger on.

No, there are much thornier plants than mere pension troubles.

"Whoever doesn't want to die, doesn't want to live," declared Seneca.[44] Though at first glance it might appear nonsensical, this is a deep teaching: How could the desire to "cure" or overcome death be antithetical to life? If life is good, and it most certainly is, then isn't it logical for the living to wish to live even longer? Why would Seneca equate the wish not to die with the wish not to live?

Here is why: The state of being alive—fully alive—is possible only in relation to an endpoint, death. It is the certainty of an end to life that allows us to appreciate sacrifice, heroism, love, beauty, the kind of virtuous life a man like Seneca lived or the self-sacrificing death of a Maximilian Kolbe. As any decent novelist or screenwriter knows, if there is nothing at stake in the story, the story is boring. If there is no final terminus to life, life loses its vitality, its zest, its drama.

Now, we know that the premodern traditions disagreed about the origins of death. For a pagan Stoic like Seneca, death was just part of the natural design of the harmonious, reason-governed cosmos. Whereas for the Christian, death was the result of our first ancestors' transgression in the Garden, a rupture inscribed into nature by human sinfulness, which God has taken upon himself to repair. Both, however, promised a decisive reunion of the human soul with the whole of which it is a part: for the pagan, a dissolving into the *Logos;* for the Christian, a face-to-face meeting with God, a chance to contemplate the Lord's infinite truth, goodness, and beauty for an eternity—heaven.

Wait, isn't that something like life without end? Shouldn't we welcome the technological breaking or deferring of the barrier of mortality? Couldn't science be realizing the vision foretold by the philosophers and prophets of antiquity?

But perpetual biological life doesn't, in fact, fulfill the longing for eternity answered by the classical and Judeo-Christian promise of a reunion with the whole. Living very, very long or forever in the here and now entails no *rest,* no final fulfillment or completion. It offers neither the abstract communion with the *Logos* envisioned by a Seneca, nor the more personal settling of accounts between God and the just and unjust that Judaism and Christianity (and Islam) say awaits us all.

Biological life extended by gene therapies and drug infusions isn't *eternal* life. Rather, as the Jewish American bioethicist Leon Kass has argued, it is an "endless present" fulfilling the "childish desire to eat one's life and keep it."[45] And an endless present means the perpetuation of all our present cares—forever: the grubby striving, the political combat, interpersonal conflict, and even pleasure made all the more tiresome by long familiarity, with nothing really new to look forward to. True, this cheap, plastic substitute for eternal life would wipe away, or long defer, the grief associated with death—but it would by the same token rob us of all the joys that find their meaning in relation to death, not least the hope in life eternal.

SO DID SENECA embrace his own death with the courage he demanded from his friends and family members? Did he manage to practice what he had spent a lifetime preaching? Yes, more or less—though his demise wasn't nearly as easy or elegant as his readers might have expected.

Nero, recall, had resolved in the year 65 to use the pretext of Piso's conspiracy to off his old mentor. The emperor dispatched a centurion to Seneca's house to offer him the usual choice: suicide or execution. There was no doubt which option Seneca would choose. It was his turn to get booted from the realm of the living, but he preferred to take his own leave.

Tacitus noted: "Seneca, quite unmoved, asked for tablets on which to inscribe his will." The centurion refused, at which point Seneca informed his friends that his true bequest to them would be "the noblest possession yet remaining to him, the pattern of his life, which, if they remembered, they would win a name for moral worth and steadfast friendship."[46]

His wife, Paulina, told him that she wished to die with him. He agreed, and they both opened the veins in their arms. But Seneca's blood didn't exactly flow, owing to his "aged frame, attenuated by frugal diet."[47] So he slashed at the veins in his knees and ankles, as well. This is the part of Seneca's story that arouses the tenderest sympathy, even as the gruesomeness makes us wince: an old man shredding through his own skin and sinew with a blade, torturing nerve-packed parts of his own body, as his wife does the same to hers.

Then, "worn out by cruel anguish, afraid too that his sufferings might break his wife's spirit . . . [Seneca] persuaded her to retire into another chamber." We don't know if his wife had similar trouble, but in the event, Nero, "not wishing to heighten the odium of his cruelty," ordered his men to put a stop to Paulina's suicide. Seneca, meanwhile, just wouldn't die. He asked for and drank poison—to no effect. "At last he entered a pool of heated water, from which he sprinkled the nearest of his slaves, adding the exclamation, 'I offer this liquid as a libation to Jupiter the Deliverer.' "[48] The hot steam of the bath, combined with the tedious loss of blood, finally put an end to the Stoic's misery. The great procession of the dead counted in its rank a new and illustrious member.

Nearly two millennia later, the inextinguishable nobility of Seneca's life and thought beckons us. Yet it appears so terribly distant amid the moral squalor and confusion of an age in which each of us risks becoming a paranoid Claudius or a gadget-wielding little Nero. It is far from clear that we might reach back and grasp something of that nobility.

A LETTER TO MAXIMILIAN

———

My dear son:

I want you in every way to be a better man than I am. When I began writing this book for you, I feared that you might inherit a life of purposeless decadence, partly born of the abundance of our society. Now, as I finish the manuscript, a viral tide you can't begin to comprehend has engulfed all of us, and it is likely to reshape the whole course of your life, inflicting pressures and sufferings on you and your sister that can't but break my fatherly heart.

I fear the absence of other kids' company and the rough-and-tumble of play in these years might misshape your early development. If social distancing becomes permanent, you will be cocooned even more tightly in the world of screens and in virtual realities. The economic devastation will take years, if not decades, to repair. Your mother and I are hanging on, but many families aren't, and I worry that you will face inequalities that make today's yawning social gaps look minuscule by comparison.

And yet I don't think that our "new normal" is all that *qualitatively* different from what came before it. Rather, the pandemic and our response have only put into hyperdrive trends that were underway long before the virus arrived in America: rule by a vast expert class; widespread economic precarity; people living restless, Sabbath-less lives; moral and cultural decay; ideological dividers partitioning off the wealthy and career-mobile from the underclass—all these were part of our social condition before you were born, before anyone had heard of COVID-19.

So, here we are. I don't quite know how to prepare you for the exact realities that will define your adulthood; most are unforeseeable. You are very young. And yet, perhaps because death is so thick in the air these days, I feel called to put to paper the best advice I can muster.

I should want you to at least avoid some of your father's (and grandfather's) mistakes.

To read old books before new ones.

To make all your big decisions by the light of sound authorities, above all that of the Holy Church.

To become not a glib man, the kind who laughs nervously when moral outrage is in order, or who preens morally rather than seek the moral way.

To at least *notice* and feel a little bad when you find yourself acting like a hypocrite.

To recognize that the moral precepts you expound demand to be acted upon—by you, in your immediate, everyday surroundings, rarely in some lofty domain of the mind.

To relate to the Blessed Virgin Mary as an uneducated peasant might. Can you do that for me? Hold her hand. She is our Mother. She will tell you everything that truly matters to a happy life. "Do as he says" (Jn 2:5).

Saint Maximilian will be there for you, too.

New York
Solemnity of the Ascension of the Lord
Sunday, May 24, 2020

ACKNOWLEDGMENTS

IN THE FALL of 2018, back in the Before Times, when we could still do such things, my agent, Keith Urbahn, and I sat down at a hotel bar somewhere in Midtown West to discuss my next book project. I told him I wanted to write a book of reportage about the rise of traditionalism among the intelligent young: twenty-something urban high-achievers who fell in love with the Traditional Latin Mass, Ivy-educated Jews who forsook conventional secular careers to become Orthodox rabbis, the Brooklyn subculture of Christian socialism, and the like.

Keith wasn't impressed. He is, in fact, rarely impressed.

"That's a long magazine article, not a book," he flatly said. "Why don't you just write a book-length case for traditionalism and explain why it would help readers live better lives? Isn't that what you really want to do?" It didn't take much more than that to persuade me. Yes, *that* was the book I really wished to write—*the book I was called to write*. Keith mentioned an editor at Penguin Random House, Derek Reed, who might just go for such a project.

A few months later, Keith, Derek, and I were on the phone. I mentioned something about how the great traditions offer answers to questions that liberal modernity doesn't even begin to ask. Derek seized on the idea: This should be a book of questions—questions, moreover, that I would explore through the lives of great thinkers. And so *The Unbroken Thread* was born.

The basic concept of this book was thus the product of a three-way mind-meld. I'm indebted to Keith for deflating my hopeless enthusiasms and discerning what was really churning my mind. And to

Derek for embracing, and carefully molding, what was an admittedly unusual book proposal. He proved a tremendous editor, from concept to comma. It has been the honor of a lifetime to work with him and his team to bring this project to life.

There are three people without whom I'd never have been able to cross the finish line. My wife, Ting, read each chapter several times (or, more often, had me read them to her while she looked after our kids), offering invaluable advice that tethered the big ideas to the ground of ordinary life. Then, as my deadline approached, and the COVID-19 pandemic turned our lives upside down, she and my indefatigable mother-in-law, Feng-Qiao, took on all of the burdens of running a household while I typed away.

Then there was our neighbor Frank Rankin, who graciously lent me his apartment across the hall as a writing space at the height of the lockdown, when the restrictions and our family circumstances meant there was quite literally nowhere else for me to do my work. In this book, I talk a lot about embracing great commitments and sacrifices. In Ting, Feng-Qiao, and Frank, I witnessed what all that means in practice.

Rusty Reno was good company during the loneliest, most grueling phase of writing. Every other afternoon or early evening, he'd invite me to go on walks with him around our neighborhood. We'd sip bourbon from plastic cups and talk politics, philosophy, and theology; he'd always leave me with a little spark of inspiration or encouragement that kept me going till the next walk. Rusty's gift for friendship is one of my life's big blessings.

Peter Kohanloo, my best and most loyal friend, was always there on the phone, to shoot the breeze, to cheer me up, to let me vent. Thanks, brother. Alex and Malise Sundstrom granted us a much-needed Floridian respite after the last of the copyedits were finished.

On to my experts and gurus, though, needless to say, all outstanding errors are mine alone:

Professor Scott Moringiello of DePaul University somehow made it through the first draft of the introduction and first chapter (which needed a lot of work, and he was kind and honest enough to say so!). Geoff Hughes, a dear friend with an infectious enthusiasm for the life of the mind, did the same thing. Professor Chad Pecknold of the Catholic University of America reviewed crucial sections of chapter 2 to make sure I didn't bungle the Angelic Doctor's ideas. It's very rare indeed to strike true, deep friendships as an adult, but I count Chad, whom I met only in 2017, among my closest friends.

Jonathan Silver of the Tikvah Fund, Rabbi Motti Seligson, and Rabbi Meir Soloveichik—all three great personal friends—read and offered feedback on chapter 3. The scholarship of Pater Edmund Waldstein deeply influenced chapter 6, and at a moment of perilous doubt, he reassured me that I was on the right track. For the same chapter, Professor Pavlos Papadopoulos of Wyoming Catholic College was likewise generous with his time and insights.

Professor Annping Chin of Yale University spent an hour on the phone shepherding me through the mountains of ancient material to locate the best sources on Confucian filiality. Bria Sandford was the guiding spirit behind my chapter on Andrea Dworkin, and she pointed me to John Cavadini's scholarship, which ended up serving as my conceptual fulcrum. At a Napa Institute event in 2019 in New York, I struck up a conversation with one of the attendees, who took an interest in my then-nascent book idea. It was he who suggested I use Hans Jonas for my chapter on the body. The advice proved enormously useful, yet sadly, I've forgotten that gentleman's name and lost his business card: Thank you, sir.

Many thanks to the patient and dedicated research librarians of the New York Public Library; Professor Gladden Pappin of the University of Dallas for assistance in nailing down a Martin Luther citation (and, more generally, for his friendship and his wit); Ryan Hendrickson at the Howard Gotlieb Archival Research Center at Boston University for helping me track down recordings of Howard Thurman's lectures on Augustine; Tobias Hoonhout, who served as my early research assistant on chapter 8, and to his teacher (and my friend) Professor Vincent Phillip Muñoz of Notre Dame's Tocqueville

Program, for placing Toby with me; and the learned Urban Hannon for triple-checking a key bit of New Testament Greek in chapter 11.

I would be remiss not to thank my *New York Post* colleagues: our editor in chief, Stephen Lynch; our editorial-page editor, Mark Cunningham; and my co-workers and comrades Adam Brodsky, Michael Benjamin, Elisha Maldonado, Kelly Jane Torrance, Brooke Rogers, Karl Salzmann, and Ashley Allen. Let's do it again tomorrow!

Finally, to fulfill a vow I made long ago to acknowledge in every book I write the three men to whom I owe my career in journalism: Thank you to Jamie Kirchick, John Podhoretz, and Bret Stephens.

NOTES

INTRODUCTION

1. Mary Craig, "Blessed Maximilian Kolbe: Priest Hero of a Death Camp," EWTN.com: https://www.ewtn.com/catholicism/library/st-maximilian-kolbe-priest-hero-of-a-death-camp-5602.

2. "Saint Maximilian Mary Kolbe" (documentary), produced by the Servant Brothers of the Home of the Mother for HM Television, YouTube, August 11, 2014, at 30:26, https://www.youtube.com/watch?v=THT5QxhCiGE.

3. Jewish Virtual Library, "Maximilian Kolbe, 1894–1941," https://www.jewishvirtual library.org/maximilian-kolbe; see also Jewish Telegraphic Agency, "Scholars Reject Charge St. Maximilian Was Anti-Semitic," January 3, 1983, https://www.jta.org/1983/01/03/archive/scholars-reject-charge-st-maximilian-was-anti-semitic.

4. Ann Ball, *Modern Saints: Their Lives and Faces—Book One* (Charlotte, NC: TAN Books, 2011), 357, 356.

5. *Ibid.*, 357.

6. See *ibid.*, 358; see also Westminster Abbey, "St. Maximilian Kolbe," https://www.westminster-abbey.org/abbey-commemorations/commemorations/st-maximilian-kolbe.

7. Craig, "Blessed Maximilian Kolbe."

8. Christopher O. Blum, "Introduction," in *Critics of the Enlightenment: Readings in the French Counter-Revolutionary Tradition,* ed. and trans. Blum (Providence, RI: Cluny Media, 2020), p. xxix.

9. Quoted in *ibid.*, p. xii.

10. Joseph B. Soloveitchik, *The Lonely Man of Faith* (Jerusalem: Maggid Books, 2018), 2, 5.

11. *Ibid.*, 81–82.

12. Joseph Ratzinger, *Introduction to Christianity,* trans. J. R. Foster (San Francisco: Ignatius Press, 2004), 53.

13. C. F. J. Martin, *Thomas Aquinas: God and Explanations* (Edinburgh: Edinburgh University Press, 1997), 203, quoted in Edward Feser, *Aquinas: A Beginner's Guide* (London: Oneworld Publications, 2018), 2.

QUESTION ONE

1. Steven R. Weisman, ed., *Daniel Patrick Moynihan: A Portrait in Letters of an American Visionary* (New York: PublicAffairs, 2010), 2.

2. Ben Shapiro, @benshapiro on Twitter, February 5, 2016, https://twitter.com/ben shapiro/status/695638866993115136.

3. C. S. Lewis, *Out of the Silent Planet* (London: HarperCollins, 2013).

4. Alister McGrath, *C. S. Lewis—A Life: Eccentric Genius, Reluctant Prophet* (Carol Stream, Ill.: Tyndale House, 2013), 234.

5. *Ibid.*

6. Lewis, *Out of the Silent Planet*, 10, 15.

7. *Ibid.*, 24.

8. *Ibid.*, 17.

9. *Ibid.*, 24.

10. J. B. S. Haldane, "Eugenics and Social Reform," in *Possible Worlds and Other Essays* (London: Chatto and Windus, 1927), 190, http://jbshaldane.org/books/1927-Possible-Worlds/haldane-1927-possible-worlds.html#Page_190.

11. Bertrand Russell, *Marriage and Morals* (New York: Liveright, 1970), 259.

12. Quoted in Neil M. Gorsuch, *The Future of Assisted Suicide and Euthanasia* (Princeton, N.J.: Princeton University Press, 2006), 35.

13. Quoted in *ibid.*, 34.

14. See Julian Quinones and Arijeta Lajka, "'What Kind of Society Do You Want to Live In?': Inside the Country Where Down Syndrome Is Disappearing," CBS News, August 14, 2017, https://www.cbsnews.com/news/down-syndrome-iceland/.

15. C. S. Lewis, *Surprised by Joy: The Shape of My Early Life* (San Francisco: HarperOne, 2017), 2.

16. McGrath, *C. S. Lewis—A Life*, 8.

17. *Ibid.*, 9.

18. Lewis, *Surprised by Joy*, 20, 23.

19. *Ibid.*, 17; see *ibid.*, 18.

20. *Ibid.*, 23.

21. *Ibid.*, 25, 40, 79.

22. *Ibid.*, 78.

23. *Ibid.*, 194.

24. See McGrath, *C.S. Lewis—A Life*, 74–75.

25. Lewis, *Surprised by Joy*, 246.

26. "The Royal Commission on Oxford and Cambridge," *The Spectator*, April 1, 1922, 6.

27. Lewis, *Surprised by Joy*, 254.

28. *Ibid.*, 249, 250.

29. *Ibid.*, 251.

30. McGrath, *C. S. Lewis—A Life*, 102, quoting C. S. Lewis, *All My Road Before Me: The Diary of C. S. Lewis, 1922–1927*, ed. Walter Hooper (San Diego: Harcourt Brace Jovanovich, 1991), 53.

31. Lewis, *Surprised by Joy*, 254.

32. *Ibid.*, 255.

33. *Ibid.*

34. McGrath, *C.S. Lewis—A Life*, 135.

35. Lewis, *Out of the Silent Planet*, 40, 41.

36. *Ibid.*, 64.

37. *Ibid.*

38. *Ibid.*, 75.

39. *Ibid.*, 94.

40. *Ibid.*, 115.

41. *Ibid.*, 123.

42. *Ibid.*

43. C. S. Lewis, *The Abolition of Man: or, Reflections on Education with Special Reference to the Teaching of English in the Upper Forms of Schools* (New York: HarperOne, 2017), 36.
44. *Ibid.*
45. *Ibid.*, 72.

Question Two

1. "Louisiana Pastor Again Holds Church Services, Defying House Arrest Orders," CBS News, April 27, 2020, https://www.cbsnews.com/news/tony-spell-louisiana-pastor-house-arrest-church-services-coronavirus-lockdown/.
2. Rozina Sini and Armen Shahbazian, "Coronavirus: Iran Holy-Shrine-Lickers Face Prison," BBC News, March 3, 2020, https://www.bbc.com/news/blogs-trending-51706021.
3. Martin Luther, *Luther's Works*, vol. 40: Church and Ministry II, ed. Conrad Bergendoff (Philadelphia: Fortress Press, 1958), 175.
4. Plato, *Phaedo*, in *Euthyphro, Apology, Crito, Phaedo*, eds. and trans. Chris Emlyn-Jones and William Preddy (Cambridge, Mass.: Harvard University Press, 2017), 451.
5. *Ibid.*
6. *Ibid.*, 453.
7. *Ibid.*
8. For a deeply learned yet accessible account of the marriage of Jewish revelation and Greek philosophy, see Pope Benedict XVI, "Faith, Reason and the University: Memories and Reflections" (Lecture of the Holy Father at the University of Regensburg), September 12, 2006, http://w2.vatican.va/content/benedict-xvi/en/speeches/2006/september/documents/hf_ben-xvi_spe_20060912_university-regensburg.html.
9. See *ibid.*; see also Hans Jonas, *The Gnostic Religion: The Message of the Alien God and the Beginnings of Christianity*, 3rd ed. (Boston: Beacon Press, 2001), 15.
10. For these biblical notes, I am gratefully indebted to Pope Benedict XVI, "Faith, Reason and the University."
11. Quoted in Étienne Gilson, *Reason and Revelation in the Middle Ages* (New York: Scribner's, 1966), 8, 9–10.
12. Quoted in *ibid.*, 13, 14.
13. *Ibid.*, 15.
14. See *ibid.*, 32–33.
15. The place of birth is now the subject of a consensus among biographers and historians. See Jean-Pierre Torrell, *Saint Thomas Aquinas*, vol. 1: *The Person and His Work*, rev. ed., trans. Robert Royal (Washington, D.C.: Catholic University of America Press, 2005), 1–2; see also Edward Feser, *Aquinas: A Beginner's Guide* (London: Oneworld Publications, 2018), 3.
16. Torrell, *Saint Thomas Aquinas*, 1:5.
17. Quoted in *ibid.*, 1:278–80.
18. Quoted in *ibid.*, 1:26.
19. Gilson, *Reason and Revelation in the Middle Ages*, 40.
20. Ibn Rushd, *The Decisive Treatise*, in *Classical Arabic Philosophy: An Anthology of Sources*, eds. and trans. Jon McGinnis and David Reisman (Indianapolis: Hackett, 2007), 309.
21. Gilson, *Reason and Revelation in the Middle Ages*, 50.
22. Thomas Aquinas, *Summa theologiae* II-II.1.5, trans. Fathers of the English Dominican Province (2017), *New Advent*, http://www.newadvent.org/summa/3001.htm#article5.
23. *Ibid.*; cf. I Cor 13:12.
24. G. K. Chesterton, *St. Thomas Aquinas*, in *The Everyman Chesterton*, ed. Ian Ker (New York: Knopf, 2011), 513, 514.

25. Quoted in Torrell, *Saint Thomas Aquinas*, 1:244.

26. See *ibid.*, 1:243.

27. Quoted in *ibid.*, 1:292.

28. Aquinas, *Summa theologiae* I.2.3.

29. See Torrell, *Saint Thomas Aquinas*, 1:73.

30. See *ibid.*, 1:113.

31. See *ibid.*, 1:49.

32. Quoted in *ibid.*, 1:289.

33. See Gilson, *Reason and Revelation in the Middle Ages*, 85–87.

34. See Robert Stern, "Martin Luther," *The Stanford Encyclopedia of Philosophy* (Fall 2020), ed. Edward N. Zalta, https://plato.stanford.edu/archives/fall2020/entries/luther/; for a more sympathetic treatment, see Jeffrey K. Mann, "Luther on Reason: What Makes a Whore a Whore," *Seminary Ridge Review* 18, no. 1 (2015): 1–17.

35. Martin Luther, "To the Christian Nobility of the German Nation," in *Three Treatises*, 2nd rev. ed., trans. Charles M. Jacobs, rev. James Atkinson (Minneapolis: Fortress Press, 1970), 92–93.

QUESTION THREE

1. James MacPherson, "North Dakota Ends Ban on Sunday-Morning Shopping," AP News, August 3, 2019, https://apnews.com/ade09bb0818b4391a81dad4af16be686.

2. *Ibid.*

3. Dominick Bouck, "Bring Back the Blue Laws," *First Things*, April 2, 2019, https://www.firstthings.com/web-exclusives/2019/04/bring-back-the-blue-laws.

4. Abraham Joshua Heschel, *The Sabbath: Its Meaning for Modern Man* (New York: Farrar, Straus and Giroux, 2005), viii.

5. "Friday Night Kiddush Text," Chabad.org, https://www.chabad.org/library/article_cdo/aid/258903/jewish/Friday-Night-Kiddush.htm.

6. Susannah Heschel, introduction to *The Sabbath*, by Abraham Joshua Heschel, ix.

7. A. J. Heschel, *The Sabbath*, 14.

8. Susannah Heschel, in *ibid.*, xii.

9. A. J. Heschel, *The Sabbath*, 3.

10. *Ibid.*, 89.

11. Edward K. Kaplan, *Abraham Joshua Heschel: Mind, Heart, Soul* (Lincoln and Philadelphia: University of Nebraska Press for the Jewish Publication Society, 2019), 4.

12. *Ibid.*, 13.

13. *Ibid.*, 18, quoting Abraham Joshua Heschel, *A Passion for Truth* (New York: Farrar, Straus and Giroux, 1973), xv.

14. Heschel, *The Sabbath*, 16.

15. Kaplan, *Abraham Joshua Heschel*, 18.

16. See *ibid.*, 20.

17. *Ibid.*, 49, quoting Abraham Joshua Heschel, "Toward an Understanding of Halacha," *Yearbook of the Central Conference of American Rabbis* 63 (1953): 386–87.

18. *Ibid.*, 46, quoting the Abraham Liessin Papers, New York YIVO Institute for Jewish Research Archives.

19. *Ibid.*, 52, quoting Heschel, "Toward an Understanding of Halacha," 389–90.

20. *Ibid.* (emphasis in original).

21. Quoted in *ibid.* (emphasis in original; Kaplan notes that this phrase appears in Hebrew in the Heschel).

22. Quoted in *ibid.*, 53.

23. *Ibid.*, 57; quoted in *ibid.*, 58.

24. *Ibid.*, 62.

25. *Ibid.*, 63, quoting material from the Abraham Joshua Heschel Archives, Jewish Theological Seminary, New York.

26. Quoted in *ibid.*, 81.

27. Heschel, *The Sabbath*, 40.

28. Kaplan, *Abraham Joshua Heschel*, 50.

29. *Ibid.*

30. See *ibid.*, 91.

31. See *ibid.*, 98.

32. *Ibid.*, 101–2, quoting Abraham Joshua Heschel, "No Religion Is an Island," *Union Seminary Quarterly Review* 21 (January 1966): 117.

33. *Ibid.*, 189, quoting Abraham Joshua Heschel, "The Spirit of Jewish Prayer," *Proceedings of the Rabbinical Assembly of America* 17 (1953): 151–77.

34. Heschel, *The Sabbath*, 13.

35. See, e.g., Joseph Cardinal Ratzinger, *The Spirit of the Liturgy*, trans. John Saward, in *The Spirit of the Liturgy* commemorative ed. (San Francisco: Ignatius Press, 2018), 29–33.

36. *Ibid.*, 28.

37. *Ibid.*, 89.

38. Susannah Heschel, in *ibid.*, xvi.

QUESTION FOUR

1. See Uwe Michael Lang's summary of the anthropology of ritual in his *Signs of the Holy One: Liturgy, Ritual, and Expression of the Sacred* (San Francisco: Ignatius Press, 2015), 17–22.

2. Tara Isabella Burton, "'Spiritual but Not Religious': Inside America's Rapidly Growing Faith Group," *Vox*, November 10, 2017, https://www.vox.com/identities/2017/11/10/16630178/study-spiritual-but-not-religious.

3. *Ibid.*

4. See, e.g., Romano Guardini, *The Spirit of the Liturgy*, trans. Ada Lane, in *The Spirit of the Liturgy* commemorative ed. (San Francisco: Ignatius Press, 2018), 335; see also Lang, *Signs of the Holy One*, 23.

5. Lang, *Signs of the Holy One*, 22, quoting S. J. Tambiah, "A Performative Approach to Ritual," *Proceedings of the British Academy* 65 (1979): 119.

6. See *ibid.*, 19, citing Émile Durkheim, *The Elementary Forms of Religious Life*, trans. J. W. Swain (London: Allen & Unwin, 1915), 47.

7. Quoted in Timothy Larsen, *The Slain God: Anthropologists and the Christian Faith* (Oxford: Oxford University Press, 2014), 179.

8. Edith Turner, *Heart of Lightness: The Life Story of an Anthropologist* (New York and Oxford: Berghahn Books, 2006), 55.

9. See Larsen, *The Slain God*, 178.

10. Quoted in *ibid.*, 175.

11. E. Turner, *Heart of Lightness*, 40, 41.

12. Larsen, *The Slain God*, 176.

13. Quoted in *ibid.*, 176, 177.

14. Quoted in *ibid.*, 178.

15. Quoted in *ibid.*, 179.

16. E. Turner, *Heart of Lightness,* 50.

17. See *ibid.,* 49–50.

18. *Ibid.,* 49

19. Larsen, *The Slain God,* 177.

20. Victor Turner, *The Ritual Process: Structure and Anti-Structure* (Chicago: Aldine, 1969), 4.

21. *Ibid.,* 3.

22. *Ibid.,* 8.

23. See E. Turner, *Heart of Lightness,* 58.

24. See V. Turner, *The Ritual Process,* 9.

25. *Ibid.,* 15–16.

26. *Ibid.,* 18, 20.

27. *Ibid.,* 15.

28. *Ibid.,* 28.

29. *Ibid.,* 37.

30. See *ibid.,* 94–95.

31. *Ibid.,* 95.

32. *Ibid.,* 125.

33. *Ibid.,* 96.

34. See Larsen, *The Slain God,* 192, citing Victor Turner, *The Drums of Affliction* (Ithaca, N.Y.: Cornell University Press, 1981), 172.

35. V. Turner, *The Ritual Process,* 97.

36. *Ibid.,* 128.

37. Victor Turner, *Chihamba, the White Spirit: A Ritual Drama of the Ndembu* (Manchester: Manchester University Press, 1969), 3.

38. See Victor Turner, "Ritual, Tribal and Catholic," *Worship* 50 (1976): 517.

39. V. Turner, *Chihamba, the White Spirit,* 22.

40. *Ibid.,* 1.

41. See *ibid.,* 31–34.

42. *Ibid.,* 5.

43. *Ibid.,* 17.

44. See *ibid.,* 15.

45. *Ibid.,* 39.

46. V. Turner, "Ritual, Tribal and Catholic," 518.

47. *Ibid.*

48. *Ibid.,* 518–19.

49. See, e.g., Christian Smith, "God and the Anthropologists," a review of Larsen's *The Slain God, First Things,* March 2015, https://www.firstthings.com/article/2015/03/god-and-the-anthropologists.

50. Larsen, *The Slain God,* 183, quoting Matthew Engelke, "An Interview with Edith Turner," *Current Anthropology* 41:5 (2000): 847.

51. *Ibid.,* 184, quoting Victor Turner, *Revelation and Divination in Ndembu Ritual* (Ithaca, N.Y.: Cornell University Press, 1975), 31.

52. *Ibid.,* quoting Edith Turner, *Among the Healers: Stories of Spiritual and Ritual Healing from Around the World* (Westport, Conn.: Praeger, 2006), xiii.

53. V. Turner, "Ritual, Tribal and Catholic," p. 516.

54. See Lang, *Signs of the Holy One,* 26, citing Roy A. Rappaport, *Ecology, Meaning, and Religion* (Richmond, Calif.: North Atlantic Books, 1979), 182.

55. *Ibid.,* 27.

56. V. Turner, "Ritual, Tribal and Catholic," 517.

57. *Ibid.*, 519.

58. See, e.g., Victor Turner, "Social Dramas and Stories about Them," *Critical Inquiry* 7:1 (1980): 141–68.

59. Larsen, *The Slain God*, 188, quoting Victor Turner, "Passages, Margins, and Poverty: Religious Symbols of *Communitas*," *Worship* 47 (1972): 392.

60. Janet Adamy and Paul Overberg, "More Than Ever, Americans Age Alone," *The Wall Street Journal*, December 12, 2018.

61. Brian Resnick, "22 Percent of Millennials Say They Have 'No Friends,'" *Vox*, August 1, 2019, https://www.vox.com/science-and-health/2019/8/1/20750047/millennials-poll -loneliness.

62. On this possibility, see Adrian Vermeule, "Liturgy of Liberalism," a review of *The Demon in Democracy: Totalitarian Temptations in Free Societies* by Ryszard Legutko, *First Things*, January 2017, https://www.firstthings.com/article/2017/01/liturgy-of-liberalism.

63. Larsen, *The Slain God*, 190.

QUESTION FIVE

1. Karl Marx, *Critique of Hegel's 'Philosophy of Right,'* ed. Joseph O'Malley, trans. Annette Jolin and O'Malley (Cambridge: Cambridge University Press, 2009), 131.

2. Howard Thurman, *With Head and Heart: The Autobiography of Howard Thurman* (San Diego and New York: Harcourt Brace, 1979), 103.

3. Howard Thurman, *Jesus and the Disinherited* (Boston: Beacon Press, 1996), 4.

4. *Ibid.*

5. *Ibid.*, 5.

6. See Thurman, *With Head and Heart*, 5.

7. *Ibid.*, 5–6.

8. *Ibid.*, 13.

9. Thurman, *Jesus and the Disinherited*, 29.

10. Thurman, *With Head and Heart*, 36.

11. Thurman, *Jesus and the Disinherited*, 33.

12. Thurman, *With Head and Heart*, 12, 36.

13. *Ibid.*

14. *Ibid.*, 21.

15. *Ibid.*

16. *Ibid.*, 18.

17. *Ibid.*, 18–19.

18. *Ibid.*, 20.

19. *Ibid.*, 20 (emphasis in original).

20. *Ibid.*, 24.

21. *Ibid.*, 35.

22. *Ibid.*, 37.

23. *Ibid.*, 45.

24. *Ibid.*, 114.

25. Thurman, *Jesus and the Disinherited*, xix.

26. *Ibid.*, 1–2.

27. *Ibid.*, 3.

28. *Ibid.*, 2.

29. The 1537 bull denounced as Satanic the notion that "the Indians of the West and the South, and other people of whom We have recent knowledge should be treated as dumb

brutes created for our service, pretending that they are incapable of receiving the Catholic Faith." Paul III, *Sublimis Dei [sic]: On the Enslavement and Evangelization of Indians* [1537], Papal Encyclicals Online, https://www.papalencyclicals.net/paul03/p3subli.htm.

30. In a largely adulatory 1961 lecture on Saint Augustine, for example, Thurman laid the blame for the mistreatment his family received after his father's death on the bishop of Hippo's teachings on the Catholic Church as the sole vehicle of human salvation. See Howard Thurman, "Saint Augustine: Architect of a New Faith," part 2, Boston University, December 10, 1961, the Howard Thurman and Sue Bailey Thurman Collections at Boston University.

31. Thurman, *Jesus and the Disinherited*, 5.

32. *Ibid.*, 7.

33. *Ibid.*

34. *Ibid.*

35. See, e.g., Benedict XVI, *Jesus of Nazareth: From the Baptism in the Jordan to the Transfiguration* (New York: Doubleday, 2007), 12–13.

36. Thurman, *Jesus and the Disinherited*, 8.

37. *Ibid.*, 12.

38. *Ibid.*, 39.

39. Thurman, *With Head and Heart*, 16.

40. Thurman, *Jesus and the Disinherited*, 39.

41. *Ibid.*, 41.

42. *Ibid.*, 72.

43. *Ibid.*, 62–63.

44. *Ibid.*, 76.

45. *Ibid.*, 77–78.

46. Thurman, *With Head and Heart*, 160–61.

47. *Ibid.*

48. *Ibid.*

49. *Ibid.*, 254–55.

50. See *ibid.*, 255.

QUESTION SIX

1. Pelagius, the British monk and later heresiarch, quoted in Peter Brown, *Augustine of Hippo: A Biography* (Berkeley: University of California Press, 2000), 287.

2. *Ibid.*

3. Quoted in *ibid.*, 288.

4. See *ibid.*, 286.

5. See Saint Augustine, *The City of God*, I.7, trans. Marcus Dods, rev. ed. Kevin Knight, *New Advent*, https://www.newadvent.org/fathers/1201.htm (table of contents and URL directory).

6. Brown, *Augustine of Hippo*, 286.

7. *Ibid.*, 296.

8. *Ibid.*, 300.

9. See *ibid.*, 301.

10. Edmund Waldstein, "Spiritual Ends and Temporal Power: An Integralist Reading of *The City of God*," in *Augustine in a Time of Crisis: Politics and Religion Contested*, eds. Boleslaw Z. Kabala, Ashleen Menchaca-Bagnulo, and Nathan Pinkoski (London: Palgrave Macmillan, forthcoming).

11. Brown, *Augustine of Hippo*, 300.

12. Saint Augustine, *The City of God*, I, pref.

13. Brown, *Augustine of Hippo*, 9.

14. Saint Augustine, *The Confessions*, ed. and trans. Philip Burton (New York: Everyman's Library, 2001), 34.

15. *Ibid.*, 38, 35.

16. Quoted in Brown, *Augustine of Hippo*, 29.

17. *Ibid.*, 46.

18. *Ibid.*, 39.

19. *Ibid.*, 40.

20. See Saint Augustine, *The Confessions*, 93.

21. *Ibid.*, 94.

22. *Ibid.*, 98.

23. Brown, *Augustine of Hippo*, 89, 88; see Brown's unsurpassable summary of the Neo-Platonic doctrine of procession in *ibid.*, 89.

24. *Ibid.*, 95.

25. Saint Augustine, *The Confessions*, 174.

26. *Ibid.*

27. *Ibid.*, 182.

28. *Ibid.*, 183.

29. *Ibid.*

30. Saint Augustine, *The City of God*, XI.1.

31. Quoted in Brown, *Augustine of Hippo*, 292.

32. Edmund Waldstein, "The City of God: An Introduction," *The Josias*, August 28, 2017, https://thejosias.com/2017/08/28/the-city-of-god-an-introduction/.

33. *Ibid.*, quoting Numa Denis Fustel de Coulanges, *The Ancient City: A Study on the Religion, Laws and Institutions of Greece and Rome*, trans. Willard Small (Baltimore: Johns Hopkins University Press, 1980), 381.

34. Waldstein, "The City of God."

35. *Ibid.*

36. See Waldstein, "Spiritual Ends and Temporal Power."

37. Cicero, *On the Republic*, in *On the Republic, On the Laws*, trans. C. W. Keyes (Cambridge, Mass.: Harvard University Press, 2000), 65.

38. Saint Augustine, *The City of God*, I, pref.

39. *Ibid.*, XIV.28.

40. *Ibid.*, XIX.23.

41. *Ibid.* (emphasis in original).

42. Virgil, *Aeneid*, in *Virgil: Eclogues, Georgics, Aeneid, Books 1–6*, trans. H. R. Fairclough, rev. G. P. Goold (Cambridge, Mass.: Harvard University Press, 1999), 437.

43. Eve Adler, *Vergil's Empire: Political Thought in the Aeneid* (Lanham, Md.: Rowman & Littlefield, 2003), 193.

44. Saint Augustine, *The City of God*, III.14.

45. *Ibid.*, VII.27.

46. Brown, *Augustine of Hippo*, 193.

47. See *ibid.*, 186.

48. Waldstein, "The City of God: An Introduction."

49. *Ibid.*

50. Saint Augustine, *The City of God*, V.19.

51. *Ibid.*, V.26.

52. *Ibid.*
53. Brown, *Augustine of Hippo,* 428.
54. See *ibid.,* 430.
55. *Ibid.,* 433, 434.
56. For a magnificently detailed account of how this vision played out in Louis IX's French kingdom, see Andrew Willard Jones, *Before Church and State: A Study of Social Order in the Sacramental Kingdom of St. Louis IX* (Steubenville, Ohio: Emmaus Academic, 2017).
57. Waldstein, "The City of God."
58. Waldstein, "Spiritual Ends and Temporal Power."
59. *Ibid.*

QUESTION SEVEN

1. Quentin Fottrell, "My Husband and I Set Up a Nonprofit for His Parents. We Charged Them $10K. When His Siblings Found Out, 'All Hell Broke Loose'—Now They Want $10K for Simply Doing Chores," The Moneyist, *Market Watch,* February 15, 2020, https://www.marketwatch.com/story/my-husband-and-i-spent-a-year-setting-up-a-nonprofit-for-his-parents-we-charged-10k-when-his-siblings-found-out-all-hell-broke-loose-they-want-10k-for-doing-chores-2020-02-06.
2. *Ibid.*
3. *Ibid.*
4. *Ibid.*
5. Annping Chin, *The Authentic Confucius: A Life of Thought and Politics* (New York: Scribner's, 2007), 6.
6. *Ibid.,* 52.
7. *Ibid.*
8. *Ibid.,* 53.
9. *Ibid.*
10. *Ibid.*
11. *Ibid.*
12. See *ibid.,* 54.
13. *Ibid.*
14. Confucius, *Analects,* trans. Annping Chin (New York: Penguin, 2014), 2.
15. *Ibid.,* 97.
16. Chin, *The Authentic Confucius,* 24.
17. *Ibid.,* 13.
18. Confucius, *Analects,* 132.
19. Chin, *The Authentic Confucius,* 39.
20. Jerry Dennerline, *Qian Mu and the World of Seven Mansions* (New Haven, Conn.: Yale University Press, 1988), 9.
21. Chin, *The Authentic Confucius,* 164.
22. *Ibid.,* 166.
23. Confucius, *Analects,* 25.
24. See Chin, *The Authentic Confucius,* 50.
25. Chin suggests that the bit about the dancing girls, for example, is interpolated from a different story. See *ibid.,* 28.
26. *Ibid.,* 23.
27. Confucius, *Analects,* 256.
28. *Ibid.,* 141–42 (brackets as in the original).

29. *Ibid.*, 133 (brackets as in the original).
30. *Ibid.*, 319.
31. *Ibid.*, 135–36.
32. Quoted in Chin, *The Authentic Confucius*, 184.
33. *Ibid.*, 13.
34. *Ibid.*, 99.
35. *Ibid.*, 97.
36. Quoted in *ibid.* (brackets as in the original).
37. Confucius, *Analects*, 4.
38. *Ibid.*, 5.
39. *Classic of Filiality (Xiaojing)*, in *Sources of Chinese Tradition*, vol. 1, comp. Wm. Theodore de Bary and Irene Bloom, 2nd ed. (New York: Columbia University Press, 1999), 326.
40. Confucius, *Analects*, 15.
41. *Ibid.*, 16.
42. *Ibid.*, 292–93 (brackets as in the original).
43. *Classic of Filiality (Xiaojing)*, 326, 328.
44. *Ibid.*, 326–27 (brackets as in the original).
45. *Ibid.*, 328.
46. Emily Yoffe, "The Debt: When Terrible, Abusive Parents Come Crawling Back, What Do Their Grown Children Owe Them?" *Slate*, February 18, 2013, https://slate.com /human-interest/2013/02/abusive-parents-what-do-grown-children-owe-the-mothers -and-fathers-who-made-their-childhood-a-living-hell.html.
47. *Ibid.*
48. *Mencius*, trans. D. C. Lau (New York: Penguin, 2004), 99.
49. *Ibid.*, 99–100.
50. Confucius, *Analects*, 54.

Question Eight

1. See, e.g., Timothy Leary, "Think for Yourself," track 4, *Sound Bites from the Counter Culture*, Atlantic, 1990, compact disc.
2. See, e.g., Timothy Leary, *Turn On, Tune In, Drop Out* (Berkeley, Calif.: Ronin, 1999).
3. Leary, "Think for Yourself."
4. On legally recognized polyamorous unions, see, e.g., Ellen Barry, "A City Gives Family Rights to Multiple-Partner Unions," *New York Times*, July 5, 2020, https://www .nytimes.com/2020/07/01/us/somerville-polyamorous-domestic-partnership.html; on self-marriage, see, e.g., Didem Tali, "Why Growing Numbers Are Saying 'Yes' to Themselves," BBC News, December 22, 2017, https://www.bbc.com/news/business -42415394.
5. John Skorupski, "Liberalism as Free Thought," in *John Stuart Mill—Thought and Influence: The Saint of Rationalism*, eds. Georgios Varouxakis and Paul Kelly (London and New York: Routledge, 2010), 147 (my emphasis).
6. Farhad Manjoo, @fmanjoo on Twitter, July 12, 2019, https://twitter.com/fmanjoo /status/1149767779270062080.
7. Emily Ekins, "Poll: 62 Percent of Americans Say They Have Political Views They're Afraid to Share," Cato Institute, July 22, 2020, https://www.cato.org/publications /survey-reports/poll-62-americans-say-they-have-political-views-theyre-afraid-share.
8. Quoted in Roland Quinalt, "Gladstone and Slavery," *Historical Journal* 52, no. 2 (2009): 368.

9. See *ibid.*, 369.

10. See Geoffrey Wheatcroft, "The Most Eminent Victorian," *The Atlantic,* January 1997, https://www.theatlantic.com/magazine/archive/1997/01/the-most-eminent -victorian/376762/.

11. *Ibid.*

12. Quoted in *ibid.*

13. Wheatcroft (*ibid.*) writes: "He was highly sexed, or even sex-obsessed. There is no reason to doubt his claim at the end of his life that he had never been in the strict sense unfaithful to his admirable wife, Catherine, and there is no doubting, either, that his motives for rescue work were, in part, sincere by his lights. If he thought that prostitution was the epitome of woman's degradation and exploitation by man, was he wrong? But there is also no denying the strong erotic overtones to his meetings with these fallen women, especially since the *Diaries* also detail his guilt-ridden dabbling in pornography (which is to say mildly spicy French novels of the kind booksellers used to class as *facetiae*) and his occasional habit of self-flagellation, scourgings marked in the *Diaries* by the sign of a little whip."

14. Quoted in *ibid.* (emphasis in the original).

15. *Decreta dogmatica concilii vaticani de fide Catholica et de ecclesia Christi* [1870], Christian Classics Ethereal Library, Creeds of Christendom, vol. 2, https://www.ccel.org/ccel /schaff/creeds2.v.ii.i.html.

16. W. E. Gladstone, *The Vatican Decrees in Their Bearing on Civil Allegiance: A Political Expostulation* (New York: Harper, 1875), 9.

17. *Ibid.*, 11.

18. *Ibid.*, 10.

19. Pope Pius IX, *The Syllabus of Errors* [1864], EWTN.com, https://www.ewtn.com /catholicism/library/syllabus-of-errors-9048.

20. Gladstone, *The Vatican Decrees in Their Bearing on Civil Allegiance*, 19.

21. *Ibid.*, 39.

22. *Ibid.*, 45.

23. John Henry Newman, *Apologia Pro Vita Sua* (New York: Penguin Classics, 2004), 25.

24. Avery Dulles, *John Henry Newman* (London and New York: Continuum, 2002), 2.

25. Newman, *Apologia Pro Vita Sua*, 43.

26. Dulles, *John Henry Newman*, 5.

27. Newman, *Apologia Pro Vita Sua*, 65.

28. Quoted in Dulles, *John Henry Newman*, 4.

29. Newman, *Apologia Pro Vita Sua*, 50.

30. *Ibid.*, 143.

31. *Ibid.*, 144.

32. *Ibid.*, 61, 177.

33. *Ibid.*, 115–17.

34. John Henry Newman, *A Letter Addressed to the Duke of Norfolk: On Occasion of Mr. Gladstone's Recent Expostulation* (London: Aeterna, 2015), 1.

35. *Ibid.*, 2.

36. See C. S. Lewis, *Mere Christianity* (London: Collins, 2012), 3–8.

37. Newman, *A Letter Addressed to the Duke of Norfolk*, 41.

38. *Ibid.*

39. *Ibid.*

40. *Ibid.*

41. *Ibid.*

42. *Ibid.*, 58.

43. *Ibid.*

44. *Ibid.*

45. See Newman, *Apologia Pro Vita Sua*, 255–56.

46. Newman, *A Letter Addressed to the Duke of Norfolk*, 55.

47. *Ibid.*, 44.

48. *Ibid.*, 45.

49. Pope Leo XIII, *Rerum novarum* (Encyclical on Capital and Labor), May 15, 1891, http://www.vatican.va/content/leo-xiii/en/encyclicals/documents/hf_l-xiii_enc_15051891_rerum-novarum.html.

50. Newman, *A Letter Addressed to the Duke of Norfolk*, 55.

51. *Ibid.*, 58.

52. Newman, *Apologia Pro Vita Sua*, 255.

53. *Ibid.*

54. Gigi Engle, "Anal Sex: Safety, How-Tos, Tips, and More," *Teen Vogue*, November 12, 2019, https://www.teenvogue.com/story/anal-sex-what-you-need-to-know; "Theme: Future Societys [sic]," TEDx event, University of Würzburg, Bayern, Germany, May 5, 2018, https://www.ted.com/tedx/events/24068.

55. Newman, *A Letter Addressed to the Duke of Norfolk*, 48.

56. *Ibid.*

57. *Ibid.*, 50.

58. Quoted in Wheatcroft, "The Most Eminent Victorian."

QUESTION NINE

1. Jack Nicas, "He Has 17,700 Bottles of Hand Sanitizer and Nowhere to Sell Them," *New York Times*, March 15, 2020, https://www.nytimes.com/2020/03/14/technology/coronavirus-purell-wipes-amazon-sellers.html.

2. *Ibid.*

3. *Ibid.*

4. Aleksandr Solzhenitsyn, *Between Two Millstones, Book 1: Sketches of Exile, 1974–1978*, trans. Peter Constantine (Notre Dame, Ind.: University of Notre Dame Press, 2018), 4.

5. *Ibid.*, 238.

6. Ronald Berman, ed., *Solzhenitsyn at Harvard: The Address, Twelve Early Responses, Six Later Reflections* (Washington, D.C.: Ethics and Public Policy Center, 1980), 3.

7. *Ibid.*, 8.

8. *Ibid.*

9. *Ibid.*, 9–11.

10. *Ibid.*, 11.

11. *Ibid.*, 12.

12. *Ibid.*, 23–24.

13. *Ibid.*, 26.

14. *Ibid.*, 31.

15. *Ibid.*, 35.

16. *Ibid.*, 62.

17. Solzhenitsyn, *Between Two Millstones, Book 1*, 230 (emphasis in original).

18. Alexander Solzhenitsyn, *One Day in the Life of Ivan Denisovich*, trans. H. T. Willetts (New York: Everyman's Library, 1995), 12.

19. *Ibid.*, 3.

20. *Ibid.*, 15.
21. *Ibid.*, 26.
22. *Ibid.*, 89.
23. *Ibid.*, 143.
24. *Ibid.*, 87.
25. *Ibid.*, 109.
26. *Ibid.*, 159.
27. Alexander Solzhenitsyn, "Letter to Soviet Leaders," *The Way of the World,* March 1974, http://www.tparents.org/Library/Unification/Publications/TWotW/TWotW-74/TWotW-7403.pdf.
28. Solzhenitsyn, *Between Two Millstones, Book 1,* 14.
29. *Ibid.*, 126.
30. *Ibid.*, 47.
31. *Ibid.*, 202.
32. *Ibid.*, 90.
33. See *ibid.*, 237.
34. *Ibid.*, 265.
35. *Ibid.*, 105.
36. Berman, *Solzhenitsyn at Harvard,* 8.
37. *Ibid.*, 16.
38. *Ibid.*
39. See *ibid.*, 18; more recently, the conservative Polish politician and academic Ryszard Legutko has further developed this critique in his *The Demon in Democracy: Totalitarian Temptations in Free Societies,* trans. Teresa Adelson (New York: Encounter Books, 2016).
40. Solzhenitsyn, *Between Two Millstones, Book 1,* 285 (emphasis in original).
41. *Ibid.*, 286.
42. Michael Kaufman, "Solzhenitsyn, Literary Giant Who Defied Soviets, Dies at 89," *New York Times,* Aug. 4, 2008, available online: https://www.nytimes.com/2008/08/04/books/04solzhenitsyn.html.

QUESTION TEN

1. See Chiara Sabina, Janis Wolak, and David Finkelhor, "The Nature and Dynamics of Internet Pornography Exposure for Youth," *CyberPsychology and Behavior* 11, no. 6 (2008), http://www.unh.edu/ccrc/pdf/CV169.pdf.
2. E.g., Amanda Taub, "#MeToo Paradox: Movement Topples the Ordinary, Not the Powerful," *New York Times,* February 11, 2019, https://www.nytimes.com/2019/02/11/world/americas/metoo-ocar-arias.html.
3. Judy Klemesrud, "Joining Hands in the Fight against Pornography," *New York Times,* August 26, 1985, https://www.nytimes.com/1985/08/26/style/joining-hands-in-the-fight-against-pronorgraphy.html.
4. Andrea Dworkin, *Heartbreak: The Political Memoir of a Feminist Militant* (New York: Basic Books, 2002), 171.
5. *Ibid.*, 203.
6. *Ibid.*, 174.
7. *Ibid.*
8. Klemesrud, "Joining Hands in the Fight against Pornography."
9. See Dworkin, *Heartbreak,* 174–75.

10. Ariel Levy, "The Prisoner of Sex," *New York*, May 27, 2005, https://nymag.com/ny metro/news/people/features/11907.

11. United Press International, "Hustler Magazine Withstands Feminist's Challenge," January 24, 1989.

12. See Klemesrud, "Joining Hands in the Fight against Pornography."

13. Levy, "The Prisoner of Sex."

14. *Ibid.*

15. Dworkin, *Heartbreak*, 6.

16. *Ibid.*, 17.

17. *Ibid.*, 11.

18. *Ibid.*, 4.

19. *Ibid.*, 81.

20. *Ibid.*, 45–46.

21. *Ibid.*, 47.

22. *Ibid.*, 114.

23. *Ibid.*, 117–19.

24. Andrea Dworkin, *Intercourse* (New York: Basic Books, 2007), 59.

25. *Ibid.*

26. *Ibid.*, 141, quoting Marabel Morgan, *The Total Woman* (New York: Pocket Books, 1975).

27. *Ibid.*, 60.

28. *Ibid.*, 157.

29. *Ibid.*, 13.

30. See *ibid.*, 64.

31. *Ibid.*, 67.

32. *Ibid.*, 25.

33. *Ibid.*, xxxiii (emphasis added).

34. *Ibid.*, 190, quoting Augustine, *The City of God*, trans. Gerald G. Walsh and Demetrius B. Zema et al., abridged (Garden City, N.Y.: Image Books, 1958), 321. As John Cavadini has pointed out, Dworkin unfortunately used a flawed, abridged translation of *The City of God*, leading her to misunderstand Augustine in crucial respects.

35. *Ibid.*, 167.

36. John C. Cavadini, "Feeling Right: Augustine on the Passions and Sexual Desire," *Augustinian Studies* 36, no. 1 (2005): 198.

37. *Ibid.*, 207–8, quoting Augustine, *The City of God*, trans. Henry Bettenson (New York: Penguin, 1984), 245–46 (translation modified by Cavadini).

38. *Ibid.*, 209.

39. Dworkin, *Intercourse*, 186.

40. *Ibid.*, 195.

41. *Ibid.*, 205, quoting Augustine, *The City of God*, 14.26 (in Cavadini's own translation from the Latin).

42. *Ibid.*

43. *Ibid.*, 206, quoting Augustine, *The City of God*, 14.26 (Cavadini's own translation).

44. Dworkin, *Intercourse*, 190–91.

45. *Ibid.*, 171.

46. *Ibid.*, 163.

47. See Cavadini, "Feeling Right," 205.

48. Dworkin, *Intercourse*, 193.

49. *Ibid.*, 174.

50. *Ibid.*, 172.

51. *Ibid.,* 175.
52. *Ibid.,* 189.
53. Cavadini, "Feeling Right," 212.
54. Dworkin, *Heartbreak,* 190.

QUESTION ELEVEN

1. See John Loftus, "Lockdown Suicides on the Rise," *National Review Online,* July 30, 2020, https://www.nationalreview.com/corner/lockdown-suicides-on-the-rise/.
2. Hans Jonas, *Memoirs,* ed. Christian Wiese, trans. Krishna Winston (Waltham, Mass.: Brandeis University Press, 2008), 49; see also 43, on Edmund Husserl's hostility to religious commitments in philosophy, which Jonas encountered firsthand.
3. For this distinctly Heideggerian account of existentialism, I'm indebted to, *inter alia,* Simon Critchley, "Being and Time, Part 1: Why Heidegger Matters," *The Guardian,* June 8, 2009, https://www.theguardian.com/commentisfree/belief/2009/jun/05/heidegger-philosophy; and "Being and Time, Part 2: On 'Mineness,'" *The Guardian,* June 15, 2009, https://www.theguardian.com/commentisfree/belief/2009/jun/15/heidegger-being-time-philosophy.
4. See Jonas, *Memoirs,* 41.
5. Hans Jonas, *The Gnostic Religion: The Message of the Alien God and the Beginnings of Christianity,* 3rd ed. (Boston: Beacon Press, 2001), xv.
6. Jonas, *Memoirs,* 61.
7. *Ibid.,* 25.
8. *Ibid.,* 56; see also Jonas, *The Gnostic Religion,* xvi.
9. Jonas, *The Gnostic Religion,* xxxi.
10. *Ibid.,* 42.
11. *Ibid.,* 18; see also Pope Benedict XVI, "Faith, Reason and the University: Memories and Reflections," September 12, 2006, w2.vatican.va/content/benedict-xvi/en/speeches/2006/september/documents/hf_ben-xvi_spe_20060912_university-regensburg.html.
12. *Ibid.,* 22, 23.
13. See, e.g., Irenaeus, *Against Heresies,* trans. Alexander Roberts and William Rambaut, rev. ed. Kevin Knight, *New Advent,* https://www.newadvent.org/fathers/0103.htm; Hippolytus, *Refutation of All Heresies,* trans. J. H. MacMahon, rev. ed. Kevin Knight, *New Advent,* https://www.newadvent.org/fathers/0501.htm; Tertullian, *Against All Heresies,* trans. S. Thelwall, rev. ed. Kevin Knight, *New Advent,* https://www.newadvent.org/fathers/0319.htm; Tertullian, *Against Marcion,* trans. Peter Holmes, rev. ed. Kevin Knight, *New Advent,* https://www.newadvent.org/fathers/0312.htm.
14. Arthur Darby Nock, "Review of Jonas, *Gnosis und spätantiker Geist I,*" *Gnomon* 12 (1936), 605–12, quoted in Michael Waldstein, "Hans Jonas' Construct 'Gnosticism': Analysis and Critique," *Journal of Early Christian Studies,* 8, no. 3 (2000): 343.
15. *Ibid.,* 342, quoting Michael A. Williams, *Rethinking "Gnosticism": An Argument for Dismantling a Dubious Category* (Princeton, N.J.: Princeton University Press, 1996), 5.
16. The Austrian scholar Michael Waldstein catalogues some of Jonas's errors and too-broad generalizations in *ibid.,* 370–71.
17. *Ibid.,* 342, quoting Hans-Martin Schenke, "Review of Hans Jonas, *Gnosis und spätantiker Geist I,*" *Theologischen Literaturzeitung* 84 (1959): 818.
18. Jonas, *The Gnostic Religion,* 327, 325, 110.
19. *Ibid.,* 49.
20. Quoted in *ibid.,* 49 (emphasis added).

21. *Ibid.*, 49, 137.
22. See, e.g., Tertullian, *Against All Heresies*.
23. See John Arendzen, "Marcionites," *The Catholic Encyclopedia*, vol. 9 (New York: Appleton, 1910), https://www.newadvent.org/cathen/09645c.htm.
24. See Tertullian, *Against All Heresies*.
25. Quoted in Jonas, *The Gnostic Religion*, 141.
26. *Ibid.*, 43.
27. Quoted in *ibid.*, 52.
28. Quoted in *ibid.*, 114.
29. Quoted in *ibid.*
30. Quoted in *ibid.*, 115.
31. See *ibid.*, 44.
32. Quoted in *ibid.*, 44, 85, 88, 64 (emphasis added).
33. *Ibid.*, 226–27.
34. *Ibid.*, 246.
35. For a handy summary of *arete*, see the translators' introduction to the *Apology*, in Plato, *Euthyphro, Apology, Crito, Phaedo*, eds. and trans. Chris Emlyn-Jones and William Preddy (Cambridge, Mass.: Harvard University Press, 2017), 99.
36. Jonas, *The Gnostic Religion*, 253.
37. *Ibid.*, 268.
38. *Ibid.*, 272.
39. Irenaeus, *Against Heresies*, I.25.4.
40. Jonas, *Memoirs*, 67.
41. *Ibid.*
42. *Ibid.*, 65.
43. *Ibid.*, 66.
44. Jonas, *Memoirs*, 101.
45. Jonas, *The Gnostic Religion*, 325, 326, 334.
46. Robert P. George, "Gnostic Liberalism," *First Things* (December 2016), https://www.firstthings.com/article/2016/12/gnostic-liberalism.
47. Holman W. Jenkins Jr., "Will Google's Ray Kurzweil Live Forever?" *Wall Street Journal*, April 13, 2013, https://www.wsj.com/articles/SB10001424127887324504704578412581386515510.
48. See, e.g., Tara Isabella Burton, "Bad Traditionalism: How I Escaped a Disastrous Engagement," *Commonweal* (July/August 2020), https://www.commonwealmagazine.org/bad-traditionalism.
49. George, "Gnostic Liberalism."
50. *Ibid.*
51. Jonas, *Memoirs*, 144.
52. *Ibid.*, 145.
53. *Ibid.*
54. *Ibid.*, 193.
55. *Ibid.*

Question Twelve

1. See Leon R. Kass, "Ageless Bodies, Happy Souls: Biotechnology and the Pursuit of Perfection," *The New Atlantis* (Spring 2003), https://www.thenewatlantis.com/publications/ageless-bodies-happy-souls.

2. Arthur L. Caplan, "Death as an Unnatural Process: Why Is It Wrong to Seek a Cure for Aging?" *European Molecular Biology Organization Reports* 6 (2005): S72.

3. Alison Abbott, "First Hint That Body's 'Biological Age' Can Be Reversed," *Nature* (September 5, 2019), https://www.nature.com/articles/d41586-019-02638-w.

4. On the therapy–enhancement distinction and its limits as an ethical concept, see Kass, "Ageless Bodies, Happy Souls."

5. Tacitus, *Annals*, in *Annals and Histories*, trans. Alfred John Church and William Jackson Brodribb (New York: Everyman's Library, 2009), 350.

6. *Ibid.*, 350–51.

7. *Ibid.*, 351.

8. *Ibid.*, 353.

9. See Francis Caldwell Holland, *The Stoic* (Enhanced Media, 2015), 88 (digital edition of Francis Caldwell Holland, *Seneca* [London: Longmans, Green, 1920]).

10. Tacitus, *Annals*, 354.

11. Caldwell Holland, *The Stoic*, 88.

12. See *ibid.*, 9.

13. Quoted in *ibid.*, 17.

14. James Romm, "Introduction," in Seneca, *How to Die*, ed. and trans. James S. Romm (Princeton, N.J.: Princeton University Press, 2018), xiv.

15. *Ibid.*, xv.

16. Quoted in Caldwell Holland, *The Stoic*, 14.

17. Quoted in *ibid*.

18. *Ibid.*, 14.

19. Seneca, *How to Die*, 8.

20. *Ibid.*, 9.

21. *Ibid.*, 15–16.

22. Caldwell Holland, *The Stoic*, 21.

23. Seneca, *How to Die*, 16, 10.

24. *Ibid.*

25. See Caldwell Holland, *The Stoic*, 21.

26. Seneca, *How to Die*, 57.

27. *Ibid.*, 224n17.

28. *Ibid.*, 58.

29. *Ibid.*, 111.

30. Quoted in Caldwell Holland, *The Stoic*, 19.

31. *Ibid.*, 19.

32. *Ibid.*, 23, 24.

33. *Ibid.*, 25.

34. See *ibid*.

35. Tacitus, *Annals*, 262.

36. Seneca, *How to Die*, 42–43.

37. Tacitus, *Annals*, 234.

38. Caldwell Holland, *The Stoic*, 37.

39. See *ibid.*, 38.

40. See *ibid.*, 39.

41. Seneca, *How to Die*, 43, 47.

42. *Ibid.*, 44–45.

43. *Ibid.*, 104.

44. *Ibid.*, 22.

45. Leon R. Kass, "L'Chaim and Its Limits: Why Not Immortality?" *First Things* (May 2001), https://www.firstthings.com/article/2001/05/lchaim-and-its-limits-why-not-immortality.

46. Tacitus, *Annals,* 364.

47. *Ibid.*

48. *Ibid.,* 365.

INDEX

ABOUT THE AUTHOR

SOHRAB AHMARI is the op-ed editor of the *New York Post*, a columnist for *First Things*, and a contributing editor of the *Catholic Herald*. Previously, he served as a columnist and editor for the *Wall Street Journal* opinion pages in New York and London, and as senior writer at *Commentary*. In addition to those publications, his writing has appeared in *The New York Times*, *The Times Literary Supplement*, *The Chronicle of Higher Education*, *The Spectator*, *Dissent*, and *America*.

ABOUT THE TYPE

This book was set in Dante, a typeface designed by Giovanni Mardersteig (1892–1977). Conceived as a private type for the Officina Bodoni in Verona, Italy, Dante was originally cut only for hand composition by Charles Malin, the famous Parisian punch cutter, between 1946 and 1952. Its first use was in an edition of Boccaccio's *Trattatello in laude di Dante* that appeared in 1954. The Monotype Corporation's version of Dante followed in 1957. Though modeled on the Aldine type used for Pietro Cardinal Bembo's treatise *De Aetna* in 1495, Dante is a thoroughly modern interpretation of that venerable face.